Letting Go

Letting Go

Feminist and Social Justice Insight and Activism

Donna King and
Catherine (Kay) G. Valentine,

EDITORS

VANDERBILT UNIVERSITY PRESS
NASHVILLE

©2015 by Vanderbilt University Press
Nashville, Tennessee 37235
All rights reserved
First printing 2015

This book is printed on acid-free paper.
Manufactured in the United States of America

Library of Congress Cataloging-in-Publication Data on file

LC control number 2014045417
LC classification HQ1155.L47 2015
Dewey class number 305.42—dc23

ISBN 978-0-8265-2065-4 (hardcover)
ISBN 978-0-8265-2066-1 (paperback)
ISBN 978-0-8265-2067-8 (ebook)

CONTENTS

Introduction

    Letting Go Feminism:
    Reconnecting Self-Care and Social Justice   1
    Catherine (Kay) G. Valentine

Part One: **Theoretical Perspectives**

   1   Toward a Feminist Theory of Letting Go   15
      Donna King

   2   On the Interdependence of Personal
      and Social Transformation   33
      David R. Loy

   3   Leaning In and Letting Go:
      Feminist Tools for Valuing Nonwork   47
      Jennifer Randles

   4   Letting Go of Normal when "Normal" Is
      Pathological, or Why Feminism Is a Gift to Men   57
      Robert Jensen

Part Two: **Personal Essays**

   5   When "Straight-Acting" Lost Its Luster:
      Letting Go of Masculine Privilege   69
      Anthony C. Ocampo

   6   The Gold Pen   81
      Deborah J. Cohan

   7   Whether Willing or Unwilling: The Personal,
      the Professional, and Two Years of Too Much   91
      Meghan M. Sweeney

8   Letting Go: How Does a Feminist Retire?   103
     Diane E. Levy

9   When Enough Is Enough:
     African American Women Reclaiming Themselves   113
     Shirley A. Jackson

Part Three: **Ethnographies**

10   What to Let Go: Insights from
     Online Cervical Cancer Narratives   127
     Tracy B. Citeroni

11   Stay-at-Home Fathers: Are Domestic
     Men Bucking Hegemonic Masculinity?   139
     Steven Farough

12   From Retail Banking to Credit Counseling:
     Opting Out and Tuning In   151
     Kevin J. Delaney

13   Keeping Up Appearances: Working Class Feminists
     Speak Out about the Success Model in Academia   161
     Roxanne Gerbrandt and Liza Kurtz

14   Letting Go and Having Fun: Redefining Aging in America   173
     Deana A. Rohlinger and Haley Gentile

Part Four: **Ecological Perspectives**

15   Letting Go and Getting Real: Applying Buddhist
     Principles to Address Environmental Crisis   187
     Janine Schipper

16   Consuming Violence:
     Oil and Food in Everyday Life   201
     Patricia Widener

17   Growing Food, Growing Justice:
     Letting Go by Holding On to the Feminine Principle   211
     Leontina Hormel and Ryanne Pilgeram

Part Five: **Visionary Feminism**

18   Dig Deep: Beyond Lean In   225
     bell hooks

     Contributors   235

Index   239

Letting Go

INTRODUCTION

Letting Go Feminism

Reconnecting Self-Care and Social Justice

Catherine (Kay) G. Valentine

What is *letting go* and how might it contribute to feminist and social justice insight and activism? In this introduction we address this question by explicitly critiquing neoliberal feminism and the radical individualism it promotes as exemplified in Sheryl Sandberg's *Lean In* (2013).

A letting go feminist perspective as we envision it demands a radical recognition that the values and structures of our neoliberal (competitive, striving, accumulating, consuming, exploiting, oppressive) society are harmful and destructive both on a personal level (something some of the more privileged of us discover when we can't "keep up" with performance demands, for example) AND, especially important, on a social and environmental level. In other words, letting go is a practice of self-awareness in the service of a more humane, interconnected, interdependent social system, and it is a critique and rejection of unreflective neoliberal individualism and its destructive social forms and structures. We argue that a feminist letting go and its attendant self-care has the potential to be a radical act of awakening to social and environmental injustice and a call to activism for more humane and sustainable alternative structures. This is our basic orientation in moving toward a feminist theory of letting go and thus the context of this book.

In what follows we briefly define neoliberal capitalism and neoliberal feminism, offer a short critique of neoliberal feminism's notion of care, further discuss the theory and practice of letting go, and show how the contributions in this collection address these issues from various perspectives. While our focus is the contemporary United States, the issues are global in their reach and consequences.

Neoliberal Capitalism

Neoliberal capitalism is an ideology and a form of political economy that favors unregulated markets and radical individualism. Neoliberalism emphasizes the necessity and desirability of "transferring economic power and control from governments to private markets" (Centeno and Cohen 2011, 1). Under neoliberalism, corporate expansion into all walks of life, from education to health care, is viewed as good for everyone ("What's good for business is good for the nation"), and individual choice and responsibility are elevated to moral imperatives ("Taking personal accountability is a beautiful thing because it gives us complete control of our destinies").[1] Neoliberalism is, in many respects, an extreme expression of the American Dream, where the heroes are the self-made men or women who can stand on their own two feet and look after themselves with minimal reliance on others. Margaret Thornton (2004, 7) captures the essence of neoliberalism—it is "the shift away from the familiar relationship of citizen and state to that of consumer/entrepreneur and market," a shift that signals the replacement of "social justice and common good" by "individual desire and private profit."[2]

Neoliberal Feminism

Neoliberal feminism (also referred to as free market or choice feminism) emerged in tandem with the normalization of neoliberalism. In the United States, neoliberal feminism took center stage with the 2013 publication of Sheryl Sandberg's *Lean In*, a New York Times bestseller for seventy weeks and counting as we write this in the summer of 2014. Reinforcing the neoliberal sanctification of self-determination, *Lean In*'s central focus is the individual woman and her responsibility for overcoming internal obstacles (e.g., lack of confidence) that prevent her from getting ahead in corporate America. "We can dismantle the hurdles in ourselves today," says Sandberg (2013, 9). Touting the neoliberal mandates for women to be successful through striving, accumulating, and attention-seeking, *Lean In* spawned a very profitable industry including the Lean In Foundation, Lean In Circles, a movie deal, and a second book aimed at women college graduates (Sandberg 2014).

It is not surprising that *Lean In* has been wildly successful in this era of neoliberalism. Although Sandberg acknowledges a few institutional barriers to women's success in the workplace (e.g., the gender pay gap), she glosses over any meaningful analysis of those barriers in favor of emphasizing her argument that individual women can rise to the top by freeing themselves from holding themselves back. Sandberg is the quintessential neoliberal. Her vision of freedom rests on women accepting full responsibility for our own well-being. Professional success (power through corporate leadership) and personal fulfillment (happiness at home and work) will come to women who follow Sandberg's prescriptions for getting ahead by becoming an entrepreneur of the self.

But *Lean In* is more than a celebration of privatization, corporatization, and the self-made woman. It is "symptomatic of a larger cultural phenomenon in which neoliberal feminism is fast displacing liberal, social justice feminism"

(Rottenberg 2013, 419) as well as feeding the ongoing marginalization of radical and socialist feminisms (see discussion below). Sidelining twentieth century feminisms built on collective identity, basic rights, and shared sacrifice, neoliberal feminism promotes the belief that gender inequality will be resolved through the hard work and generosity of the entrepreneurial women (supported by entrepreneurial "husbands") who climb the ladder (or jungle gym, per Sandberg) to success. The social inequalities that undergird that ladder are never questioned by Sandberg. Catherine Rottenberg (2013) astutely summarizes the flawed thinking underlying Sandberg's lean in philosophy: "her feminism is so individuated that it has been completely unmoored from any notion of *social* inequality and consequently cannot offer any sustained analytic of the structures of male dominance, power, or privilege" (224–25, emphasis in the original).

Care-Lite and Faux Feminism

Care, a major theme across the essays in this book and historically a central concern of feminism and other social justice movements, is one of the victims of neoliberalism and its feminist proponents. Judith Butler (2012) reminds us that care is a precondition of life, an absolute necessity for a livable life, but care is diminished and degraded by the neoliberal ideology of radical individualism. Butler observes that, "Our very bodily existence depends upon systems of support that are both human and non-human" (165). We are vulnerable, all of us, and our vulnerability is key to our need for social relations and institutions that make life worth living. Butler continues, "Vulnerability not only designates a relation to the world, but asserts our very existence as a relational one. To say that any of us are vulnerable is thus to establish our radical dependency not only on others, but on a sustaining and sustainable world" (184). However, the profit-driven machinery of unfettered capitalism and capitalism's radical individualism rely on women and men who have learned to believe that success (and failure) is in their own hands, even though neoliberal success, in fact, rests on others performing the caretaking and life-sustaining work that enables success or, when absent, is responsible for deprivation.

To elaborate, at the heart of care is empathy, a feeling and enactment of intentional regard for the well-being of others and by extension the support systems (e.g., universal health care and a living wage) that insure well-being. Empathy, a fundamental human emotion, moves us to examine our connections to others, and if we are privileged by social class, race, gender, and other divisions, "to examine our excess, access and privileges as contributing factors" to the experiences of oppression in the lives of others (Moore 2013). But empathy, and thus care, in the fullest sense are antithetical to the enactment of radical individualism. The self-made woman (or man) must contain, restrict, and redirect empathy so that the social class, race, and other inequalities that produce personal, social, and ecological ill-being are "explained away" as individual failings (she's poor because she made poor choices) or as problems that can best be fixed by privatized, corporatized strategies (such as replacing welfare with "workfare" at poverty wages). Finally, locked inside the punitive logic of neoliberalism, the neoliberal women and men who fail to live up to performance demands are left to twist in the wind with only themselves to blame for their failure to succeed. In neoliberal consumer capitalist America, our emotional, embodied ties to others and their well-being are rerouted to profitable sources, especially consumer goods and services, and to "doing good" if it is profitable and fits the culture of radical individualism. For example, campaigns such as Pink Ribbon and Product Red have persuaded many of us that consuming products (e.g., Starbucks Red; Pink Ribbon T-shirts) will solve extraordinarily complex social and global problems while skillfully hiding the fact that corporations themselves create and amplify many of the problems in the first place (Eikenberry 2009; Sulik 2012).

The neoliberal feminist embrace of radical individualism and free market capitalism has created a version of feminism, a faux feminism according to many critics, in which care is truncated and twisted. The well-documented facts that women in the United States and globally do the lion's share of unpaid and paid care work and that women constitute the majority of those living in poverty or on the brink of poverty are "disappeared" in the neoliberal feminist agenda. Returning to Sheryl Sandberg's "feminist manifesto," the reader finds that care shrinks to the hope that adding a few more women to positions of power and leadership in corporate America will translate into fairer treatment for all women. Sandberg's neoliberal feminism models the top-down, trickle-down approach to inequality that is characteristic of the larger neoliberal transformation of the United States.[3] It's notable that *Lean In* contains only a few brief paragraphs that acknowledge, in the vaguest terms possible, the need for flexible workplaces, better maternity leave policies, and affordable child care. Not a single chapter is devoted to analysis of these critical issues or the neoliberal capitalism that has eroded social democracy and the benefits of social welfare citizenship in the United States. This is care-lite, lacking in substance and seriousness. Care writ large is off the table in the neoliberal feminist worldview. There is no room for social movements for universal health care, strong labor unions, or generous parental leave policies. There is, as well, no central place in the neoliberal feminist worldview for serious and sustained attention to issues such as the continuing high rates of violence against women in the United States and the rolling back of women's access to abortion services. Tellingly, the word "rape" appears twice in *Lean In*, each time framed as a problem for women in developing countries, specifically Afghanistan, Sudan, and Liberia, not as an everyday experience for many American women. One has the sense, as pointed out by Rottenberg (2013, 432), that neoliberal feminism is in the business of bolstering the belief in American exceptionalism while "(re)inscribing an impe-rialist logic," a logic that narrows the critique of gender inequality in the United States to a few acceptable issues while asserting US (neoliberal capitalist) supe-riority on the global stage.

Toward a Feminist Theory of Letting Go

As we stated at the beginning of this introduction, the theory and practice of letting go challenges neoliberal feminism and argues that we can't change so-ciety without changing ourselves, and we can't change ourselves without recog-nizing our embeddedness and interconnectedness in social and environmental structures and processes. This understanding of letting go is grounded in the sociological proposition that there is no self without society (self and society are mutually constitutive); the feminist understanding that the personal is political (and the practice of feminist consciousness-raising); the Buddhist emphasis on the interdependence of all things; and recognition of the inextricable link be-tween personal transformation and social transformation.

A feminist letting go reconnects self-awareness and social responsibility. From this perspective, self-care practices such as meditation and consciousness-raising can make internal and external dynamics of power relations visible, creating a pathway between an individual woman's or man's sense of injustice and her or his participation in feminist, social justice, and environmental move-ments.[4] In and of itself, self-care has the potential to subvert patriarchal capitalist structures of oppression that consign women—in particular Black, immigrant, and poor women—to constant labor, both paid and unpaid. Black feminists have vigorously made this point:

> It's subversive to take care of ourselves because for centuries black women worldwide have been taking care of others, from the children of slave masters to those of business executives, and often serving today as primary caregivers for the elderly as home health workers and nursing home employees. Black women's self-care is also subversive because to take care of ourselves means that we disrupt societal and political paradigms that say that Black women are disposable, unvalued. Indeed, people and things that aren't cared for are considered expendable. So when we don't take care of ourselves, we are affirming the social order that says black women are disposable. (Brooks-Tatum 2012)

Refusing to be or become disposable by engaging in activism, including radical self-care, is not the self-care of neoliberal feminism. It is the self-care of let-ting go of modes of life (e.g., individual striving, accumulating, and attention-seeking) based on hierarchical and exploitative values such as power-over and competitive opposition. Letting go theory and practice open up the possibilities of learning to relate as equals based on an ethic of care, and it supports and promotes the radical democratic principle of an equal claim to a livable life.

Letting Go and Liberal, Radical, and Socialist Feminisms

Letting go theory can be understood in relation to three major strands of feminist theory and practice: liberal feminism, radical feminism, and socialist feminism. It picks up threads and exposes limitations from each. Below we summarize these feminist frameworks in relationship to letting go. The summaries emphasize key ideas only; in practice, schools of thought overlap and individual feminists may move among them over time (Lorber 2009; Cobble, Gordon, and Henry 2014).

Liberal feminism argues that women should have the freedom to live lives of their own choosing with rights equal to those of men. Liberal feminists have invested in movements to dismantle legal barriers to women's equality with men in institutions such as education, marriage, and the military. They have advocated for laws and policies that facilitate reproductive choice, parental leave, quality day care, and flexible work schedules. Notably, liberal feminists have argued that the state has a major role to play in guaranteeing women's autonomy and ensuring equal rights. It is at this juncture that neoliberal feminism departs significantly from liberal feminism. Rottenberg (2013, 428) puts it this way: neoliberal feminism has no orientation toward the common good and, with its emphasis on the self-made woman, defines a feminist as a woman who "no longer demands anything from state or government."

Letting go acknowledges contributions of liberal feminism to women's liberation but also recognizes the limits of the liberal approach. For example, liberal feminism takes hierarchy as a given and acritically accepts corporate, military, and other forms of what is termed "power-over," or systems of domination and subordination. The goal of liberal feminism in the United States has been integration of women into power structures so that some women have power-over other women (and men), and some nations, specifically the United States, have power-over other nations. The liberal feminist stance on the military is illustrative. By and large, liberal feminists do not question militarism and have supported the inclusion of women at all levels in the military. Letting go, as emphasized previously, begins with a critique of neoliberal capitalist hierarchies and thus the militarism and violence associated with maintaining those hierarchies. Letting go moves toward imagining and creating sustaining bonds that do not produce disposable people in a precarious and threatening world.

Radical feminism rests on the premise that patriarchy is the basis of women's oppression and a foundation for other forms of oppression such as those based on class and race. Radical feminists identify the core principles of patriarchy as male dominance, male centeredness, male identification, and control (Johnson 1997). Rooting out the complex sources of patriarchy and its intersections with other forms of privilege and domination such as racial inequality is part of contemporary radical feminist work. However, women's oppression "as a class" remains a centerpiece of this school of thought. Radical feminists have scrutinized the sexual objectification of women through everyday mass media images, pornography, and prostitution. They have contributed to the establishment of women's health care services, safe houses for survivors of abuse, and counseling and legal services for rape victims. Their examination of men's control over women via violence and its threat has been crucial to movements for women's liberation.

Feminist letting go theory has a direct link to this school of thought through the radical feminist argument that the personal is political and the development of consciousness-raising groups as a tool for exploring the relationship between the personal injuries of sexism and the political causes of sexism in women's lives. In addition, the radical feminist emphasis on the significance of embodiment (e.g., how our bodies are involved in creating gender differences and inequalities through clothing and conformity to other gendered appearance norms) in gender inequality is foundational to letting go.

Letting go departs from radical feminism in several ways. For example, we understand that hierarchies of oppression (e., racism, sexism, and classism) are intertwined and that there is no primary form or structure of dominance and subordination. Letting go also departs from radical feminist theorizing that valorizes mothering and embraces beliefs that women are naturally more nurturing and caring than men. Not only does this mode of thinking slide into essentialism, it gives rise to impossible barriers between women and men, securing notions not too far removed from those of neoliberal feminists such as Sandberg who argue that women in positions of power will naturally care for other women.

Socialist feminism examines the interlocking dynamics of capitalism and patriarchy, focusing primarily on the problems facing poor and working class women and strategies to end the oppression and exploitation of women in those classes by moving away from capitalism and toward socialism. In her article in *Dissent*, Sarah Jaffe (2013), a contemporary socialist feminist, makes the argument that feminists should be spending their time doing analysis and participating in organizing on behalf of the "struggle for respect and better treatment for workers, mostly women, who 'make all other work possible,'" that is, for the disproportionate number of women in the booming sectors of the economy which pay poverty wages (e.g., retail sales, food service, and home health care). Jaffe (2013), writing in *Jacobin*, also urges feminists to challenge the dangerous belief that care work should be provided for love, not money, hiding the fact that care is work. Out of this line of thinking comes the call for "caring or care worker strikes" that demonstrate "what happens when women stop working."

Feminist letting go draws from socialist feminist critiques of neoliberal capitalism and its negative consequences for all but the most privileged women. Laurie Penny (2011, 2–3) a critic of neoliberal feminism, sums it up: "While we worry about the glass ceiling, there are millions of women standing in the basement—and the basement is flooding." Socialist feminist attention to valuable political strategies such as the care worker strikes and other forms of organizing across boundaries, including the nation-state, expand our understanding of how to let go of neoliberal capitalist relationships that prioritize individual success, growth, class privilege, and the exploitation of others over the promotion of a sustainable and livable life for all.

Letting go feminist thought diverges from socialist feminist theory, which like radical feminist theory identifies a primary form of domination and subordination. In the case of socialist feminism, capitalism and social class exploitation are the center of analysis. We argue that attempts to reduce oppression and exploitation to one set of power dynamics—classism or sexism—ends up fueling divisions and estrangements between groups working toward mutuality and solidarity. Rose M. Brewer (2014) expresses the letting go viewpoint: "In a movement for social transformation we simply cannot be race, class, gender reductionists but must move with a mediated understanding of the deep interrelationality of social forces to center our movement building."

Contributions in This Collection

Essays in this collection are exploratory and lay the groundwork for scholars, students, and activists to further develop the theory and practice of letting go. Contributors to Part One take up the sociological, feminist, and contemporary Buddhist principles that are the point of departure for critiquing neoliberal values that encourage individuals to think of themselves primarily as "mini-corporations," entrepreneurs, and consumers, who must endlessly work and strive to be number one (Martin 2000). Together, these essays argue that we can no longer afford the belief (delusion) that we are separate, autonomous selves with self-interests that trump the universal human right to a decent, dignified life and the necessity of living sustainably on the planet.

In Part Two, contributors uncover the intricacies of the connections between personal experience and the networks of power in which those experiences are embedded. They offer rich narratives of the process of letting go, of suffocating ways of life rooted in systems of oppression that have driven painful and dangerous wedges between groups, and the radical individualism that pits us against one another in the "battle to get ahead."

Part Three details the ways in which ordinary people, individually and collectively, employ letting go strategies to counteract the harmful neoliberal structuring of social relationships in a variety of everyday settings. The price we pay, individually and collectively, for our participation in neoliberal relationships and social structures that emphasize exploitation of all "resources," human and natural, is most dramatically apparent in our collapsing ecosystem.

Contributions in Part Four analyze the links between global inequalities and the environmental crisis. They also provide a wide range of strategies for letting go of neoliberal values and practices while moving toward sustainability and livability. The book concludes with bell hooks' call for us to dig deep and move beyond the "faux feminism" of Sandberg's *Lean In* to a more radical and visionary feminism that encourages all of us to let go of neoliberalism and its white capitalist patriarchal systems of inequality and to do our part to change the world so that freedom and justice and the opportunity to have optimal well-being can be equally shared by everyone.

NOTES

1. Heather Schuck (2013) quoted in Eldon Taylor's (2013) *Huffington Post* blog "Personal Best." Taylor and Schuck are perfect examples of contemporary self-help proponents whose ideas reinforce the radical individualism of neoliberalism.
2. Neoliberalism is a complex and wide-reaching concept. See for example: Centeno & Cohen (2010); Chomsky & McChesny ([1999] 2011); Duggan (2004); Eisenstein (2009); Foucault (2008); Fraser (2013); Giroux (2008); Harvey (2005); Stiglitz (2012); Wacquant (2009).
3. The failure of trickle-down is highlighted in Bryce Covert's (2014) report on the results of a recent study of the outcomes of Norway's 2003 requirement that public companies make their boards at least 40 percent female. The study shows that increasing women's board participation has had no impact on increasing women's ranks at levels below the top of the hierarchy. In addition, there have been no improvements in the gender wage gap or work environments for women in those Norwegian companies.
4. Letting go reveals the neoliberal feminist co-optation of Eastern spirituality practices for what it is, another way to separate self-awareness from social responsibility and another way to make money. Similarly, letting go highlights the distortion of feminist consciousness-raising groups by neoliberal feminist advocates such as Sheryl Sandberg (2013) whose Lean In Circles are superficially linked to consciousness-raising but are designed to promote self-advancement not revolutionary change.

REFERENCES

Brewer, Rose M. 2014. "From Feminist Critique to Social Transformation: Lessons from Social Forum." *Feminist Wire*, April 8. *thefeministwire.com/2014/04/social-transformation-beyond-critique*.

Brooks-Tatum, Shanesha. 2012. "Subversive Self-Care: Centering Black Women's Wellness." *Feminist Wire*, November 9. *thefeministwire.com/2012/11/subversive-self-care-centering-black-womens-wellness*.

Butler, Judith. 2012. "Bodily Vulnerability, Coalitions and Street Politics." In *The State of Things*, edited by Marta Kuzma, Pablo Lafuente, and Peter Osborne, 161–97. London: Office for Contemporary Art Norway and Koenig Books.

Centano, Miguel A., and Joseph N. Cohen. 2010. *Global Capitalism: A Sociological Perspective*. Cambridge, UK: Polity.

———. 2011. "The Arc of Neoliberalism: Prepared for the *Annual Review of Sociology*," September 1. *scholar.princeton.edu/sites/default/files/annual_review_centeno_and_cohen_final_draft_0.pdf*.

Chomsky, Noam, and David McChesney. (1999) 2011. *Profit Over People*. New York: Seven Stories Press.

Cobble, Dorothy Sue, Linda Gordon, and Astrid Henry. 2014. "What *Lean In* Leaves Out." Chronicle Review. *Chronicle of Higher Education*, September 22. *chronicle.com/article/What-Lean-In-Leaves-Out/148843*.

Covert, Bryce. 2014. "What Happened When One Country Required All Corporate Boards to Be 40% Women." *Bryce Covert* (blog), *Nation*, July 7. *www.thenation.com/blog/180528/what-happened-when-one-country-required-all-corporate-boards-be-40-women*.

Duggan, Lisa. 2004. *The Twilight of Equality: Neoliberalism, Cultural Politics, and the Attack on Democracy*. Boston: Beacon Press.

Eikenberry, Angela M. 2009. "The Hidden Costs of Cause Marketing." *Stanford Social Innovation Review* 18 (Summer): 1–11. *www.ssireview.org/articles/entry/the_hidden_costs_of_cause_marketing*.

Eisenstein, Hester. 2009. *Feminism Seduced: How Global Elites Use Women's Labor and Ideas to Exploit the World*. Boulder, CO: Paradigm.

Foucault, Michel. 2008. *The Birth of Biopolitics: Lectures at the Collège de France, 1978–79*. New York: Palgrave Macmillan.

Fraser, Nancy. 2013. *Fortunes of Feminism: From State-Managed Capitalism to Neoliberal Crisis*. New York: Verso.

Giroux, Henry. 2008. *Against the Terror of Neoliberalism*. Boulder: Paradigm.

Harvey, David. 2005. *A Brief History of Neoliberalism*. New York: Oxford University Press.

Jaffe, Sarah. 2013. "Trickle-Down Feminism." *Dissent* (Winter) *www.dissentmagazine.org/article/trickle-down-feminism*.

———. 2013. "A Day Without Care." *Jacobin: A Magazine of Culture and Polemic* 10 (Spring): n.p. *www.jacobinmag.com/2013/04/a-day-without-care*.

Johnson, Allan. 1997. *The Gender Knot: Unraveling our Patriarchal Legacy*. Philadelphia: Temple University Press.

Lorber, Judith. 2009. *Gender Inequality: Feminist Theories and Politics*. New York: Oxford University Press.

Martin, Emily. 2000. "Mind-Body Problems." AES Presidential Address. *havenscenter.wisc.edu/files/mind_body.pdf*.

Moore, Darnell L. 2013. "On Love, Empathy, and Pleasure in the Age of Neoliberalism." *Feminist Wire*, July 9. *www.thefeministwire.com/2013/07/on-love-empathy-and-pleasure-in-the-age-of-neoliberalism*.

Penny, Laurie. 2011. "Don't Worry about the Glass Ceiling—The Basement is Flooding." *New Statesman*, July 27, 2011. *www.newstatesman.com/blogs/laurie-penny/2011/07/women-business-finance-power*.

Rottenberg, Catherine. 2013. "The Rise of Neoliberal Feminism," *Cultural Studies* 28 (3): 418–37. *dx.doi.org/10.1080/09502386.2013.857361*.

Sandberg, Sheryl. 2013. *Lean In: Women, Work, and the Will to Lead*. New York: Knopf.

Sandberg, Sheryl. 2014. *Lean In for Graduates*. New York: Knopf.

Schuck, Heather. 2013. *The Working Mom Manifesto*. Chicago: Voyager Media.

Stiglitz, Joseph. 2012. *The Price of Inequality*. New York: Norton.

Sulik, Gayle. 2011. *Pink Ribbon Blues: How Breast Cancer Culture Undermines Women's Health*. New York: Oxford University Press.

Taylor, Eldon. 2013. "Personal Best: Prosperity Power." *The Blog, Huffington Post*. July 19. *www.huffingtonpost.com/eldon-taylor/do-your-best_b_3619965.html*.

Thornton, Margaret. 2004. "Neoliberal Melancholia: The Case of Feminist Legal Scholarship." *The Australian Feminist Law Journal* 20:7–24.

Wacquant, Loic. 2009. *Punishing the Poor: The Neoliberal Government of Social Insecurity*. Durham, NC: Duke University Press.

Part One

Theoretical Perspectives

1

Toward a Feminist Theory of Letting Go

Donna King

During an interview on NPR's *All Things Considered* (2011), David Greene asked Brian Henneman of the band The Bottle Rockets, "You've played with some pretty big names . . . you guys have become big. [But] you're not as commercial . . . as big as Wilco . . . I mean, what takes you to the next level?" Henneman laughed and replied, "It's too late to go to the next level. We're too comfortable where we're at. Why would we want to move now if everything will just be more of a pain in the butt? So, yeah . . . this is a real awesome comfortable place, and we like it. And by golly, that's our story, and we're sticking to it."

Setting aside the self-conscious coda, what strikes me about this exchange is Henneman's genuine satisfaction with his band's level of success. You can hear it in his voice, he means it. He is okay exactly where he is, with his band and in his life. He does not want to get to the top; he does not have to be the best. In fact, he foresees only headaches (or worse) lying in wait should he strive for bigger commercial success. Surely Henneman's social position—as a middle-aged working class musician from the Midwest, fronting a band that has played mostly in bars for over twenty years—has shaped his aspirational goals. I find it refreshing, nonetheless, to hear him say out loud and proud, "No thanks. I don't need to reach the top. I'm okay exactly where I am."

But then there is that conditional addendum, with its self-deprecating, defensive posturing, undercutting the message that good-enough is fine and implying instead that one must justify, explain, or make excuses for being satisfied with one's life as it is.

I question the core American imperative that says we must endlessly strive to be the best. My interest in this issue is both intellectual and personal. Like many women, I struggle to balance work life, home life, professional pursuits, crea-

A version of this essay was originally published in 2012 in *Frontiers: A Journal of Women's Studies* 33 (3): 53–70. Reprinted by permission of the University of Nebraska Press.

tive endeavors, self-definition, and cultural mandates. And I ask: Does feminism provide theoretical supports for women who want to (or must) slow down, grow quiet, and let go of striving? Can one be simultaneously feminist and nothing special, a strong woman and a woman in touch with her real limitations?

I use the somewhat jarring term "nothing special" not to minimize or denigrate women, but rather to highlight cultural contradictions I see in a mainstream, white, affluent, "free market feminism" that promotes the relentless pursuit of personal and professional achievement while uncritically adopting a neoliberal ideology that conflates "female empowerment [with] the accompanying baggage of consumerism, individualism, radical inequalities of life chances [and] environmental degradation" (Eisenstein 2009, 221).[1]

As Hester Eisenstein (2009) argues in *Feminism Seduced*, "feminist energies, ideologies, and activism have been manipulated in the services of the dangerous forces of [a] globalized corporate capitalism" (viii) that views the majority of the world's women as "the cheap workforce of choice," (11) and co-opts privileged professional women, including many academic feminists, into an acritical (or defeatist) acceptance of the neoliberal agenda and its attendant "flight from the body" (220). As antidote to this cooptation, Eisenstein calls for a revitalized feminist critique of capitalism that "transcend[s] . . . the differences between Third World and First World women to create a united international women's movement that can be a force for political and social change" (68). Primary among these forces for change, says Eisenstein, is a return to the body and to a social ethic of compassion, nurturance and care that "transform[s] maternalism, not as an essentialist definition of women's roles, but as a set of claims on the state" (x–xii) to provide child care, health care, sufficient nutrition, and adequate housing for all (229).

As Eisenstein's critique makes clear, there are contradictions in our culture, and within feminism, about how women should live our lives, particularly in terms of economic and cultural demands for high productivity, fast pace, pushing past limits, and denying the body. These pressures cut across race, class, work, and home. Many women are stuck in dead-end jobs with low wages, no job security, no autonomy, no respect, no control over their schedule, and unrelenting performance expectations. Professional women, despite their relative privilege, often face extraordinary demands on their time and energy. Home life, for many women, is rarely a safe haven from stress. Bearing and raising small children, dealing with teenagers, sending kids off to college, living with a partner or a dependent that is disabled or unhappily unemployed or clinically depressed or battling addiction—any potentially overwhelming experience that stretches us beyond our physical, mental, and emotional capacities leaves us ripe for a confrontation between so-called ideal and real women's lives.

We all face potential devaluation by family, friends, colleagues, peers, bosses, and perhaps most importantly by ourselves, when we do not "pull our weight" or "measure up" to socially defined standards of achievement. Many, if not most, women internalize impossible performance expectations, and it takes a tremendous force of will, or paradoxically, a complete letting go, to liberate ourselves from them.

I use Zen insight as a complement to Eisenstein's structural analysis of global neoliberal capitalism to explore how close attunement to bodily experience allows some women with invisible chronic illness to let go of unreasonable expectations of productivity and pace. While Eisenstein is scathing in her criticism of feminist "postmodern analyses that focus on individual and private acts of resistance" (2009, 212), I argue that, much like a breaching experiment in which one consciously and publicly violates a behavior in order to make obvious its structure and social power, studying how women with invisible chronic illness navigate achievement expectations—under physically and mentally debilitating conditions—highlights oppressive and often unacknowledged productivity norms in a dramatic way and further supports Eisenstein's call for a broader social commitment to compassion and care.

I focus here on two explicitly feminist accounts of the chronic illness experience, Cheri Register's *Living with Chronic Illness* and Susan Wendell's *The Rejected Body*, and draw from Barbara Hillyer's *Feminism and Disability*. Reading the works of feminist women with disabilities reveals that they are uniquely positioned to address dominant cultural dictates in the most concrete and experiential way, through both their bodies and minds. As their bodies transform from reasonably healthy to seriously unwell, these women's lives and sense of self transform as well, sometimes in radically new and improbable ways. Many women with chronic illness live a path that moves from pain, fear, fatigue, frustration, and grief, through a gradual and often grudging acceptance of unwelcome and disabling limitations, toward a new found sense of inner peace and self-acceptance. They learn the hard way, through mortal necessity, how to let go.

Zen and the Art of Letting Go

> When you are hungry, eat.
> When you are tired, rest.
> —Zen instruction

Writing as an exhausted new mother, Zen teacher Karen Maezen Miller offers this paean to bone-tiredness:

> It is not something you would choose, like a spa vacation, but is something you can use, like a humidifier. . . . It is a cure and a balm. Fatigue helps you forget. When you are tired, you let go. You drop what you no longer need

and you do not pick it up again. You slow down. You grow quiet. You take comfort. You appreciate the smallest things. You stop fighting. (quoted in Harris 2006)

The idea that fatigue might be useful, rather than a problem to be solved, is counter-intuitive in our multitasking, wired, and information-overloaded world. Zen advice that we eat when hungry and rest when tired goes directly against American cultural norms that dictate we push past our limits in a tireless quest to succeed. What is it we drop when we slow down, grow quiet, and appreciate small things?

The Zen of letting go suggests a practice of paying attention to immediate experience and responding appropriately, including listening to the body and meeting bodily needs as they arise. This is emphatically not the same as seeking complete comfort and ease in life; an appealing but unattainable goal whose quixotic pursuit ironically leads directly to what Buddhists call *dukkha*, a Pāli word most commonly translated as "suffering" but perhaps better understood as anguish, fear, clinging, and/or dissatisfaction. We are all destined to feel multiple kinds of pain at multiple points in our lives, and for some this becomes a chronic mental, physical, and/or emotional state. But none of these kinds of pain need necessarily lead to suffering. For Buddhists, suffering is an add-on, a social construction that most often takes the form of chronic dissatisfaction with life as it is (see Loy 1996).

Letting go, in Zen terms, means dealing skillfully with whatever is going on without adding any storyline. Freedom from suffering comes from total involvement in simply being with what is—and in constantly letting go of our attachment to having things go a certain way. For the Zen practitioner, none of this is easy or ever fully accomplished. In fact, it is not even a goal. It is an ongoing practice and process with no end in sight (Beck 1989).

Far from simple passive acquiescence, however, Zen practice can explicitly critique the forces of corporate global capitalism and advocate for a political economy organized around care, compassion, and social justice (Loy 2003). As media activist and Buddhist practitioner David Edwards (2005) notes:

When society subordinates its humanity to maximized revenues at minimum cost, then that society is well on the way to becoming lost, falsified, and in fact inhuman. If we are serious about combating selfishness and promoting compassion in the world, then is it not vital that we develop the tools of intellectual self-defense to deal with these assaults on our minds and hearts? The solution must lie in reversing the priorities, in subordinating dead things—money, capital, profits—to life: people, animals, the planet. . . . The antidotes to systemic greed, I am convinced, are political movements motivated by unconditional compassion for suffering.

Thus there is real potential for radical social change when we incorporate Buddhist insights with incisive critiques of neoliberal ideologies and practices that are colonizing our consciousness and the planet. We need not choose between inner awareness, listening to the body, and political activism for social justice. Activism can take many forms, and humanizing the global political economy and revitalizing a feminist commitment to a society based not on striving and "success" but on compassion and care may be just what is called for at this historical moment. But, as some feminists with invisible chronic illness attest, mainstream free-market feminism has not always accommodated the very real human need for retreat, reflection, and rest.

Living with Chronic Illness

In the mid-1980s, Patricia Fraser, a Harvard University Medical School physician working with chronically ill patients at Brigham and Women's Hospital in Boston, recognized that women with lupus—an invisible chronic illness that includes among other symptoms debilitating pain and extreme fatigue—face unique and painful challenges living up to the contradictory expectations society ascribes to all women:

> For most of us non-superwomen in good health, the discrepancy between the real and the ideal is clear and the ideal is used as a guideline to modify our lives. During periods of high energy and heightened motivation we may attempt to emulate features of the superwomen, but as we fatigue we drop back to somewhere near or slightly above where we started. Nothing is lost and something is gained in the experience; no harm is done. With lupus the issues and stakes are always higher, the risks magnified (Aladjem 1986, 61–62).

The risks Fraser refers to here include the very real, potentially fatal risks women with lupus and similar chronic illnesses face when they push themselves beyond their physical, mental, and emotional capacities and attempt to ignore their need for rest.

Irving Zola has noted that most research on illness narratives usually ignores any "detailed descriptions of the physical disability itself, especially its chronic aspects" (cited in Hillyer 1993, 37). Barbara Hillyer describes this omission as a "cultural silencing of embodied disability" (37). Susan Wendell agrees that "people with disabilities and illnesses learn that most people do not want to know about the suffering they experience because of their bodies . . . interest in the subjective experience is rare" (1996, 91). But as Hillyer notes, "to disguise the pain denies the human connection, whether the disguise is meant to satisfy the demands of scholarly objectivity or those of political activism" (1993, 41). Thus it is important to look closely at the embodied subjectivity of women living with chronic illness as we trace the path of their self-transformation and its social implications. The precipitating event is a body that breaks down.

Living with Pain, Letting Go of Suffering

Pain can be a path to body knowing and self-centering like no other. For most healthy people feeling pain is a wake-up call. We look for the source, we seek relief, and we expect the pain to go away. Our experience of pain is not simply physical, however, as David Morris (1993, 3) makes clear when he observes that "pain is never the sole creation of our anatomy and physiology . . . it emerges . . . at the intersection of bodies, minds, and cultures." For women with chronic illness, living in pain brings body awareness into complete and total focus and initiates mental, emotional, and social challenges that require extraordinary effort to manage. As one woman reports:

> It seems to take everything in me to manage what I'm going through . . . like people are going to suck some energy out of me that I don't have to give to them because I have to stay on top of this for myself. I think it takes such tremendous amounts of energy to have pain. (Register 1987, 81)

While the intensity and scope can vary, pain that never goes away is a fact of life for most women with chronic illness. Unrelenting opportunity and bitter necessity force many women, such as Eileen Radziunas (1989), to become "connoisseurs" of their pain. She describes in exquisite detail experiences that are invisible to others, who, over time and in the face of no firm diagnosis, may be inclined to deny their reality.

> Unlike other patients who I'd heard say "pain is pain," I knew there were different ways to describe it, because I felt it at such different levels. I detailed the deep, penetrating muscle pain, as opposed to the intense burning pain on the surface of my skin. I named the specific joints which ached routinely, and I pointed out that my tendons also hurt relentlessly, causing me as much pain at rest as during activity. I mentioned my transient blurry vision and excessive hair loss. It seemed superfluous to mention the bright red rash which ran across my cheeks and nose. (84)

For some, pain is so unpredictable and intense that it takes on a "terroristic" quality. Cheri Register (1987) describes her acute flare ups this way:

> I feel [like] concrete [is] filling my liver until it bursts and spills into my abdominal cavity, hardening as it is poured so that its rough edges grate against my diaphragm and the muscles between my ribs. I can't breathe, I can't lie down, and I can't imagine anything worse . . . the knowledge that

pain like this can come on at any time never leaves me, though I have good stretches when I don't have to dwell on it. Thus the threat of pain determines, to a great extent, how I live my life, even though nothing I do can prevent it. Starting out the day is a little like heading down a dark street where a rape and an armed robbery have recently taken place. (180–81)

At these moments, when pain is the dominant mode of her existence, Register finds the possibility of acceptance and transformation remote, if not impossible: "When pain grows intense enough to force recognition, it demands complete attention. As I know it, severe pain is isolating and totally absorbing. I can't do anything but hurt. I simply have not learned how to "accept" these awful experiences. They undo me every time" (181).

But dealing with pain and rationing energy are at the heart of letting go and self-transforming for many women with chronic illness. Some women reach the point where their suffering and torment transmutes into "just pain":

From my own and other people's experiences of chronic pain, I have learned that pain is an interpreted experience . . . For example, it is a fascinating paradox that a major aspect of the painfulness of pain, or I might say the suffering caused by pain, is the desire to get rid of it, to escape from it, to make it stop. A cultivated attitude of acceptance toward it, giving in to it, or just watching/observing it as an experience like others, can reduce the suffering it usually causes. (Wendell 1996, 181)

Susan Wendell's description here is reminiscent of a form of Zen meditation. Notice the pain (thought, sensation, emotion), recognize without attachment or resistance, and let it go. Watch as it changes or transforms. Perhaps this is how/why some women with chronic illness seem eventually to become happier than they were before their illness. Perhaps this focused attention to their bodies, coupled with their acceptance that they can't will their pain or bodily uncertainty away, but must learn to live with it, functions as a sort of an untutored and natural Zen practice. There seems to be a transformation of consciousness that comes through awareness and acceptance of the body in pain, as Wendell goes on to explain. "It is difficult for most people who have not lived with prolonged or recurring pain to understand the benefits of accepting it. Yet some people who live with chronic pain speak of 'making friends' with it as the road to feeling better and enjoying life" (109).

Paying more attention to our experience of our bodies can wake us up to what we are thinking, feeling, sensing, and provide an opportunity to choose how we will respond to the stimulus. But, according to Wendell, such an effort requires restructuring our lives to include more time for contemplation and rest. "In a sense I discovered that experiences of the body can teach consciousness a certain freedom from the sufferings and limitations of the body. . . . Of course, it requires structuring my life so that I can rest and withdraw my attention into my body much more than healthy people my age normally do" (172).

Making time to rest becomes crucial for women with chronic illness who live with unrelenting pain and profound fatigue that is unpredictable and invisible to others. But how do they deal with unremitting social pressure in a neoliberal environment that tells them to push on, prove themselves, and be "productive"?

Fatigue and the Pressure to Push On

For most chronically ill women, the unexpected move from health to sudden, inexplicable illness creates an energy vacuum that is unrelieved by rest:

> It is not the good tiredness after a game of tennis. The invigorating tiredness of a morning spent digging in the garden. Or even the satisfying tiredness of swimming thirty-six pool laps. This tiredness is in a class all its own. Every cell feels like it's coated with some thick matter, making my blood heavy and sluggish, a weight. It's like there's a thin grey mesh throughout my body and the blood has to push its way through this mesh to give me the energy just to move. Every cell is exhausted with the effort. It is the tiredness of a body at odds with an element, a body trying to swim upstream against the current. At the beginning, in my twenties, I wake up in the morning feeling this way. I carry this fatigue through every part of every day, soldier on smiling, and inside, feel more and more distanced from everything and everybody around me. (Clarke 2002, 53–54)

The bone-crushing fatigue that artist and writer Jude Clarke—who has lupus—describes so devastatingly is unlike any most able-bodied women will ever know. It is the kind of exhaustion that makes lifting a coffee cup a supreme effort of will; the kind of exhaustion that is unrelieved by rest. Here the body takes center stage in a radically different context than one of body image or even of women's control over our bodies. For women with invisible chronic illnesses such as lupus that flare-up unexpectedly, the experience of being a body, an embodied woman, is centrally an issue of confronting radical bodily uncertainty coupled with excruciating pain and profound fatigue. Suddenly and for no apparent reason the body rebels, and formerly normal everyday activities become impossible to achieve.

Yet as these memoirs by feminist women with invisible chronic illness attest, many struggle initially to maintain former levels of activity. They do this, no doubt, in part because those activities have been rewarding and intrinsically important in their lives. But the heroic effort of many women, including those who can afford to take time off, to "soldier on" in the midst of profound bodily crisis indicates to me that there may also be cultural pressures to sustain impossible standards of high productivity even in the face of overwhelming fatigue and pain. Cheri Register talked to many women in this very predicament. One describes her experience this way:

> [M]y department head came to me and said I had to go on full time or lose my job. They couldn't justify three quarter time anymore. He said, "Are you OK now?" Of course, I said, "Yes, I'm OK. I'll do it." In my heart, I really think it's self-destructive. It scares me to death to think about going public with something like I can't work full time. It scares me to death that somebody's going to say, "What are you talking about? Who do you think you are?" I don't know why, but I'm really afraid of that. I'd rather risk my own happiness and be exhausted every day and bitchy at night. (Register 1987, 89)

Hers is not a hypothetical or paranoid fear. Even women who accept their limitations and honor their need to slow down run into resistance, particularly when their symptoms are invisible:

> [W]hen I had recovered enough strength to return to work part time, I no longer looked very ill although I still fought a daily battle with exhaustion, pain, nausea, and dizziness, and I used a cane to keep my balance. I was struggling and since people could not see that I was struggling I was constantly explaining to them that I was struggling, that I could no longer do things that I had done before and that I did not know when or even if I would ever be able to do them again. I simply wanted my friends and the people I worked with to recognize my limitations and to accept as I had that they might be permanent, but it is hard to describe the invisible reality of disability to others without feeling that you are constantly complaining and asking for sympathy . . . others resisted believing that I might never regain my previous health and ability. They tried to talk me out of attitudes and actions that they saw as "giving up hope" and that I saw as acceptance and rebuilding my life. (Wendell 1996, 27)

Here Susan Wendell deals with overt interpersonal and institutional pressures that explicitly reject her efforts to accept her own limitations and rebuild a slower, quieter life. For women such as Jude Clarke, whose recurring symptoms are debilitating yet invisible, this can create an increasing sense of isolation from others who cannot see, much less feel, what she is experiencing, and can inaugurate an increasing alienation from self and other:

> Glancing over at the other art students and seeing their energy, the energy I used to have, I feel separate. Different. This disease is not going to go away.

I will never feel like myself again. I will have to work twice as hard to be the
person I want to be. Thus begins the charade . . . to the rest of the world I
present a different front. I'm not even honest with my doctors. I rarely talk
about the physical pain I'm in. I can hide (or think I can) this fatigue from
people. Rise to the occasion. And inside, be desperate to just lay my head
down, to allay a profound weariness. (Clarke 2002, 54)

There are many reasons why women with invisible chronic illness may want
to hide their difficulties, including a desire for privacy, resistance to being la-
beled or judged, and just wanting to be treated like everybody else. But I wonder
if for some of us there might also be at work, in our competitive, achievement-
oriented, advertising-driven, neoliberal consumer capitalist society, an unspoken yet internalized mandate that says we are never good enough and must
always prove our worth. Ever-accelerating, unreasonable cultural standards push
not only women with chronic illness, but all of us to ignore or hide our pain and
need for rest. As Wendell explains:

Other ideals can sneak up on us, becoming standards of normality because
they enter into a society's competitive structure. For example when the pace
of life increases, stamina becomes more important to participation in every
aspect of society, and what was once regarded as an ideal level of energy
gradually comes to be regarded as normal. Everyone who cannot keep up is
urged to take steps (or medications) to increase their energy, and bodies that
were once considered normal are pathologized. In my society, I have noticed
that it has become increasingly unacceptable to "slow down" as one ages,
when not long ago it was expected. (1996, 39)

Cultural pressure to perform competitively and keep up the pace ignores
and/or denigrates the intrinsic value of all people, including people in advanced
age, with their long years of experience and attendant wisdom. A colleague preparing to retire pulled me aside to tell me that he would have liked to stay on
and believed he still had much to offer our students but had come to feel that
too many of the faculty in the department discounted the value of his thirty-plus
years of experience because he had stopped publishing research. Such relentless
performance norms also remain in place even when our bodies and minds demand that we rest. Wendell notes, "much of the public world is . . . structured as
though everyone were physically strong . . . as though everyone could work and
play at a pace that is not compatible with any kind of illness or pain, as though
no one . . . ever . . . simply needed to sit or lie down" (39).
People dealing with advanced age, illness, and/or physical pain are not the
only ones who suffer in a culture that pushes them relentlessly and provides

inhumanely designed public spaces that deny opportunities for rest. The unreasonable expectation of fast pace and high productivity is continually replicated in neoliberal capitalist institutions, including universities. I think of this whenever I see exhausted college students stretching out as best they can on the second hand benches in our drab institutional hallway. It reminds me of Buddhist sociologist Inge Bell's admonition that "Rest when tired" should be engraved above the entrance to every dorm building in every college and university (Bell, McGrane, and Gunderson 2011). But more commonly, "push past your limits" is the message that drives our culture, and it can be particularly frightening for women with invisible chronic illness, such as Cheri Register, who may be inclined to "overcompensate" for their apparent shortcomings:

> Having your capacity to work threatened also makes you take your commitment to work more seriously. You quickly learn to compensate for your shortcomings. If your pace is slowed, you work longer hours, if the job allows it, to keep up your output. For every responsibility you have to drop, you take on another that you can handle. If your symptoms are intermittent rather than constant, you work in a frenzy on the healthy days. Work that is transportable goes along to the sickbed. . . . This approach does not always allay the fears. . . . There is no clear line of demarcation between working to maintain a reasonably normal and healthy life and the fairly common phenomenon of overcompensation, defying limits at some risk to your health. (1987, 98–99)

When Is Good-Enough Good Enough?

Finding a healthy balance between working productively and taking care of one's health ought not to be a terrifying experience. Cheri Register's poignant account of her own difficulty tells me there may be an irrational aspect to the work that we do in the United States. The achievement imperative continues even in the face of diminishing returns. For the chronically ill more work often equals less health. In this era of seemingly permanent economic crisis for all but the wealthy, the so-called "new normal" with its stagnant or non-existent job opportunities, depressed wages, frozen salaries, and decreased elite political support for investment in the public good (which everyday working Americans still very much favor)—higher performance expectations are incommensurate with higher pay, and most of us are asked to do more for less.[2]

In this political, economic, and cultural context, listening to the body, self-defining what is good-enough, and resisting unreasonable interpersonal and institutional demands feels like a radical and even dangerous act. What might this process look like for non-chronically ill women, and what outcomes might they expect? Feminist critic and practicing Buddhist bell hooks (2003) describes her experience in a secure position as a distinguished full professor. As she explains, promotion and tenure do not necessarily free a woman in academia to pursue a balanced life that includes rest, recreation, or intellectual play:

> Like many professors I naively believed that the more I moved up the academic ladder the more freedom I would gain, only to find that greater academic success carried with it even more pressure to conform, to ally oneself with institutional goals and values rather than with [radically open creative and critical] intellectual work. . . . Being an intellectual is not the same as being an academic. (23)

> As an intellectual working as an academic I often felt that my commitment to radical openness and devotion to critical thinking, to seeking after truth, was at odds with the demands that I uphold the status quo if I wanted to be rewarded. My integrity was as much at risk in the academic world as it had been in the non-academic work world, where workers are expected to obey authority and follow set rules. While much lip service is given to the notion of free speech in academic settings, in actuality constant censorship—often self-imposed—takes place. (22)

For hooks, letting go began with a two year unpaid leave of absence from her academic position to go on a lecture tour and refuel her emotional tank. She subsequently quit her tenured position at the City University of New York and spent some time free of institutional constraints (and supports) until she accepted a non-traditional teaching position at Berea College in her home state of Kentucky. Hooks was physically strong, economically secure, and socially well positioned to radically reframe her life in a more personally satisfying way, yet she still struggled in a long process to recognize her needs and take action.

How much harder, then, for working class women who can't afford it? Even relatively affluent women, including those with chronic illness, grapple with the question, "When is good-enough an acceptable and respectable position?" Cheri Register characterizes her relationship to her work ambivalently:

> Consciousness of mortality has lowered my ambition for a stellar career and altered my sense of worthwhile rewards. . . . I have chosen to live with spotty employment among family and old friends, and in sight of lakes, deciduous trees, and cumulus clouds. I take on temporary projects . . . and do my own research and writing at a pace that allows me to stay healthy and productive and also make the best of single motherhood. Temporary alimony gives me the financial cushion required to do this, but I will soon have to find a steadier source of income. To my colleagues inside academe, I may seem passive or even blasé, but I am quite passionate about the work itself.

I must admit, however, that I am still occasionally tripped up by unfulfilled expectations of grandiosity. They come in the form of self-accusations like . . . what have I done with my life? (1987, 101–2)

Register creates a manageable and personally satisfying life that includes research, writing, motherhood, and the support of family, natural beauty, and good friends, and yet remains prone to self-doubts about her worth. Gradually her ongoing experience with chronic illness (and reading the work of other women dealing with disability) helps her shift her perspective and ease up on her internalized demands for relentless production and performance. Here she quotes a passage from May Sarton's *Journal of a Solitude*:

I always forget how important the empty days are, how important it may be sometimes not to expect to produce anything, even a few lines in a journal. I am still pursued by a neurosis about work inherited from my father. A day where one has not pushed oneself to the limit seems a damaged damaging day, a sinful day. Not so! The most valuable thing we can do for the psyche, occasionally, is to let it rest, wander, live in the changing light of a room, not try to be or do anything whatever. (103)

As I mentioned earlier, my interest in letting go is both professional and personal. I have known for a while, both intuitively and intellectually, this way of being that Sarton describes, and have practiced it ambivalently since becoming an academic, often feeling the sense of someone looking over my shoulder and judging me as unproductive and unworthy. And I have been challenged to understand why others don't subscribe to Sarton's very sensible advice. It sometimes seems to me as though universities believe the only way to motivate faculty to remain productive after tenure is to pressure them to achieve more and to use negative evaluations as prods. This approach has been completely counterproductive in my case. Instead, giving myself the gift of "unproductive" restful, creative, and meditative time has paradoxically allowed me to enjoy researching exactly this question: "Why don't we allow ourselves more rest, recreation, and play in our lives?" Cheri Register seems to be asking the same thing: "Letting psyche and body rest together certainly seems like a healthy response to debilitating symptoms of illness, and I am practicing it more and more. I only wish that it didn't take pain or fever to force me to 'stop and smell the roses'" (103).

In her personal life and through her research with other women with chronic illness, Register eventually recognizes that serenity can occur when we listen to the body, let go of internalized compulsions about time and work, and redefine our life and self at a slower, quieter pace. As Peggy Evans, one of Register's interviewees, reports:

One thing I have gained in place of some of the losses is time—a very precious commodity. Sometimes I think it's too bad I'm not doing something marvelous with it, like writing a book or painting pictures, but I'm not, and it doesn't really bother me. What do I do with all this time? I spend a lot of it looking out the windows, at that beautiful scenery. I enjoy the birds and the rabbits and the cats that come and drink from the birdbath and the people jogging. I feel very much a part of all the joggers. It makes me feel less inactive. I've gotten to know people that I wouldn't have known before. I have time to spend with other people who have more time, and some of them have been handicapped in a way. They have a lot to share and offer. I have a thing I just delight in doing, and I could do it all day and all night, and I sometimes do, and that is fooling around with designs. . . . It's so much fun to be able to do it without feeling guilty. (104)

How refreshing to hear someone celebrate so genuinely a satisfying and "guilt-free" life of just being, watching, listening, playing, and sharing. Here physical losses bring unanticipated rewards. Peggy doesn't have to be or do anything special to justify her place in the world. She is at peace with herself and her life.

Going Beyond the Bright Side

But this is not a happier-ever-after fairytale. We are not talking about sainthood or martyrdom or the phony heroic illness narratives our culture finds so comforting. It is a long process of discovering ultimately that letting go of the illusion of control and being with what is, is the only way to stay alive. For women with chronic illness, it is a hard won and constantly challenging freedom. Some women who were striving to prove their worth in the world are forced through circumstances outside their control to accept that everything changes, that healthy bodies can become incapacitated without warning, and that our illusions of control are just that, illusory. These women learn the Serenity Prayer as a way of life, because they have no choice.[3] They learn what to let go and when to let go. Knowing themselves to be sometimes vulnerable and weak, they grow compassion for themselves and others and immunity to trivial pursuits. Their energy wanes for drama, competition, gossip, comparing, or striving. They let go of the future and the past and live in the moment of everyday life. Without seeking for it they find a path to freedom. Theirs is a Zen life without the Zen.

And with this letting go something unexpected takes place: an inner quiet and freedom from social expectations that formerly held one in their grip. As Susan Wendell describes, the unanticipated consequence of living with chronic, invisible, unpredictable illness can be a new sense of self grounded in bodily awareness and the surrender of unrealizable social norms:

When I look back on the beginning of my illness, I still think of it, as I did then, as an involuntary violation of my body. But now I feel that such violations are sometimes the beginnings of a better life, in that they force the self to expand or be destroyed. Illness has forced me to change in ways that I am grateful for, and so, although I would joyfully accept a cure if it were offered me, I do not regret having become ill. Yet I do not believe that I became ill *because* I needed to learn what illness has taught me, nor that I will get well when I have learned everything I need to know from it. (1996, 175)

Wendell has not been "bright-sided" by her illness experience, yet she is grateful for how it has transformed her in unexpected ways.[4]

Transforming Selves, Transforming Societies

The lessons from Zen and women with invisible chronic illness seem to indicate that once we know ourselves in a deeply embodied way, we have the potential to free ourselves—from achievement mandates that tell us we are never good enough, accumulation mandates that tell us we will never have enough, attention mandates that tell us we don't count unless we are looked at and admired. Letting go of control over things we can't control, such as incurable illness, may enact a transformative process that allows for the rejection of social norms that have functioned to limit and constrain or push and exhaust, and for the rewriting of a new set of possibilities of being and time. A key transformative moment occurs when women accept "This is my body, these are my limits, these are my priorities, there is only this moment, I can let go of everything else." Is this a feminist breakthrough?

On its face letting go in this way challenges basic feminist tenets that women (as opposed to men) should control all aspects of women's lives and (more covertly) that women should excel in all pursuits. Superwoman expectations that emerged in the wake of feminist gains did and do exist for some women who "want to have it all." And some feminists who also happen to be disabled or responsible to care for someone who is disabled have written about this issue. As Barbara Hillyer (1993) notes:

[In American culture] rushing from one activity to another is highly valued by others and oneself. It is not surprising, then, that "supercrip" and "superwoman" are roles that the movements for disability and women's rights are ambivalent about. We deplore the apparent necessity to be superhuman (stronger than able-bodied white males) but admire people who can do it and demand as much of ourselves. Better to be a superwoman than to be weak or dependent. (52)

Hillyer writes about the mainstream feminist bias for strong, highly productive, politically-active roles for women in society. She calls for a feminist theory that also acknowledges that "human beings are limited; that some losses cannot be repaired; and above all, that female strength and weakness must be integrated" (15). All of us are destined to age, decline, and die, says Hillyer, and women need a more intimate and grounded experience of body knowing and self-centering to help us navigate this inevitable developmental path. Hillyer describes a grief that arises from "being in touch with one's limitations," feeling less safe, recognizing one's vulnerability, and exploring

> the nature of one's own "real" condition—not idealized or misinterpreted by the culture. . . . In a culture like ours that values optimism and a cheery willingness to minimize difficulties, it is very difficult to see oneself as a person with a serious problem . . . recognition that she is a person with a serious difficulty defined from within forces a woman to find significance in her life as it is. (16)

Acknowledging human vulnerability and finding significance in life as it is has the potential not only for radical self-transformation, but for radical social transformation as well. As Hester Eisenstein argues, returning to the body is a crucial component in revitalizing a feminist politics that is critical of so-called "free-market" economies and advocates instead for a broad social compact committed to compassion and care. A feminist theory of letting go necessitates a radical rethinking of what it means to live as a woman in a culture that mandates we give it our all. And for some women, accepting limitations and rebuilding lives based on a slower, quieter and self-determined pace has—as an unintended consequence—not only self-transformation and the seeds of social transformation, but increased joy in life as it is.

NOTES

1. Hester Eisenstein (2009:14) credits Jaqui Alexander and Chandra Talpade Mohanty for coining the term "free market feminism" to describe how in the 1990s the "Clinton administration was using mainstream feminism to sell 'free market' capitalism to the world."
2. See for example, John Ydstie, "The New Normal," *All Things Considered*, NPR, July 12, 2011. *www.npr.org/2011/07/12/137708256/what-the-new-normal-means-for-americans*.
3. The serenity prayer is attributed to Reinhold Niebuhr and is recited at Alcoholics Anonymous meetings (*www.aahistory.com/prayer.html*). It goes like this:
    [G]rant us the serenity to accept the things we cannot change,
    courage to change the things we can, and wisdom to know the difference.
4. See for example, Barbara Ehrenreich, *Bright-Sided: How Positive Thinking is Undermining America* (New York: Metropolitan Books, 2009).

REFERENCES

Aladjem, Henrietta. 1986. *Understanding Lupus*. New York: Charles Scribner.

Beck, Charlotte Joko. 1989. *Everyday Zen: Love and Work*. San Francisco: Perennial/Harper & Row.

Bell, Inge, Bernard McGrane, and John Gunderson. 2011. *This Book is Not Required: An Emotional and Intellectual Survival Manual for Students*, 4th edition. Thousand Oaks, CA: Pine Forge.

Clarke, Jude. 2002. *The Language of Water: A Woman's Struggle with Systemic Lupus Erythematosus*. Saskatchewan, Canada: Thistledown.

Edwards, David. 2005. "Life or Death." *Tricycle Magazine*, Fall 2005. *www.tricycle.com/ my-view/life-or-death*.

Eisenstein, Hester. 2009. *Feminism Seduced: How Global Elites Use Women's Labor and Ideas to Exploit the World*. Boulder, CO: Paradigm.

Harris, Leah. 2006. "If the Buddha Gave Birth: Review of *Mama Zen: Walking the Crooked Path of Motherhood*." *Literary Mama*, December 21. *www.literarymama.com/reviews/ archives/2006/12/if-the-buddha-gave-birth.html*.

Hillyer, Barbara. 1993. *Feminism and Disability*. Norman, OK: University of Oklahoma.

hooks, bell. 2003. *Teaching Community: Toward a Pedagogy of Hope*. New York: Routledge.

Loy, David R. 1996. *Lack and Transcendence: The Problem of Death and Life in Psychotherapy, Existentialism, and Buddhism*. Amherst, NY: Humanity Books.

———. 2003. *The Great Awakening: A Buddhist Social Theory*. Boston: Wisdom.

Morris, David. 1993. *The Culture of Pain*. Berkeley: University of California.

National Public Radio (NPR) Staff. 2011. "The Bottle Rockets: Heartland Tales of Heartbreak." *All Things Considered Weekend Edition*, August 14. *www.npr. org/2011/08/14/139586886/the-bottle-rockets-heartland-tales-of-heartbreak*.

Radziunas, Eileen. 1989. *Lupus: My Search for a Diagnosis*. Claremont, CA: Hunter House.

Register, Cherry. 1987. *Living with Chronic Illness: Days of Patience and Passion*. New York: Free Press.

Wendell, Susan. 1996. *The Rejected Body: Feminist Philosophical Reflections on Disability*. New York: Routledge.

2

On the Interdependence
of Personal and Social Transformation

David R. Loy

> The mercy of the West has been social revolution.
> The mercy of the East has been individual insight
> into the basic self/void. We need both.
> —Gary Snyder, *Earth House Hold*

The highest ideal of the Western tradition has been the concern to restructure our societies so that they are more socially just. The most important goal for Buddhism is to awaken and let go of the delusion of a separate self by (to use the Zen phrase) realizing one's true nature, thus putting an end to suffering. Today it has become more obvious that we need both social justice and individual awareness: not just because these ideals complement each other, but because each project needs the other.

Abrahamic emphasis on justice, in combination with the Greek realization that society can be restructured, has resulted in our modern concern to pursue social justice by reforming political and economic institutions. This has involved, most obviously, various human rights movements (the abolition of slavery, the civil rights movement, feminism, LGBT liberation), which have not been an important concern of traditional Asian Buddhism. As valuable as these reforms have been, the limitations of an institutional approach, by itself, are becoming evident. Even the best possible economic and political system cannot be expected to function well if the people within that system are motivated by greed, aggression, and delusion—the "three fires" or "three poisons" that Buddhism identifies as unwholesome motivations that need to be transformed into their more positive counterparts: generosity, loving-kindness, and wisdom.

Bringing together the Hebrew concern for social justice with the Greek realization that society can be restructured has resulted in what seems to me the highest ideal of the West, actualized in revolutions, reform movements, the development and spread of democracy, human rights—in short, social progress. We are all too aware of the shortcomings of this progress, but our concern with those shortcomings itself testifies to our social justice principles, which we understand to be universal but which are actually historically conditioned and not to be taken for granted.

Even with the best ideals (what might be called our collective intentions), our societies have not become as socially just as most of us would like, and in some ways they are becoming more unjust. An obvious economic example is the gap between rich and poor in the United States, which today is not only obscenely large but increasing.[1] How shall we understand this disparity between ideal and reality? One obvious reply is that our economic system, as it presently operates, is still unjust because wealthy people and powerful corporations manipulate our political systems for their own self-centered and shortsighted benefit. We need to keep working for a more equitable economic system and for a democratic process free of such distortions.

I would not want to challenge that explanation, but is it sufficient? Is the basic difficulty that our economic and political institutions are not structured well enough to avoid such manipulations, or is it also the case that they *cannot* be structured well enough—in other words, that we cannot rely only on an institutional solution to structural injustice? Can we create a social order so perfect that it will function well regardless of the personal motivations of the people within it? Or do we also need to find ways to address those motivations? In short, can the social transformations that our ideals seek be successful enough without also considering the challenge of personal transformation?

Perhaps this helps us to understand why so many political revolutions have ended up replacing one gang of thugs with another gang. Suppose, for example, that I am a revolutionary leader who successfully overthrows an oppressive regime. If I have not also worked on my own motivations—my own greed, aggression, and delusion—I will be sorely tempted to take personal advantage of my new situation, inclined to see those who disagree with me as enemies to be eliminated, and (the number one ego problem?) disposed to see the solution to social issues in my superior judgment and the imposition of my will. Unsurprisingly, the results of such motivations are unlikely to bring about a society that is truly just. And of course these distortions are not restricted only to authoritarian rulers. Beginning with the earliest Greek experience, and certainly supported by contemporary experience in the United States, there is plenty of evidence that democracy does not work very well if it simply becomes a different system for certain individuals and groups to manipulate and exploit—again, usually motivated by the three poisons.

If we can never have a social structure so just that it obviates the need for people to let go of their own greed, aggression, and delusion of a separate self, then our modern emphasis on social transformation—restructuring institutions to make them more just—is necessary but not sufficient. That brings us to the Buddhist focus on personal transformation.

Ignorance versus Awakening

Of course, moral behavior is also important in Buddhism, most obviously observing the five precepts (for laypeople) and the hundreds of additional rules prescribed for monastics.[2] But if we view them in an Abrahamic fashion, we are liable to miss the main point: because there is no God telling us that we must live this way, they are important because living in accordance with them means that the circumstances and quality of our own lives will naturally improve. They can be understood as exercises in mindfulness, to train ourselves in a certain way.

The precepts can also be compared to the training wheels on the bicycle of a young child, which eventually can be removed because they are necessary only until the child knows how to ride a bike. For Buddhism the fundamental axis is not between good and evil, but between ignorance/delusion and awakening/wisdom. The primary challenge is not ethical but cognitive in the broad sense: becoming more aware. In principle, someone who has awakened to the true nature of the world (including the true nature of oneself) no longer needs to follow an external moral code because he or she *naturally* wants to behave in a way that does not violate the spirit of the precepts. (If only it worked so well in practice . . .)

Another way to express the interrelationship between the Western ideal of social transformation (social justice that addresses social suffering) and the Buddhist goal of personal transformation (an awakening that addresses individual suffering) is in terms of different types of freedom. The emphasis of the modern West has been on individual freedom from oppressive institutions, a prime example being the Bill of Rights appended to the US Constitution. The emphasis of Buddhism (and many other Indian traditions) has been on what might be called psycho-spiritual freedom: freedom from the (ego)self. Today we can see more clearly the limitations of each freedom by itself. What have I gained if I am free from external control but still at the mercy of my own greed, aggression, and delusions? Awakening from the delusion of a separate self will not by itself free me, or all those with whom I remain interdependent in so many ways, from the suffering perpetuated by an exploitative economic system and an oppressive government. Again, we need to actualize both ideals to be truly free.

The Suffering of Economic Injustice

From the above, one might conclude that contemporary Buddhism simply needs to incorporate a Western concern for social justice. Yet that would overlook the distinctive social consequences of the Buddhist understanding of suffering. To draw out some of those implications, let us consider our economic situation today.

Until the modern era, economic theory was understood to be part of social philosophy and, in principle, subordinate to religious authority (e.g., Church prohibitions of usury). Today the academic profession of economics is concerned with modeling itself on the authority of the hard sciences and becoming a social science by discovering the fundamental laws of economic exchange and development, which are assumed to be objectively true in a similar way to Newton's laws of motion.

What this has meant, in practice, is that such a focus tends to rationalize the kind of system we have today, including the increasing gap between rich and poor. Despite many optimistic new reports about economic recovery (for banks and investors, at least), in the United States that disparity is now the greatest it has been since the great depression of the 1930s. We have become familiar with evidence that, for example, the wealthiest four hundred families in America now have the same total wealth as the poorest half of Americans—over 150 million people.[3] If it is argued, however, that this is happening in accordance with the basic laws of economic science—well, we may not like this development and may try to limit it in some way, but fundamentally we need to adapt to big disproportions. In this way such a disparity is normalized, with the implication that it should be accepted.

"But it's not *fair!*" In opposition to such efforts to justify the present economic order, there are movements that call for social justice—in this case, for distributive justice. Why should the wealthy have so much, and the poor so little? For an economic system to be just, its benefits should be distributed much more equitably. And I would not disagree with that. But can the Buddhist emphasis on delusion versus awakening provide an alternative perspective to supplement such a concern for social justice?

I conclude by offering what I believe to be two implications of Buddhist teachings. One of them focuses on our *individual* predicament—one's personal role in our economic system—and the other implication considers the structural or *institutional* aspect of that system.

What I have to say about our personal economic predicament follows from what is perhaps the most important teaching of the Buddha: the relationship between suffering and *anatta*, "not-self" or "nonself." *Anatta* challenges our usual but delusive sense of being a separate self; it is the strange, counterintuitive claim that there is no such self. One way to understand this teaching is that there is a basic problem with the sense of a "me" *inside* that is separate from other people, and from the rest of the world, *outside*. In contemporary terms, this sense of self is a psychological and social construction. Although the development of a sense of self seems necessary in order to function in the world, Buddhism emphasizes the suffering associated with it. Why?

Because the self is a construct; it does not have any self-existence, any reality of its own. The sense of self is composed of mostly habitual ways of thinking, feeling, acting, intending, remembering, and so forth; the ways these processes interact is what creates and sustains it. The important point is that such a construct is inevitably shadowed by suffering. Because all those processes are impermanent and insubstantial, the self is not only ungrounded but ungroundable, thus inherently insecure.

One way to express this is to say that the sense of self is usually haunted by a sense of lack: the feeling that something is wrong with me, that something is missing or not quite right about my life (Loy 1996). Normally, however, we misunderstand the source of our discomfort and believe that what we are lacking is something outside ourselves. And this brings us back to our individual economic predicament, because in the "developed" world we often grow up conditioned to understand ourselves as consumers and to understand the basic problematic of our lives as getting more money (power, fame, sex) in order to acquire more things (control, attention, satisfaction), because this is what will eventually fill up our sense of lack.

Thus there is an almost perfect fit between this fundamental sense of lack that unenlightened beings have, according to Buddhism, and our present economic system, which uses advertising and other devices to condition us into believing that the next thing we buy will make us happy—which it never does, at least not for long. In other words, a consumerist economy exploits our sense of lack, and often aggravates it, rather than helping us resolve the root problem. The system generates profits by perpetuating our discontent in a way that leaves us always wanting more.

Such a critique of consumerism is consistent with some recent studies by psychologists, sociologists, and even economists, who have established that once one attains a certain minimum income—enough food and shelter at a pretty basic level—happiness does not increase in step with increasing wealth or consumerism. Rather, the most important determinate of how happy people are seems to be the quality of one's relationships with other people. (See, for example, Gilbert 2007, Lyubomirsky 2008, and Ricard and Goleman 2007).

Notice that this Buddhist perspective does not mention distributive justice or any other type of social justice, nor does it offer an ethical evaluation. The basic problem is delusion rather than injustice or immorality. Yet this approach does not deny the inequities of our economic system, nor is it inconsistent with an Abrahamic ethical critique. Although an alternative viewpoint has been added, the ideal of social justice remains very important, necessary, but not sufficient.

What does this imply about our economic institutions, the structural aspect? The Buddha had little to say about injustice per se, but he had a lot to say about the three roots of evil, also known as the three poisons: greed, aggression, and delusion. When what we do is motivated by any of these three (and they tend to overlap), we create problems for ourselves (and often for others too, of course). Given the Buddha's emphasis on volition as the most important factor in generating karma, this may be the key to understanding karma: if you want to transform the quality of your life—how you experience other people and how they relate to you—transform your motivations.

We not only have individual senses of self, we also have collective selves: I am a man not a woman, American not Asian, and so forth. Do the problems with the three poisons apply to collective selves as well? To further complicate the issue, we also have much more powerful institutions than in the time of the Buddha, in which collective selves often assume a life of their own, in the sense that such institutions have their own motivations built into them. Elsewhere I have argued that our present economic system can be understood as institutionalized greed; that our militarism institutionalizes aggression; and that our (corporate) media institutionalize delusion because their primary focus is profiting from advertising and consumerism, rather than educating or informing us about what is really happening (Loy 2003, 2008).

If greed, aggression, and delusion are the main sources of suffering and injustice, and if today they have been institutionalized in this fashion . . . well, you can draw your own conclusions. I finish with a few words on how our economic system promotes structural suffering by institutionalizing greed.

What is greed? One definition is "never enough." On the individual level, it is the belief that next thing one buys will fill up one's sense of lack. But greed works just as well to describe what happens on an institutional level: corporations are never large enough or profitable enough, the value of their shares is never high enough, our national GDP is never big enough. . . . In fact, we cannot imagine what "big enough" might be. It is built into these systems that they must keep growing, or else they tend to collapse. But why is more always better if it can never be enough?

Consider the stock market, high temple of the economic process. On the one side are many millions of investors, most anonymous and unconcerned about the details of the corporations they invest in, except for their profitability and its effects on share prices—that is, the return on their investments. In many cases investors do not know where their money is invested, thanks to mutual funds. Such people are not evil, of course: on the contrary, investment is a highly respectable endeavor, something to do if you have some extra money, and successful investors are highly respected, even idolized (e.g., "the sage of Omaha").

On the other side of the market, however, the desires and expectations of those millions of investors become transformed into an impersonal and unremitting pressure for growth and increased profitability that every CEO must respond to, and preferably in the short run. If a CEO does not maximize profitability, he or she is likely to get into trouble. Consider, for example, the CEO of a large transnational corporation who one morning suddenly wakes up to the imminent dangers of climate change and wants to do everything he (it is usually a he) can to address this challenge. But if what he tries to do threatens corporate profits, he is likely to lose his job. And if that is true for the CEO, how much more true it is for everyone else further down the corporate hierarchy. Corporations are legally chartered so that their first responsibility is not to their employees or customers, nor to the members of the societies they operate within, nor to the ecosystems of the earth, but to the individuals who own them, who with few exceptions are concerned only about return on investment—a preoccupation, again, that is not only currently socially acceptable but socially encouraged.

What is responsible for this situation—our collective fixation on growth? The important point is that the system has attained not only a life of its own but also its own volitions, quite apart from the motivations of the individuals who work for it and who will be replaced if they do not serve that institutional motivation. And all of us participate in this process in one way or another, as workers, consumers, investors, pensioners, and so forth, although with very little if any sense of personal responsibility for the collective result. Any awareness of what is actually happening tends to be diffused in the impersonal anonymity of this economic process. Everyone is just doing their job, playing their role.

In short, any genuine solution to the economic crisis cannot simply involve better redistribution of wealth, necessary as that is. We must also find ways to address the personal suffering built into the delusions of consumerism, and the structural suffering built into institutions that have attained a life of their own. It has become obvious that what is beneficial for those institutions (in the short run) is very different from what is beneficial for the rest of us and for the biosphere.

Can Mindfulness Change a Corporation?

Let me conclude with a letter I wrote to William George, a Goldman Sachs board member and proponent of meditation in the service of corporate profits. I want to emphasize that I'm not attacking Mr. George himself, who (according to what I've read and heard) seems to be a nice, well-intentioned fellow. The basic problem is that one can be well intentioned and yet play an objectionable role in an economic system that has become unjust and unsustainable—in fact, a challenge to the wellbeing of all life on this planet. Mr. George is an important figure in the "mindfulness in business" movement. As well as being a professor in Harvard's MBA program, he has written some influential books that emphasize the importance of ethics and mindfulness in the marketplace. His position therefore highlights concerns I have about the role of the "mindfulness movement" in a neoliberal economy. And it has broad implications for socially engaged Buddhism.

16 October 2012
William George
George Family Office
1818 Oliver Ave.
S. Minneapolis, Minnesota 55405

Dear Mr. George,

We haven't met, but I'm taking the liberty of contacting you because you are in a position to contribute in a valuable way to an important debate that is developing within the Buddhist community in North America. (I'm a professor of Buddhist and comparative philosophy, and also a Zen student/teacher.)

The UK *Financial Times* magazine of August 25–26 included an article on "The Mind Business" that begins: "Yoga, meditation, 'mindfulness.' . . . Some of the west's biggest companies are embracing eastern spirituality—as a path which can lead to bigger profits." You are mentioned on p. 14:

> William George, a current Goldman Sachs board member and a former chief executive of the healthcare giant Medtronic, started meditating in 1974 and never stopped. Today, he is one of the main advocates for bringing meditation into corporate life, writing articles on the subject for the *Harvard Business Review*. "The main business case for meditation is that if you're fully present on the job, you will be more effective as a leader, you will make better decisions and you will work better with other people," he tells me [the author, David Gelles]. "I tend to live a very busy life. This keeps me focused on what's important" (Gelles 2012).

I was initially struck by your position (since 2002) as a board member of Goldman Sachs, one of the largest and most controversial investment banks. Researching online, I learned that you have also been on the corporate board of Exxon Mobil since 2005 and Novartis since 1999. I also read that you participated in a "Mind & Life" conference with the Dalai Lama and Yongey Mingyur Rinpoche, on "Compassion and Altruism in Economic Systems." These discoveries led to my decision to contact you, in order to get your perspective on what is becoming a crucial issue for Western Buddhists.

The debate within American Buddhism focuses on how much is lost if mindfulness as a technique is separated from other important aspects of the Buddhist path, such as precepts, community practice, awakening, and living compassionately. Traditional Buddhism understands all these as essential parts of a spiritual path that leads to personal transformation. More recently, there is also concern about the social implications of Buddhist teachings, especially given our collective ecological and economic situation. The Buddha referred to the "three poisons" of greed, ill will, and delusion as unwholesome motivations that cause suffering, and some of my own writing argues that today those three poisons have become institutionalized, taking on a life of their own.

I do not know how your meditation practice has affected your personal life, nor, for that matter, what type of meditation or mindfulness you practice. Given your unique position, my questions are: how has your practice influenced your understanding of the social responsibility of large corporations such as Goldman Sachs and ExxonMobil? And what effects has your practice had personally on your advisory role within those corporations?

Hundreds of taxpayers rallied outside the Goldman Sachs [Washington] DC office in November 2009 to deliver a letter for its CEO, Lloyd Blankfein, demanding he forgo paying out its multi-billion dollar bonus pool and instead use that money to help the millions of families facing foreclosure.

Those questions are motivated by the controversial—I would say problematical—role of those two corporations recently in light of the various ecological, economic, and social crises facing us today. As you know, the pharmaceutical giant Novartis has also received much criticism. (In 2006 Novartis tried to stop India developing affordable generic drugs for poor people; in 2008 the FDA warned it about deceptive advertising of Focalin, an ADHD drug; in 2009 Novartis declined to follow the example of GlaxoSmithKline and offer free flu vaccines to poor people in response to a flu epidemic; in May 2010 a jury awarded over $253 million in compensatory and punitive damages for widespread sexual discrimination, a tentative settlement that may increase to almost $1 billion; in September 2010 Novartis paid $422.5 million in criminal and civil claims for illegal kickbacks.) However, my main interest is with your role on the corporate board of Goldman Sachs and ExxonMobil, and how your meditation practice may or may not have influenced that.

Since you have been on the Goldman Sachs board for a decade, you are no doubt very aware of the controversies that have dogged it for many years, and especially since the financial meltdown of 2008. There are so many examples that one hardly knows where to begin. In July 2010 Goldman paid a record $550 million to settle an SEC civil lawsuit, but that is only the tip of the iceberg. In April 2011 a Senate Subcommittee released an extensive report on the financial crisis alleging that Goldman Sachs appeared to have misled investors and profited from the mortgage market meltdown. The chairman of that subcommittee, Carl Levin, referred this report to the Justice Department for possible prosecution; later he expressed disappointment when the Justice Department declined to do so, and said that Goldman's "actions were deceptive and immoral." Perhaps this relates to an ongoing issue: a "revolving door" relationship with the federal government, in which many senior employees move in and out of high level positions, which has led to numerous charges of conflict of interest. It may be no coincidence that Goldman Sachs was the single largest contributor to Obama's campaign in 2008.

In July 2011 a suit to fire all the members of Goldman's board—including you—for improper behavior during the financial crisis was thrown out of court, for lack of evidence.

Controversy ignited again this year when a senior Goldman employee, Greg Smith, published an Op Ed piece in the *New York Times* on "Why I Am Leaving Goldman Sachs" (March 14, 2012), writing that, "the environment [at Goldman Sachs] now is as toxic and destructive as I have ever seen it." He blames poor leadership for a drastic decline in its moral culture—which is especially interesting, given your own teaching emphasis on the importance of leadership. In just the few months since that Op Ed, however, Goldman has been fined in the UK for manipulating oil prices, and in separate US cases has paid $22 million for favoring select clients, $16 million for a pay-to-play scheme, $12 million for improper campaign donations, and $6.75 million to settle claims about how it handled option claims. Such fines seem to be acceptable as simply another cost of business, rather than a spur to change how the company conducts business.

Please understand that I'm not criticizing you for these illegal activities. Being on the board, you are not usually involved in day-to-day management. However, I would like to know how you view the "toxic environment" at Goldman Sachs, and the larger social responsibilities of such a powerful firm, in light of your own meditation practice. And since you have been on the Goldman board since 2002, how do you understand the responsibility of a board member in such a situation, and what role have you been able to play in affecting its problematical culture?

I am also curious about your position as a board member of ExxonMobil since 2005. It is reportedly the world's largest corporation ever, both by revenue and profits. According to a 2012 article in the *Daily Telegraph*, it has also "grown into one of the planet's most hated corporations, able to determine American foreign policy and the fate of entire nations" [Thomson 2012]. It is regularly criticized for risky drilling practices in endangered areas, poor response to oil spills (such as the Exxon Valdez in 1989), illegal foreign business practices, and especially its leading role in funding climate change denial.

ExxonMobil was instrumental in founding the first skeptic groups, such as the Global Climate Coalition. In 2007 a Union of Concerned Scientists report claimed that between 1998 and 2005 ExxonMobil spent $16 million supporting forty-three organizations that challenged the scientific evidence for global warming, and that it used disinformation tactics similar to those used by the tobacco industry to deny any link between smoking and lung problems, charges consistent with a leaked 1998 internal ExxonMobil memo.

In January 2007 the company seemed to change its position and announced that it would stop funding some climate-denial groups, but a July 2009 *Guardian* newspaper article [Adam 2009] revealed that it still supports lobbying groups that deny climate change, and a 2011 Carbon Brief study concluded that nine out of ten climate scientists who deny climate change have ties to ExxonMobil [Hunt 2011].

Even more important, the corporation's belated and begrudging acknowledgement that global change is happening has not been accompanied by any determination to change company policies to address the problem. Although there has been some recent funding for research into biofuels from algae, ExxonMobil has not moved significantly in the direction of renewable sources of energy such as solar and wind power. According to its 2012 *Outlook for Energy: A View to 2040* [ExxonMobil 2012], petroleum and natural gas will remain its main products: "By 2040, oil, gas and coal will continue to account for about 80 percent of the world's energy demand" (p. 46). This is despite the fact that many of the world's most reputable climate scientists are claiming that there is already much too much carbon in the atmosphere, and that we are perilously close to "tipping points" that would be disastrous for human civilization as we know it.

In response to this policy, I would like to learn how, in the light of your meditation practice, you understand the relationship between one's own personal transformation and the kind of economic and social transformation that appears to be necessary today if we are to survive and thrive during the next few critical centuries. How does your concern for future generations express itself in your activities as a board member of these corporations (among others)? Are you yourself skeptical about global warming? If not, how do you square that with your role at ExxonMobil?

Let me conclude by emphasizing again that this letter is not in any way meant to be a personal criticism. From what I have read and heard, you are generous with your time and money, helping many nonprofits in various ways. What I'm concerned about is the "compartmentalization" of one's meditation practice, so that mindfulness enables us to be more effective and productive in our work, and provides some peace of mind in our hectic lives, but does not encourage us to address the larger social problems that both companies (for example) are contributing to. Today the economic and political power of such corporations is so great that, unless they became more socially responsible, it is difficult to be hopeful about what the future holds for our grandchildren and their grandchildren.

What is the role of a corporate board member in critical times such as ours? I would much appreciate your reflections and your experience on this issue.

Sincerely yours,
David Loy
www.davidloy.org

Conclusion

The Western (now worldwide) ideal of a social transformation that institution-alizes social justice has achieved much, yet, I have argued, is limited because a truly just society cannot be realized without the correlative realization that personal transformation is also necessary. In the present generation—thanks to globalization, widespread transportation and digital communications—these two worldviews, with different but not conflicting ideals, are in conversation with each other. If I am correct, they need each other. Or more precisely, we need both.

This does not mean merely adding a concern for social justice to Buddhist teachings. Applying a Buddhist perspective to structural suffering implies an alternative evaluation of our economic situation. Instead of appealing for dis-tributive justice, this approach focuses on the consequences of individual and institutionalized delusion: the suffering of a sense of a self that feels separate from others, whose sense of lack consumerism exploits and institutionalizes into economic structures that assume a life (and motivations) of their own. Although fairness remains important in terms of equal opportunity and more equitable distribution, Buddhist emphasis on greed as a motivation—"never enough"—implies that, when institutionalized, greed ends up subverting the purpose of any economic system, which is to promote widespread and sustainable human flourishing.

Here the traditional Western concern for social justice is complemented by the Buddhist focus on ending suffering. Thus the role of greed must be ad-dressed not only individually, in our personal lives, but also its structural forms.

NOTES

1. Documentation and examples of this growing inequality abound. See Annie Lowrey, "The Wealth Gap in America is Growing Too," *economix.blogs.nytimes.com/2014/04/02/ the-wealth-gap-is-growing-too*.

2. The five Buddhist precepts include no killing or harming of sentient life; no stealing or taking what is not given; no sexual misconduct; no false speech; no taking of intoxicants (*online.sfsu.edu/rone/Buddhism/FivePrecepts/fiveprecepts.html*)

3. For yet another example of growing inequality see *currydemocrats.org/in_perspective/ american_pie.html*.

REFERENCES

Adam, David. 2009. "ExxonMobil Continuing to Fund Climate Skeptic Groups, Records Show." *Guardian*, July 1. *www.theguardian.com/environment/2009/jul/01/ exxon-mobil-climate-change-sceptics-funding*.

Hunt, Christian. 2011. "Analysing the '900 papers Supporting Climate Scepticism': 9 Out of Top 10 Authors Linked to ExxonMobil." *Analysis* (blog), *Carbon Brief*, April 15. *www. carbonbrief.org/blog/2011/04/900-papers-supporting-climate-scepticism-exxon-links*.

ExxonMobil. 2012. *The Outlook for Energy: A View to 2040. corporate.exxonmobil.com/en/ energy/energy-outlook*.

Gellas, David. 2012. "The Mind Business." *Financial Times*, August 24. *www.ft.com/cms/s/2/d9cb7940-ebea-11e1-985a-00144feab49a.html*.

Gilbert, Daniel. 2007. *Stumbling on Happiness*. New York: Knopf.

Loy, David R. 1996. *Lack and Transcendence: The Problem of Death and Life in Psychotherapy, Existentialism and Buddhism*. Amherst, NY: Humanities Books.

———. 2003. *The Great Awakening: A Buddhist Social Theory*. Boston: Wisdom Publications.

———. 2008. *Money Sex War Karma: Notes for a Buddhist Revolution*. Boston: Wisdom Publications.

Lyubomirsky, Sonja. 2008. *The How of Happiness: A New Approach to Getting the Life You Want*. New York: Penguin.

Ricard, Matthieu, and Daniel Goleman. 2007. *Happiness: A Guide to Developing Life's Most Important Skill*. New York: Little, Brown and Company.

Smith, Greg. 2012. "Why I Am Leaving Goldman Sachs." *New York Times*, March 14. *www.nytimes.com/2012/03/14/opinion/why-i-am-leaving-goldman-sachs.html*.

Snyder, Gary. 1969. *Earth House Hold: Technical Notes and Queries Follow Dharma REvolutionaries*. New York: New Directions.

Thomson, Ian. 2012. "Book Review: *Private Empire: Exxon Mobil and American Power* by Steve Coll." *Daily Telegraph*, July 30. *www.telegraph.co.uk/culture/books/bookreviews/9429215/Private-Empire-ExxonMobil-and-American-Power-by-Steve-Coll.html*.

Union of Concerned Scientists. 2007. *Smoke, Mirrors and Hot Air: How ExxonMobil Uses Big Tobacco's Tactics to Manufacture Uncertainty on Climate Science*. *www.ucsusa.org/global_warming/solutions/fight-misinformation/exxonmobil-report-smoke.html*.

3

Leaning In and Letting Go
Feminist Tools for Valuing Nonwork

Jennifer Randles

When Sheryl Sandberg, Chief Operating Officer of Facebook, published her 2013 book, *Lean In: Women, Work, and the Will to Lead*, it reinvigorated the debate over why women continue to lag behind men in leadership positions. In what she claims is a "sort of feminist manifesto" (9), Sandberg writes:

> In addition to the external barriers erected by society, women are hindered by barriers that exist within ourselves. We hold ourselves back in ways both big and small, by lacking self-confidence, by not raising our hands, and by pulling back when we should be leaning in. We internalize the negative messages we get throughout our lives—the messages that say it's wrong to be outspoken, aggressive, and more powerful than men. We lower our expectations of what we can achieve. . . . Getting rid of these internal barriers is critical to gaining power. (8)

Sandberg's central claim that women need to break down internal barriers to occupational success provoked strong resistance from many. Feminists were some of the loudest voices among this critical group. Their claims for social justice tend to focus on dismantling external institutional barriers that prevent women's rise to the top, such as workplace discrimination and the gendered division of family labor through which women still bear the brunt of unpaid housework. In stressing the importance of family-friendly workplace policies like parental leave and the value of empowering men at home to be equal nurturing caregivers, Sandberg acknowledges these external constraints. However, most of her advice to women entails encouraging them to reshape themselves rather than the workplace by developing stronger individual tendencies to take initiative, negotiate, and speak up. As for balancing work and family, she argues that the having-it-all ideal is a myth that leads to unattainable and guilt-inducing expectations, a reality to which Sandberg—the mother of two young children—could attest.

Instead of advocating that women scale down their tendencies to overexert themselves at home *and* work, Sandberg encourages women to manage their guilt as well as their time and focus on priorities, including raising healthy children who more often than not thrive when their mothers work outside the home. By urging women to let go of perfectionism in their personal lives, Sandberg reasons that they can invest more of themselves at work. Research shows, she claims, that to flourish children generally need love, support, and resources. They don't necessarily require the kind of "intensive mothering"—an ideology described by sociologist Sharon Hays (1996)—that demands a woman's full-time attention and all-encompassing identification with the role of maternal caregiver devoted exclusively to a child's every whim and momentary need.

This advice that women first need to dismantle internal barriers to success to circumvent external ones resonated loudly. Within months of its publication, *Lean In* topped both the *New York Times'* non-fiction and Amazon.com bestsellers lists and sold over half a million copies. So many people purchased copies for young women in celebration of their high school and college graduations that it prompted a follow-up book, *Lean In for Graduates*, in April 2014.

Yet, Sandberg's call to women to lean in was not well-received by all. Writing in *Dissent*, Kate Losse (2013), author and former Facebook employee, challenges Sandberg's core proposition that to rise to the top women must invest even more of their time, effort, and sense of self into work and ascending the career ladder. Losse writes:

> If resistance to working harder is the problem, then it follows that work, in Sandberg's book, is a solution. Work will save us; but, the reader may be asking, from what? By taking note of the forms of human activity that do not appear in *Lean In*, we see that what work will save us from is not-work: pleasure and other nonproductive pastimes. . . . There is no not-work, or pleasure, in *Lean In*. . . . Sandberg assumes instead that the feminist question is simply, how can I be a more successful worker?

Losse's main critique is that Sandberg encourages women to be more committed to the workplace without also demanding that workplaces maintain a similar commitment to them in the form of fair and equal wages and gender-neutral hiring and promotion practices. Consequently, she claims, *Lean In* will likely benefit capitalism and the corporate workplace much more than it will women, their families, or any sphere of social life that isn't focused on generating profit.

This critique speaks to a central conflict in feminist struggles for justice and equality. All too often in mainstream feminism, pursuing equality has come to mean fighting specifically for workplace equality and equitable access to the positions of political and economic leadership understandably prized by Sandberg. Many feminists have described the limitations of this important, but myopic, political goal. They urge us not to downplay the importance of equally valuing both paid and non-paid labor as we focus on fighting for women's and other minorities' access to positions of power on equal footing with white men. Thus, the important feminist question for some is how to be more successful in the workplace. But the key question for others is: how do we adequately value, both economically and ideologically, the unpaid labor and care that women, especially low-income women and women of color, disproportionately provide?

Of course, these are not conflicting political goals. The devaluation of care and unpaid household labor makes it more likely that women and minorities will continue to perform it. It also justifies paying them less for doing so than for other kinds of work that are considered more skilled and more valuable to the capitalist economy. As the feminist sociologist Arlie Russell Hochschild (1997) has argued, the "stalled revolution" in gender equality is the result of two interrelated trends: men have not picked up the slack at home since the influx of women into the paid labor market that began in the 1960s, nor has the American workplace changed to accommodate more working mothers and dual-career families. As evidenced by her choice to devote an entire chapter to urging women to avoid "maternal gatekeeping" and let men be equally involved at home, Sandberg acknowledged the importance of the former while implying that she saw little need for the latter. This perpetuates the struggles that women, and increasingly men, endure to balance work and family commitments, an issue to which feminists have drawn much-needed attention.

And yet there is an important third sphere of life that even feminists often continue to overlook in the quest for social justice and gender equality, the one that includes neither the paid labor we do at work nor the unpaid labor we do at home. It is best understood as a form of *being* rather than *doing*. That ostensibly unproductive aspect of life—the sphere of pleasure to which Losse refers—is not missing only in Sandberg's feminist manifesto. It hasn't historically occupied a central place in feminist theorizing about equality and social justice. Other, seemingly more important concerns—challenging inequitable wages, sexist behavioral norms, and the denial of social and economic rights—have understandably occupied more feminist attention in campaigns for social justice.

This third sphere—what we tend to think of as pleasure or leisure—is also rife with gender inequality. The United States has one of the largest gendered leisure gaps in the world. According to a 2013 Pew Research Center report, men in the United States spend on average five more hours per week engaged in leisure activities such as sports, playing games, and watching television than American women (Drake 2013). Women's "free" time, especially mothers', is also more likely to be interrupted by others and spent multitasking. This study reminds us that we shouldn't conflate leisure with being, or not doing, as leisure activities included attending/hosting social events, exercising, and computer use for nonwork related activities. Socializing and exercising can be both relaxing and pleasurable, but as anyone who has ever organized a social event or struggled to consistently exercise can attest, such activities are not necessarily experienced as *nonwork*.

One of the ironies of encouraging women to work harder to be more competitive so they can get into the highest positions of power is that we often assume if we have enough women at the top, they can help change society to be less work focused, less competitive, and less power hungry. Many people want women in leadership positions because they believe that women are uniquely qualified to reshape social institutions toward more equality, fairness, and justice. But women and men who share this goal must often reshape themselves in the process and work harder, be more competitive, and take advantage of inequalities (such as outsourcing poorly paid household labor) as they pursue those coveted positions. Individuals can change institutions, but often institutions change people in the process.

My main goal is not to criticize Sandberg who, by writing *Lean In* and starting a national dialogue on what holds women back, is understandably pursuing the noble goal of getting more women into influential positions of power. But I do question the costs of the strategies she advocates for doing so. As many working caregivers know all too well, doing it all often comes at the expense of poorer health, strained interpersonal relationships, and existential crises that compel us to question what "having it all" really means. We often internalize impossible performance expectations because we live in a society that teaches us to value *having it all* at the same time that it leaves us to our own devices to *do it all*. The United States is one of only a handful of countries in the world that does not have universal, mandatory paid family leave, while Americans work more hours than employees in most other industrialized countries (Schor 1993). In this context, as with Sandberg's *Lean In*, demands for gender parity in the workplace have often translated into prescriptions for doing more with less. The problem with Sandberg's call for women to "internalize the revolution" is that it urges them to devote themselves even more to work in the absence of public supports for care and any activity understood as nonwork.

I had been thinking a lot about this concept of nonwork when I first read Donna King's (2012) essay that inspired this edited collection. In it, she questions the "core American imperative that says we must endlessly strive to be the best," and asks "Does feminism provide theoretical supports for women who want to (or must) slow down, grow quiet, and let go of striving?" (53) The key feminist question for King is not how can women *lean in*, but how can they *let go*. In a society where dominant definitions of success and strength entail having and doing, even when it comes to leisure, how can we create the social and ideological conditions in which not doing, just being, is valued? In response to King, I argue that, if one knows where to look, feminism provides conceptual tools for those who desire to or must slow down and let go of socially patterned tendencies to be tethered to striving and achievement.

But first let me take a brief sociological digression. In his influential 1959 text, *The Sociological Imagination*, C. Wright Mills described how individuals often experience their lives as series of traps. We feel trapped, he claimed, because though we are often blind to the larger social problems that shape our personal troubles, we often have this nagging sense that much of how our life unfolds and the stress of our day-to-day lived experience is somehow not entirely within our control. To overcome this sense of constraint, Mills advocated that individuals adopt a sociological imagination that would allow them to understand how the most intimate aspects of their lives were shaped by social and historical forces. Accepting this was, to use Mills's words, both a "magnificent" and "terrible" lesson. In adopting a sociological worldview we had to accept the terrible realization that our lives largely play out as a result of social circumstance over which we have little choice, while simultaneously embracing the magnificent idea that our seemingly private problems are not entirely our fault. Mills ultimately advocated that we let go of the tendency to individualize our personal successes and private failures.

Aware of this intricate connection between the personal and the social, even feminist sociologists are often quick to dispense personal advice when social change is unlikely. I recently attended a panel discussion at a sociology conference about how women professors balance work and family obligations. After almost an hour of discussing the challenges of having and doing it all in academe, someone humorously joked that our best bet was to marry a feminist who did half the housework, secure a job with supportive supervisors and colleagues who respect personal commitments, and move to Sweden where they have family-friendly policies and a real public safety net. Everyone in the room was a member of a discipline founded on the idea that success (or failure) is a result of both individual effort and social circumstance. But, as is the tendency in our highly individualistic society, even we were guilty of embracing the idea that personal behavior is more amenable to change than larger social forces that all too often seem completely out of our control. This is a trap of the kind Mills so poignantly described.

As individuals shaped by socially shared ideas of worth and value, our inclination in the United States is to think that the way to be and have more is to work harder and accumulate accolades and things. The old adage "less is more" does not characterize the national mindset about how to define and create a well-lived life. We live in a competitive culture where it's now common to brag about how little sleep we get, how busy we are, and how much we still have yet to do. The perpetually unfinished to-do list has become a badge of honor. It's as though the person with the most stress wins some illusory social game in which flaunting how much responsibility we have and how much we're getting done allows us to make legitimate claims to being necessary and valuable. We live in a society where the tendency is to believe that only through doing are we worthy of being.

But where has doing more—and even leaning in—gotten us? As Hochschild (2001) describes, when women work for pay outside the home, they tend to do so as part of a "first shift" of paid labor, only to be followed by a "second shift" of unpaid labor. Many often perform a "third shift" of emotional labor as they cope with conflicting demands generated by the first two. Because the majority of American families must send all of their adult members into the paid workforce, we collectively face a time bind in which there are more things to do but less time in which to do them. What strategies do we use to cope? Hochschild argues that we tend to emotionally downsize our understanding of what family members need to thrive—for example, we start to think "kids don't need a home-cooked dinner *every* night." We also create imagined selves, identities based on all those things we would do and be if only we had the time. Even if we can't have and do it all, we still hold tightly to the idea that maybe we just can't have it all at once. If we must sacrifice family for paid work and career now, the logic often goes, it's all in the service of creating an imagined future where we finally have the time to prioritize family, friends, care, and leisure. We tend to imagine future versions of ourselves who have let go of accumulating and striving, but only after we've already spent most of our lives hanging on and leaning in.

Of course, some are forced to let go somewhere en route to this imagined future. In recounting the illness narratives of women with invisible chronic health problems, King (2012) describes a process of letting go that begins with a bodily taking away. Similarly, Toni Bernhard (2010) writes in *How to Be Sick* about her experience living with an incurable viral infection that left her permanently bedridden:

> I blamed myself for not recovering from the initial viral infection—as if not regaining my health was my fault, a failure of will, somehow, or a deficit of character. This is a common reaction for people to have toward their illness. It's not surprising, given that our culture tends to treat chronic illness as some kind of personal failure on the part of the afflicted—the bias is often implicit or unconscious, but it is nonetheless palpable. (59)

Bernhard also writes of the physical, and even more so psychological, suffering she endured before she was able to feel compassion for herself and the illness that had forcibly required her to let go of a distinguished career as a law professor and an active personal life. As I read Bernhard's account of learning to be sick, one that insightfully framed living with chronic illness as an important life skill, I was reminded of how Talcott Parsons ([1951] 1991)—one of the most notable, if now disputed, social theorists of the twentieth century—described the social experience of being sick. He argued that we are content to let people occupy what he called the *sick role* and excuse them from their other responsibilities such as work and family care, but only as long as we are convinced they are committed to getting well and understand their condition as *undesirable*. According to Parsons, illness is a time-limited form of social deviance that the sick individual has an obligation to overcome by seeking care from competent healthcare professionals and following doctors' orders to rest, take prescribed medications, and refrain from unnecessary physical and mental activity. Thus, we're content to let people be sick and let go of normal responsibilities when we believe that doing so will help them recover and be back to work and family as soon as possible.

Parsons's theory of illness as a deviant and dysfunctional state reinforces the idea that illness is bad primarily because it keeps us from all the doings of daily life that define our being—all the activities we perform as part of our responsibilities as employees, students, parents, partners, and caregivers. From this perspective, sickness is bad because it keeps us from doing those things that society deems valuable. In being sick, we have permission, even if only briefly, to let go. But this perspective gives us permission to let go only as long as it allows us to hold more tightly to achievement mandates once we recover, that is, if we ever do. Many have critiqued Parsons's theory for not accounting for the experience of sufferers of chronic illness for whom being sick is not a "role" temporarily occupied but a lifestyle involuntarily imposed. In a competitive, capitalist culture of accumulation and overwork, being sick—or any form of nonwork—seems to lack all merit when it's not in the service of recuperating for yet even more work.

We may tell ourselves that value and meaning are intrinsically defined, but this ignores how much we as social beings seek affirmation, acceptance, and recognition of our own value from other people who provide the validation we seek. This is another kind of trap to which Mills alluded. *Value* has no inherent or inevitable meaning. It is subjective and what sociologists would call a social construction; how we as a society define value and achievement is a result of human choices. This doesn't mean that these definitions of success and value are not very real in their consequences, but it does suggest they are amenable to change. This also points to perhaps the main dilemma we confront in letting go. From a sociological perspective, what is challenging about letting go is that we have few social scripts that help us do so. Social scripts consist of norms about how to act in particular situations. A classic example is of a diner at a restaurant who just somehow knows to sit down, use table manners, order from the menu, and leave a tip, not because someone directly tells her to do so, but because she's learned from years of socialization and conditioning that that's just the way it's done. We all carry behavioral norms around in our heads that allow us to create some semblance of social order. When we look around our social world and see validation heaped on those getting stuff done and getting more stuff—the kids in school who win the sports trophies and earn the A's, the colleague at work who got the latest promotion, the friend who just bought that big, new house—it's difficult to let go of striving toward those things that most often bring social recognition.

Where, then, might we look for help in letting go? Many have turned to spiritual and religious teachings that promote compassion toward and acceptance of a self that is inherently valuable, not because of what one does, but simply because of what one is—a perfectly imperfect entity that is part of the intricate web of life that connects us all. Feminism provides another script for letting go by revealing the inadequacies of social institutions that have let go of their reciprocal responsibilities to institutionalize the value of care, pleasure, and simply being.

Feminism is a particularly good place to look for conceptual tools that help us learn to let go because it—as both a social movement and area of theoretical inquiry—has been at the forefront of valuing activities that seem to have little worth because they do not directly create a profit. By revealing the value of things that do not readily lend themselves to an easily commodifiable metric, feminism provides a social script for how to recognize usefulness and worth in care and even nonwork. It is largely because of feminist writings on unpaid care work that we better understand how devalued reproductive labor creates economic value by sustaining a productive work force (see Hartmann 1981). Feminism also has many lessons about the value of activity that is neither paid nor unpaid labor. It teaches us to value activities that simply bring us pleasure, help us generate meaning, and enable us to feel connected to one another. Ultimately, feminism helps us understand that central to our drive to strive for more often lies a narrow understanding of value that allows our work—and ultimately our worth—to be quantified and commodified. In doing so, it helps us let go of impossible achievement mandates that equate highly-paid work with worth and narrow economic definitions of success with significance.

Specifically, feminist writings on family, work, and care provide useful conceptual and practical tools for letting go because they teach us to understand our inherent limitations, not as shortcomings of the self, but as inadequacies of institutional caregiving arrangements, including those focused on self-care and other forms of nonwork. These tools help us challenge the idea that if we just work hard enough and get enough done, we are valuable. Hochschild (2001) for example, recommends that we need an organized time movement to challenge the increasing demands that both work and home make on our limited time. This would entail defying many of the basic premises of capitalist work culture. Instead of measuring workplace productivity and success only in terms of financial profit, we could use metrics that better reflect overall organizational well-being, including that of employees whose labor generates profit. To do so, we would need to focus on the *process* of work as well as its result. Devising alternative measures of workplace success, such as how many employees report that they have ample time to spend with their family, would be one way to let go of unduly burdensome work expectations. We could also implement similar metrics at home and in our unrelenting internal self-assessments. Instead of asking "How much did I earn or get done?" as a barometer of a day well lived, we might instead ask, "How much joy did I experience today? With how many loved ones did I meaningfully connect? Was I grateful? Did I laugh enough? Did I adequately rest?" This kind of time movement—organized efforts to fundamentally rethink how we spend and value our time and ultimately ourselves—would be one way of practicing and institutionalizing alternative definitions of value that circumvent a singular focus on doing and earning more.

Feminist political scientist Joan C. Tronto (1993) offers another conceptual tool for letting go: a political ethic of care. She argues that instead of standard economic measures like Gross Domestic Product (GDP), we should instead use the quality and availability of care as indicators of social well-being. We typically devalue care to mask our inevitable dependency on others. Consequently, care work is usually provided by the least powerful individuals in society, women and no- or low-wage workers, and is often rendered invisible. Following Tronto's lead to use care as a "tool for critical political analysis . . . to reveal relationships of power," we could also extend this ethic of care to ourselves (172). By "self-care" people usually mean brief respites from the harried bustle of working life. Adopting a true self-care ethic akin to the kind Tronto proposes entails letting go of definitions of personal value and achievement embedded in capitalist relations of power, that is, valuations of worth tied solely to work and profit. Thus, letting go entails more than taking a weekly yoga class, stealing a nap, or indulging in a hobby. It involves fundamentally reconsidering how the devaluation of interdependence and care—of both others and the self—is born of capitalism, the inequalities that support it, and workplace and family ideologies that often push us beyond our limits.

One of these ideologies is the pull toward intensive mothering described by sociologist Sharon Hays (1996) who argues that capitalism benefits when we all believe that the "troubles of the world can be solved by the individual efforts of superhuman women" (177). We all benefit when we recognize that the ideology of intensive mothering persists, not because it effectively serves the interests of mothers, children, and families, but those of people in positions of power, including men, capitalists, the state, the middle class, and whites. Though Sandberg urged mothers to let go of these superhuman expectations when it comes to mothering, *leaning in* props up ideologies of intensive work that primarily serve those capitalist interests.

These theoretical tools offered by Hochschild, Tronto, and Hays allude to why letting go is a difficult and revolutionary act. Letting go does not serve the interests of the most powerful groups in society. It does not serve capitalism. It does not generate financial profit. It does not therefore seem to have legitimate value. By revealing the ideological and political underpinnings of our drives to do and have more, these feminist scholars compel us to confront the external forces that keep us hanging on rather than letting go. In doing so, feminist tools for letting go reveal the necessity of collective solutions for change, such as a society-wide time movement and a socially shared care ethic. To be truly effective, letting go cannot be a lone pursuit.

These tensions between leaning in and letting go point to a persistent struggle at the heart of feminist goals for social change and justice: if feminism is about promoting equality among women and men, we need further to ask ourselves, *equal to what?* Do we aspire to have equitable access to workplace stress and the competitive strivings of the marketplace? Or are we fighting to make the workplace, and social life in general, less about work and more about those things we claim to value above all else—family, friends, connection, and a sense of purpose? Feminism offers us the tools to recognize that there is value in ascending the corporate ladder and making money, just as there is value in doing the laundry, holding a loved one's hand, being sick—and even just being. Ultimately, one of feminism's most important insights is that there is great value in both leaning in and letting go.

REFERENCES

Bernhard, Toni. 2010. *How to be Sick: A Buddhist-Inspired Guide for the Chronically Ill and Their Caregivers*. Boston: Wisdom Publication.

Drake, Bruce. 2013. "Another Gender Gap: Men Spend More Time in Leisure Activities." Pew Research Center, June 10. *www.pewresearch.org/fact-tank/2013/06/10/another-gender-gap-men-spend-more-time-in-leisure-activities*.

Hartmann, Heidi I. 1981. "The Family as the Locus of Gender, Class, and Political Struggle: The Example of Housework," *Signs* 6 (3): 366–94.

Hays, Sharon. 1996. *The Cultural Contradictions of Motherhood*. New Haven, CT: Yale University Press.

Hochschild, Arlie Russell, with Anne Machung. 1997. *The Second Shift: Working Families and the Revolution at Home*. New York: Penguin.

Hochschild, Arlie Russell. 2001. *The Time Bind: When Work Becomes Home and Home Becomes Work*. New York: Holt.

King, Donna. 2012. "Toward a Feminist Theory of Letting Go," *Feminist Frontiers* 33 (3): 53–70.

Losse, Kate. 2013. "Feminism's Tipping Point: Who Wins from Leaning In?" *Dissent Magazine*, March 26. *www.dissentmagazine.org/online_articles/feminisms-tipping-point-who-wins-from-leaning-in*.

Mills, C. Wright. 1959. *The Sociological Imagination*. London: Oxford University Press.

Parsons, Talcott. (1951) 1991. *The Social System*. New York: Routledge.

Sandberg, Sheryl. 2013. *Lean In: Women, Work, and the Will to Lead*. New York: Knopf.

Sandberg, Sheryl. 2014. *Lean In for Graduates*. New York: Knopf.

Schor, Juliet. 1993. *The Overworked American: The Unexpected Decline of Leisure*. New York: Basic Books.

Tronto, Joan C. 1993. *Moral Boundaries: A Political Argument for an Ethic of Care*. New York: Routledge.

4

Letting Go of Normal when "Normal" Is Pathological, or Why Feminism Is a Gift to Men

Robert Jensen

I have never been normal. For years I struggled and failed to be normal, until I finally just gave up. Since then, I am doing much better. I feel better, in large part, because of feminism, and more specifically radical feminism, the kind of feminism that is relentlessly harsh in evaluating men's behavior—especially men's violence and sexual exploitation of women—in a patriarchal world. I embrace radical feminism, which sounds crazy to some people but is the sanest place a man can land. I recommend it for all men, not just on principle—because it's the right thing to do morally and politically, though I believe that it is—but because it is in our own self-interest.

Here's why I can say this with confidence to another man: I am not normal, and you shouldn't be either. The quest for normal in patriarchy is a losing game. All this likely will seem counter-intuitive to many men, since most of us were trained to be afraid of feminism. What are feminists? I was taught most of my life that feminists were ugly women who couldn't get dates and as a result had a grudge against men, wanted revenge against men, and would do unpleasant things to men given the chance.

That's what I was socialized to think, and that's what I thought for my first thirty years. But then I started to actually read feminist writing and talk to lots of feminists. Over the next couple of years, I kept reading and talking, and I took seriously the feminist critique of patriarchy. Slowly, I was persuaded by the intellectual and moral power of the arguments they made, but probably more important was the way those arguments resonated with me personally. I realized that radical feminism would allow me to let go of my failed quest to be normal.

Definitions

It is important to be clear about what I mean by terms that are used in different ways by different people. *Patriarchy* is a social system based on the assertion that males and females were created or evolved differently for different purposes, with men taking their rightful place on top (Lerner 1986). In patriarchy, the differences in male and female biology are assumed to produce significant moral, intellectual, and emotional differences between men and women, which are used to justify men's subordination of women. Whether grounded in God or evolution, patriarchal systems claim that the differences are immutable, an odd idea given that patriarchy is a relatively recent phenomenon in human history.

The development of patriarchy is tied to agriculture and the domestication of animals, when the communal and cooperative ethic of gatherer-hunter societies was replaced with ideas of private ownership and patrimony that led to men controlling women's reproduction and claiming ownership of women. In the 200,000-year history of the modern human, patriarchy is less than 10,000 years old; in this sense, patriarchy is not only not universal and not timeless but a relatively recent shift away from a considerably more just and sustainable gender system.

∽

Feminism analyzes the ways in which women are oppressed as a class—the ways in which men as a class hold more power, and how those differences in power systematically disadvantage women in the public and private spheres. Gender oppression plays out in different ways depending on social location, as men's oppression of women is affected by other systems of oppression—heterosexism, racism, class privilege, and histories of colonial and postcolonial domination (Hunter College 2014).

Radical feminism is the analysis of the ways that, within this patriarchal system in which we live, one of the key sites of this oppression—one key method of domination—is sexuality. One of the most powerful radical feminists, the late writer Andrea Dworkin (1981, 1983, 1988), was central to the feminist anti-pornography movement in which I have worked. The radical feminist philosophy that has shaped my thinking is most clearly articulated by Marilyn Frye (1983, 1992), while Catharine MacKinnon (1987, 1989) has been influential in my understanding of the law's role, and Audre Lorde (1984, 2009) challenged many of my naïve assumptions about gender and race.

I also understand radical feminism not just as a way of critiquing men's domination of women but also as a way to understand systems of power and oppression more generally. Hierarchies of any kind are inconsistent with human flourishing unless a compelling argument can be made that the hierarchy is necessary to help those with less power in the system, a test that can rarely be met. Feminism is not the only way into a broader critique of the many types of oppression, of course, but it is one important way, and was for me the first route into such a framework.

∽

The feminist movement with which I identify is not satisfied with improving the conditions for women within other hierarchical systems. The contempo-

rary United States is still a white-supremacist society—even after the significant achievements of the civil-rights and liberation movements—and so radical
feminism must critique the current manifestations of that racial hierarchy and
reject the common claim that the country is "post-racial" (Bonilla-Silva 2013).
Capitalism is a profoundly inhuman, anti-democratic, and unsustainable system (Jensen 2009, 150–156)—a threat to the health of people and planet—and
so radical feminism must articulate a different ecological and economic vision
(Mies and Shiva 2014) and reject the current capitalist triumphalism, often referred to as "neoliberalism" or "market fundamentalism" (Schweickart 2002).

Radical feminists can, of course, work pragmatically to improve the conditions for all women within existing systems, but the ultimate objective is the
abolition of those hierarchies. The work, in short, is not to lean into hierarchy
but to eliminate it.

Because there are different approaches to feminism (just as in any intel-
lectual/political movement), everyone has to make choices and cannot simply endorse all feminist views. Although men should be hesitant to weigh in
on disputes within feminism—and there are times when men's voices are not
terribly important in intra-feminist debates—we have to be clear about our
commitments.

In the past three decades, radical feminism has lost ground to traditional
liberal feminism (which I believe offers a weak critique not only of patriarchy
but of other hierarchies), a surging libertarian feminism (a weak critique of patriarchy and no critique of other hierarchies), and postmodern feminism (which
I have always found either perplexing and/or counter-productive). Twenty-five
years after my introduction to feminism, I continue to find radical feminism the
most compelling way to understand the contemporary world, and I believe that
this radical approach has been marginalized—not only in the culture at large but
also within feminism and women's studies—precisely because it is compelling
and calls for significant changes in all our lives.

⁓

Normal can be purely descriptive, meaning an idea or practice that is common,
the norm for a particular society or group. Normal can also be used normatively,
to convey moral or social approval of an idea or practice. Care for children, for
example, is normal and normal—it is a common practice, and it is a practice we
endorse. Problems arise when normal behaviors (in the sense of being common)
that also are considered normal (in the sense of socially approved) are actually
deeply pathological and destructive. Therein lies the problem with the dominant
patriarchal masculinity in contemporary US culture: Men are assumed to be
naturally competitive and aggressive, and being a "real man" is therefore marked
by the struggle for control, conquest, and domination. A man looks at the world,
sees what he wants, and takes it. That's normal, and in this case what's normal is
dangerous.

Patriarchal Masculinity

Men who don't measure up are suspect—they are wimps, sissies, fags, girls. The worst insult one man can hurl at another, whether among boys on the playground or at corporate executive gym, remains the accusation that a man is like a woman (or is gay, which is assumed to be too much like a woman). Although the culture allows men in some situations to exhibit traits traditionally associated with women (such as caring, compassion, and tenderness), in the end it is men's strength-expressed-as-toughness that defines us and must trump any woman-like softness. Those aspects of masculinity must prevail for a man to be a real man, to be normal.

To identify this dominant definition of what it means to be a man is not to suggest that every male lives by the exact same rules. Scholars and activists often talk of "masculinities," plural (Kimmel, Hearn, and Connell 2004)—the idea that different men and groups of men fashion different conceptions of what it means to be a man in different social locations. That's a positive development when it helps us understand how other forms of hierarchy (especially race, class, and sexual orientation) affect men in patriarchy, in what has become known as intersectional analysis. But this trend is diversionary when it undermines the focus on patriarchy, for it always is crucial to remember that all masculinities are a masculinity-in-patriarchy. Our goal should not be to redefine masculinity but to leave it behind.

Men who oppose patriarchy and strive honestly, albeit imperfectly, for equality are not performing/doing/enacting a form of masculinity, but are stating a commitment to the end of masculinity. I need not pretend I am always successful in this venture or that by this declaration of resistance I can magically walk in the world without the unearned privileges that society accords to men. But there is a difference between this commitment to the abolition of masculinity and a reformist project. Even a pro-feminist masculinity is a masculinity, and masculinity, no matter how it is defined, is always about dominance. A kinder-and-gentler masculinity is still patriarchal.

And whatever the variation in how men live masculinities, there remains a dominant conception of masculinity to which virtually all males are exposed and with which a significant percentage (likely a substantial majority) identify in some fashion. Many men who claim to be challenging the dominant conception of masculinity are simply putting a new face on the same system, the key components of which are the struggle for supremacy in interpersonal relationships and social situations; avoidance of any activities too closely connected to women; and repression of emotions connected to women. (Men do not repress all emotion; in certain situations men freely express anger, for example.)

King of the Hill

This conception of masculinity can be explained through the children's game King of the Hill, in which the object is to be the one who remains on top of the hill (or, if not an actual hill, a large pile of anything or the center of any designated area). To do that, one has to repel those who challenge the king's supremacy. That can be done in a friendly spirit with an understanding that a minimal amount of force will be used by all, or it can be violent and vicious, with both the king and the challengers allowed to use any means necessary. Games that start with a friendly understanding can often turn violent and vicious.

In my experience, both male and female children can, and did, play King of the Hill, but it was overwhelmingly a game of male children, one that trains male children to be men. No matter who is playing, it is a game of masculinity. King of the Hill reveals one essential characteristic of the dominant conception of masculinity: No one is ever safe, and everyone loses something.

Most obviously, this King-of-the-Hill masculinity is dangerous for women. It leads men to seek control over "their" women and define their own pleasure in that control, which leads to pandemic levels of rape and battery. But this view of masculinity is toxic for men as well. One thing is immediately obvious about King-of-the-Hill masculinity: Not everyone can win. In fact, there can be only one really real man at any given moment. In a system based on hierarchy, by definition there can be only one person at the top of the hierarchy. There's only one King of the Hill.

In this conception of masculinity, men are in constant struggle with each other for dominance. Every other man must in some way be subordinated to the king, but even the king can't feel too comfortable—he has to be nervous about who is coming up that hill to get him. This isn't just a game, of course. A friend who once worked on Wall Street, one of the preeminent sites of masculine competition in the business world, described coming to work as like "walking into a knife fight when all the good spots along the wall were taken." Every day you faced the possibility of getting killed—figuratively, in business terms—and there was no spot you could stand where your back was covered. This is masculinity lived as endless competition and threat. Normal guys don't have to play this game every moment of their lives, but no guy can be normal if he challenges the basic rules of the game.

Again, to be clear: There is not a single standard for masculinity or a central committee that sets the rules. As in any system there is variation. But it is crucial to remember that the study of men and masculinity will not be meaningful politically—that is, a potentially useful intervention into the way power operates—unless it is grounded in the study of patriarchy. Scholarship, like pop culture, is susceptible to de-politicization and faddishness, both problems of what Michael Schwalbe (2014, 38) calls "the masculinities industry," which can "take men off the feminist hook by talking about masculinity instead of talking about men's oppressive behavior."

Whatever the short-term, material benefits of masculinity, whatever power it gives one over others, it's also exhausting and, in the end, unfulfilling. No one man created this system. Perhaps no man, if given a real choice, would choose it. But we live our lives in that system, and it deforms men, narrowing our emotional range and depth and limiting our capacity to experience the rich connections with others—not just with women and children, but also with other men—which require vulnerability but make life meaningful. The Man Who Would Be King is the Man Who Is Broken and Alone. A normal guy is typically a miserable guy.

Yet this toxic conception of masculinity continues to dominate. We teach our boys that to be a man is to be tough, to be acquisitive, to be competitive, to be aggressive. We congratulate them when they make a tough hit on the football field that takes out an opponent. We honor them in parades when they return from slaughtering the enemy abroad. We put them on magazine covers when they destroy business competitors and make millions by putting people out of work. We train boys that it is normal to be cruel, to ignore the feelings of others, to be violent. US culture's most-admired male heroes reflect those characteristics: they most often are men who take charge rather than seek consensus, seize power rather than look for ways to share it, and are willing to be violent to achieve their goals. Victory is sweet. Conquest gives a sense of power. We close the deal. The occasional rush crowds out the always-present isolation.

And then there is sex, where victory, conquest, and dealing come together, typically out of public view. Masculinity played out in sexual relationships, straight or gay, brings King of the Hill into our most intimate spaces. This doesn't mean that every man in every sexual situation plays out this dominance, but simply that there exists a pattern, and that it is the rare man who doesn't struggle with these feelings. The cruel and degrading sexualized images of women so routine in pornography, and the routine way men use women through pornography, is painful testimony to this reality (Jensen 2007).

Again, for emphasis: the fact that this toxic masculinity hurts men doesn't mean it's equally dangerous for men and women. As feminists have long pointed out, there's a big difference between women dealing with the constant threat of being raped, beaten, and killed by the men in their lives, and men not being able to cry. But we can see that the short-term material gains that men get in patriarchy are not adequate compensation for what we men give up in the long haul, which is to surrender part of our humanity to the project of dominance.

This doesn't mean, of course, that in this world all men have it easy. Those other systems of dominance and oppression—white supremacy, heterosexism, and predatory corporate capitalism—mean that non-white men, gay men, poor and working class men suffer in various ways. A radical feminist analysis doesn't preclude us from understanding those problems but in fact helps us see them more clearly.

Beyond Normality

So, embracing radical feminism and critiquing patriarchy's toxic conception of masculinity does not solve all the problems men have. And, again for emphasis, rejecting the pathology of patriarchy does not allow one to transcend magically one's own training or the real-world manifestations of it. I still routinely fight my own patriarchal tendencies and still have to navigate in a patriarchal world. And no matter how successful I am in that struggle, I still am a man in a patriarchal world that gives me unearned privilege and power in many situations. Such privilege and power cannot be given away by an individual; it comes with the identity.

That decision to embrace radical feminism opened up a process that led to similar processes of challenging norms around sexual orientation, race, class, and nationality. Each process, like each system of power, was similar in outline and different in details. My experience with feminism provided a framework for working through the rejection of normal in each of those arenas.

As a result, I no longer try to be normal. For me, that has included some things that are relatively trivial (no longer pretending to care about football and instead openly critiquing its routine brutality), some that can be uncomfortable (challenging other men when they use women in the sexual-exploitation industries of pornography, prostitution, and stripping), and some that are life-changing (finally dealing openly with my shifting sexuality from straight to gay and back to straight). Most crucially, it has meant committing some of my time/energy/money to feminist organizing and doing my best to bring a feminist consciousness into other progressive political activities, efforts that are not a sacrifice but an opportunity for me to enrich my life.

I may inadvertently get pulled into a game of King of the Hill at work or have to contend with unexpected urges to be the King of the Hill. But on a day-to-day basis, I don't have to keep trying to be a normal pathological man. Giving up on the failed project of being normally pathological has made me a healthier person. Apart from whatever contribution this may allow me to make to political movements that fight hierarchies, apart from any positive effect I have on my students by exposing them to these ideas, apart from any moral claim I can make to being on the right side of history—I am a saner person than I was when I was trying to be normal.

But a caveat: sane does not necessarily mean upbeat and happy. Understanding the nature of hierarchy and the injuries it visits upon people, engaging in activities that put those injuries in plain view, committing some part of one's daily life to these issues—that doesn't leave one happy. But it creates the possibility of finding joy.

Letting go of normal means letting go of the cheap and easy pleasures that can numb the pain of facing the world honestly. I have nothing against pleasure, and there are pleasures in my life. But the quick routes to feeling happy are cut off when one chooses to let go of normal. Instead of a superficial happiness, letting go of normal offers new ways to experience a deeper joy. And as that capacity for joy deepens, so does the capacity for grief.

Letting go of normal changes the equation. It makes daily life harder, but it makes life more meaningful. James Baldwin (cited in Bayley 2009), as he so often did, got to the heart of this in a comment that is often quoted:

> I think the inability to love is the central problem, because the inability masks a certain terror, and that terror is the terror of being touched. And, if you can't be touched, you can't be changed. And, if you can't be changed, you can't be alive.

That's why I repeat, over and over, to as many men as I can reach: We are told that feminism is a threat, and in some sense that is accurate. Feminism is a threat to our ability to hang onto normal. But once we let go of the pathology of normal, we can more easily embrace change, touch, and love. When we let go of normal, we can see that feminism is, in fact, a gift to men.

REFERENCES

Bayley, Michael. 2009. "Knowing What To Do, Knowing Why To Stay." *The Wild Reed: Thoughts and Reflections from a Progressive, Gay, Catholic Perspective* (blog), November 16, *thewildreed.blogspot.com/2009/11/knowing-what-to-do-knowing-why-to-stay.html*.

Bonilla-Silva, Eduardo. 2013. *Racism without Racists: Color-Blind Racism and the Persistence of Racial Inequality in America*, 4th edition. Lanham, MD: Rowman & Littlefield.

Dworkin, Andrea. 1981. *Pornography: Men Possessing Women*. New York: Perigee.

———. 1983. *Right-wing Women*. New York: Perigee.

———. 1988. *Letters from a War Zone: Writings 1976–1987*. London: Secker & Warburg.

Frye, Marilyn. 1983. *The Politics of Reality*. Freedom, CA: Crossing Press.

———. 1992. *Willful Virgin*. Freedom, CA: Crossing Press.

Hunter College Women's and Gender Studies Collective. 2014. *Women's Realities, Women's Choices*, 4th edition. New York: Oxford University Press.

Jensen, Robert. 2007. *Getting Off: Pornography and the End of Masculinity*. Boston: South End Press.

———. 2009. *All My Bones Shake: Seeking a Progressive Path to the Prophetic Voice*. Berkeley, CA: Soft Skull Press.

Kimmel, Michael S., Jeff Hearn, and Robert W. Connell. 2004. *Handbook of Studies on Men and Masculinities*. Thousand Oaks, CA: Sage.

Lerner, Gerda. 1986. *The Creation of Patriarchy*. New York: Oxford University Press.

Lorde, Audre. 1984. *Sister Outsider*. Freedom, CA: Crossing Press.

———. 2009. *I Am Your Sister: Collected and Unpublished Writings of Audre Lorde*, edited by Rudolph P. Byrd, Johnnetta Betsch Cole, and Beverly Guy-Sheftall. New York: Oxford University Press.

MacKinnon, Catharine A. 1987. *Feminism Unmodified: Discourses on Life and Law.* Cambridge, MA: Harvard University Press.

———. 1989. *Toward a Feminist Theory of the State.* Cambridge, MA: Harvard University Press.

Mies, Maria, and Vandana Shiva. 2014. *Ecofeminism: Critique, Influence, Change,* 2nd edition. London: Zed Books.

Schwalbe, Michael. 2014. *Manhood Acts: Gender and the Practices of Domination.* Boulder, CO: Paradigm Press.

Schweickart, David. 2002. *After Capitalism.* Lanham, MD: Rowman & Littlefield.

Part Two

Personal Essays

5

When "Straight-Acting" Lost Its Luster

Letting Go of Masculine Privilege

Anthony C. Ocampo

In the summer of 2010, I attended the thirtieth birthday celebration of Gregory, one of my closest friends from college.[1] During our college years (from 1999 to 2003), Gregory and I shared countless memories, everything from pulling all-nighters in the library to lifting weights at the gym to partying on the weekends with our fraternity brothers. However, Gregory and I drifted apart after college. The year after we graduated, I came out as gay, and I felt the need to cut myself off from many of my old college friends, particularly straight male friends like Gregory who had assumed that I was heterosexual. At the time, I felt a tremendous amount of guilt and shame for the many times I had pretended to share their commiserations about dating women. Three years after we graduated, I finally came out to Gregory. I viewed the invitation to his thirtieth birthday as a gesture of his acceptance.

Gregory told me that he had only invited his closest friends to his birthday, and I was honored to be one of them. Out of the fifteen invitees, I happened to be the only gay person. To my surprise, my sexuality turned out to be a topic of interest to the dinner guests, and with a little bit of liquid courage, the other guests (primarily the men) began to ask some very personal questions. *When did you first know you were gay? How is it dating someone of the same sex? How does sex work? How does your family feel about your being gay?* Despite the invasiveness of some of their questions, I did not mind volunteering a few intimate details from my own experience as a gay man. I was happy to provide a teachable moment, especially for the men in the group, who, before finding out I was gay, were more than willing to make homophobic comments in my presence.

As the dinner conversation progressed, I became more and more impressed at the other men's willingness to look at the world from a gay person's perspective. Some even apologized for having pejoratively used the word "gay" in the past. Toward the end of the celebration, however, one of Gregory's friends made a troubling comment. "Man, I'm just happy you're not one of *those* gay guys," he said, clearly intending his remark to be a compliment. I looked at the other guests at the dinner table to see if they were as shocked by the comment as I was. None seemed to be. Instead, I found that a few others were nodding their heads in agreement with this "compliment."

I was at a proverbial fork in the road. At the beginning of the dinner, I had tacitly signaled my sexuality to the other guests by telling them I was a bit tired from spending the previous evening partying in the Castro, one of the most famous gayborhoods in the United States. In this sense, I had no intention to try to pass as a straight man. However, what I realized at this moment was that my presentation of self gave me the ability to *cover*. Sociologist Erving Goffman was the first to conceptualize covering as a strategy for navigating social life for individuals from marginalized populations: "It is a fact that persons who are ready to admit possession of a stigma (in many cases because it is known about or immediately apparent) may nonetheless make a great effort to keep the stigma from looming large. . . . This process will be referred to as *covering*" (Goffman [1963] 2009, 103).

Legal scholar Kenji Yoshino applies Goffman's concept to the case of gay men. "Gays are increasingly permitted to be gay and out so long as we do not 'flaunt' our identities," Yoshino writes. In other words, society tells gay men, "Fine, be gay, but don't shove it in our faces" (Yoshino 2006, 19). At this dinner table, I was adhering to this "covering demand," as Yoshino puts it. I was disclosing my gay identity, and I was able to achieve acceptance and applause from the straight men at the table, precisely because I had not violated their conceptions of how a man is supposed to act—masculine, unflamboyant, and confident. They considered me to be "straight-acting," the idea that I could seamlessly fit in with a group of heterosexual men, so long as I continued to "tone down [the behaviors of] a disfavored identity to fit into the mainstream" (Yoshino 2006, ix).

I found myself in a catch-22. To acknowledge the compliment would be to further cement my acceptance among a contingent of men who, at one point in my life, had provoked fear and feelings of inadequacy. At the same time, doing so would simultaneously condone a practice of conditional acceptance among this group of heterosexual men, who might subconsciously learn that it is okay to only accept gay men who adhere to the gender performance of the stereotypical masculine man. On the other hand, pointing out the insulting nature of the compliment risked alienating myself from a group of heterosexual men whose acceptance I had subconsciously yearned for. In this moment, I chose neither fight nor flight. I simply froze. The consequence of this act was shame for not adhering to the ethos of the LGBT movement, which is to be loudly "out and proud" in all social situations and to immediately come to the defense of all members of the LGBT community (Connell 2014). In this moment, acceptance and authenticity seemed like mutually exclusive choices. In this moment, choice felt like a misnomer.

In the early stages of my own coming out process, I would have worn the label of straight-acting as a stamp of approval, confirming that I could fit in with other real (read heterosexual *and* masculine) men. Even within the context of gay social spaces, straight-acting functions as a badge of honor among gay men, who themselves unproblematically participate in the "fag discourse" (Ocampo 2012; Pascoe 2007). Sociologist C. J. Pascoe (2007) found that young heterosexual boys regularly employ gay epithets as a means of policing each other's masculinity. In my own research on queer men of color from immigrant families, I have found that even gay men are guilty of using this fag discourse as a way to win back masculinity points among other gays and make themselves appear as attractive partners within gay social scenes (Ocampo 2012, 2014). In fact, there is a long tradition of this practice among gay men since the gay liberation movement. The late Martin Levine, a pioneering scholar of gay masculinities, documented how gay men who subscribed to heteronormative masculine ideals monitored everything from their build to their attire to their voice inflections in order to avoid being seen as "failed men" (Levine and Kimmel 1998). In the process, they would also openly denigrate effeminate gay men in order to maintain their standing as the exceptional gay man who could fit in in any heteronormative context minus the minor technicality of sexual orientation.

To use the logic of neoliberal individualism, it was as if these men were leaning in to the most problematic aspects of masculinity. Embracing the idea of being the exceptional gay or the supergay or the gay guy who fits in with straights simultaneously embraces the ethos of individual striving and competition. When gay men use covering as a strategy—whether it be through working out, maintaining a masculine presentation of self, or valorizing sexual experiences as conquests—they fail to question, let alone undermine, the institutional mechanisms that continue to facilitate symbolic and physical violence to large segments of the LGBT community (Meyer 2012; Stockdill and Danico 2012). As Yoshino succinctly put it, "covering is a hidden assault on our civil rights" (2006, xi).

Feminist sociologist Donna King highlights how the promotion of neoliberal and capitalistic frameworks in our society has paved the way for individual striving at the expense of one's community, as well as one's mental and physical well-being. In her essay "Toward a Feminist Theory of Letting Go," King critiques "the core American imperative that says we must endlessly strive to be the best" (2012, 53). In her piece, she is referring to the temptation for women to be superwomen, but there is much applicability to the case of gay men, who many researchers have shown, strive to be exceptional rather than ordinary—whether in terms of their masculinity, their workplace, or their families (Cantú, Naples, and Vidal-Ortiz 2009; Connell 2014; Decena 2011; Levine and Kimmel 1998; Ocampo 2014). King argues that the celebration of female empowerment and valorization of female trailblazers—the underlying logic of leaning in, a concept recently popularized by Facebook executive Sheryl Sandberg—imposes a tremendous amount of psychological and physical distress to the vast majority of women who are structurally, or even physically, unable to become superwomen.

Expanding on the critiques of another feminist sociologist, Hester Eisenstein, King notes the inherent contradictions within certain segments of feminism that demand "high productivity, a fast pace, pushing past limits, and denying the body" in a society where women's ability to succeed is severely structurally constrained (King 2012, 54). She then draws on the narratives of women with chronic physical illnesses to demonstrate the impactfulness of letting go of these demands, something she argues is a *cultivated practice*. Physically unable to compete within a lean in paradigm of feminism, these women divest completely and instead begin focusing on the limitations of their own bodies, rather than social and cultural demands of other societal institutions (which would include feminist movements). For these women, pain—both physical pain and the pain of falling short of externally imposed expectations—unexpectedly becomes a pathway to transformation, self-centering, and inner peace (King 2012). As King's essay illustrates, women with chronic physical illnesses lose the capacity to engage in covering, and rather than feeling limited, they ironically become more whole. In this respect, King's discussion of this segment of women provides a lesson for me in the benefits of divestment.

Psychologist Alan Downs, who has counseled countless gay men through their own coming out processes, has documented the plethora of strategies that gay men have employed to remain invested in a game of masculinity, which, by its very nature, has relegated them to second-class citizens. In his book *The Velvet Rage*, he argues that gay men compensate for the shame of their sexuality by becoming supermen at their jobs, in the gym, in the dating circuit, or at the clubs (Downs 2006). In the end, none of these strategies adequately overcome the emotional "pain of growing up in a straight man's world." Despite its limited discussion of race and class divisions among gay men, Down's hypothesis resonated with me greatly, particularly as I reflect about my academic career. In retrospect, the success of my academic career was in part a byproduct of my desire to win back "masculinity points" with my parents, my friends, and my classmates.

However, now that I am a full-fledged university professor, I have come to realize how gay men's continued investment in a straight man's version of masculinity, one that relies entirely on a neoliberal ethos of competition and individual striving, directly hurts other members of the LGBT community—gay women, effeminate gay men, working class gay men, undocuqueers (queer undocumented immigrants), and transgender men and women, particularly trans people of color (McBride 2005; Meyer 2012; Schilt 2011; Ward 2008). In the second half of this essay, I discuss how my decision to let go of my masculine privilege—and my inclination to cover—facilitated invaluable intellectual and personal transformations for two of my male students.

Letting Go of Covering

When it comes to navigating their identities as both sexual minorities and educators, LGBT teachers constantly face the type of impossible choices iterated by King in her essay on letting go. Sociologist Catherine Connell (2014) argues that LGBT teachers feel tremendous pressure to adhere to two contradictory scripts associated with their competing identities. As Connell notes, "since the 1960s, the prevailing politics of gay pride have increasingly demanded that its constituents be 'out and proud' *in all contexts*" (2, emphasis mine), yet the profession of teaching generally frowns upon the idea of introducing teachers' sexual lives into classroom discussion. "The clashing expectations of pride and professionalism force gay and lesbian teachers into a no-win struggle between their political and professional obligations," she adds (2). In other words, the demands of covering are particularly significant for LGBT teachers, whose sexual lives constitute a central part of their core identity.

Though Connell's work focuses mainly on secondary school teachers, her argument can also be extended to LGBT professors. For example, there are countless examples of gay, lesbian, and transgender professors encountering hostility from their colleagues and the administration, as well as being suspiciously denied tenure, when they make the decision not to tone down their identity as sexual minorities (Stockdill and Danico 2012). In my own department's not so distant past, this type of hostility contributed to one gay male professor's decision to leave his faculty post. While the colleagues and administrators that I have encountered have been nothing short of accepting, this was not the case for that professor.

As such, coming out as a gay professor and choosing not to cover was not a decision I took lightly. Before I began my position as an assistant professor, the possibility of encountering hostility and harassment—from colleagues, administrators, or even students—loomed in my mind for months. Fortunately, most of those I encountered, including the department chair and the search chair in charge of my hire, explicitly signaled their support and celebrated the addition of a faculty member who was both gay and a person of color. Throughout my experience as a junior faculty member, I have not experienced any hostility, nor any microaggressions, from my colleagues on account of either my ethnicity or sexuality—a testament to the antiracist, antisexist, and antihomophobic environment that some of my colleagues have worked very hard to create (Stockdill and Danico 2012).

When it came to the students, however, my fears manifested rather differently than it did with my colleagues. One of the greatest aspects of the public university is that I have the privilege of teaching a diverse group of students.

They are not only racially diverse, but they are also diverse in terms of their social position. Some are working class, undocumented, LGBT, working parents, or veterans of war. However, for the most part, the students converge in terms of age—the majority of them are only a few years separated from high school. Standing in front of the classroom for the first time as a professor in the fall of 2011, I was newly thirty years old. Though I was more than ten years separated from my own high school experiences, the faces of my students triggered my impulse to cover my sexuality, just as I did in my teens and early twenties. In particular, many of the men triggered my own memories of being harassed for being gay.

What my first experiences as a university professor showed me was that covering was my habit. While I had not engaged in covering my sexuality among the mostly liberal social circles in graduate school, I did not yet have the same assurance of antihomophobic support from the random groups of students that I encountered as a first-year professor. In his *New York Times* bestselling book *The Power of Habit*, Pulitzer Prize winning journalist Charles Duhigg (2014) writes of the deeply embedded nature of habits—when people encounter triggers, they almost automatically engage in a set of behaviors, which then lead to a reward. Applied to my first few months as a professor, I regularly found myself looking into the audience of students, seeing men who physically resembled bullies from high school (trigger), felt the need to cover my sexuality (the behavior), in the hopes of evading gossip about my being gay (the reward). I became aware of this very quickly, and I decided, as Duhigg and many behavioral psychologists suggest, to intervene in this problematic feedback loop. With no guarantee of a "reward," I decided to *signal* my sexuality—by talking about my same-sex friends and partner, by discussing my research on gay minority communities, or by explicitly identifying as gay.

It was truly terrifying.

In doing so, however, I discovered new rewards I never believed possible. Many of my students—both male and female, both straight and LGBT—expressed to me that my choice not to cover helped them become more comfortable with their own vulnerabilities. Within the classroom and during my office hours, students began coming out, not just in terms of their sexual identity, but also with respect to their socioeconomic background, their family situation, their legal status, and even the state of their physical and mental health. In addition, students were not just coming out, they were also covering less. The most poignant examples of this occurred when students were willing to share their vulnerabilities, not as a means of garnering sympathy, but rather as an empirical point of departure to understand larger systems of social inequality within the United States and beyond.

Some students, upon reaching a certain comfort level with me, note that they "had no idea" that I was a gay man. At times, I admit that such comments trigger my desire to revert back to covering—to embrace the idea of being the straight-acting gay professor. While this strategy is at times necessary for LGBT professors in more hostile institutional environment, I have found that the personal costs of doing this, for me, are too emotionally taxing. More importantly, I have also reflected on how covering might have robbed me of two of the most fulfilling moments in my teaching career.

Andres

I met Andres, a thirty-year-old Mexican American undergraduate, in my upper division statistics course. Statistics was the first course I had ever taught as a professor, and Andres was one of twenty-four students in the class. Unlike a qualitative research course, statistics is a class where the relevance of my social position might not be as readily apparent, given that statistics relies on data collected from surveys, not face-to-face interaction. Nonetheless, I decided before I began my position to share bits of personal information to my students—my biography, my educational background, my research interests—as a means of being transparent about my social position and as a strategy for building rapport with my students. The majority of the class was comprised of students of color (many from immigrant families), and I thought that sharing my own background as a son of an immigrant might help them become more comfortable with me as their instructor.

Though I had no concerns about sharing my ethnic background, I had a great deal of anxiety sharing my sexual identity. Despite my initial hesitation, I decided that it was important for me to let students know that I was gay, and that my own experiences as a gay man had inspired me to pursue research on the gay children of immigrants. One of the main reasons that I did so was because I had admired one of my own undergraduate professors for coming out in the classroom, especially because I was closeted at the time. The revelation of my sexual identity to my statistics class came and went without incident, and my worries quickly faded.

Five weeks into the course, Andres approached me after class to solicit some help for a research proposal he was developing for a different course. Before he had approached me, I had my assumptions about Andres. Andres was a quiet student who generally only spoke out in class if I called on him. Given his shy demeanor, I was surprised that he had approached me for something unrelated to the class material.

Andres handed me a short two-page draft of a research proposal. In the proposal, Andres wrote about his interest in studying the romantic relationships of gay Latino immigrants. Throughout the document, there were idiosyncratic bits of information that suggested to me that Andres was familiar with the Los Angeles gay scene. He alluded to different gayborhoods and night clubs that were frequented mainly by gay Latino men (many of which I was familiar with due to my own research). He had also mentioned in the proposal that he was gay himself. As I kept reading his proposal, it dawned on me that I had assumed Andres was heterosexual throughout the duration of the class thus far!

Andres informed me that a major reason he approached me was because I had come out on the first day of class. He admitted that he was generally hesitant about approaching professors outside of class, but that my identity as a gay man prompted him to overcome his reticence. Andres decided to pursue his proposed research through the Ronald E. McNair Scholars Program, a federally funded initiative that aims to recruit working class minority students into doctoral programs. Over the next two years, I worked closely with Andres on his research on the romantic relationships of gay Latino immigrants. Rather than dismiss his research as mere navel-gazing, as is often the case for minorities who choose to study their own communities, my intimate knowledge of gay immigrant experiences helped me train Andres' sociological imagination and research abilities. I was able to create a safe space in which Andres was also able to teach me. As a native Spanish speaker, Andres had greater access to gay venues that were predominantly comprised of Latino immigrants. Through his own research of these communities, he taught me about the way undocumented status shapes the process by which certain gay Latino immigrants navigate their social relationships. Andres' research eventually earned him a place in one of the most competitive sociology doctoral programs in the University of California, where he is currently conducting research for his dissertation project.

The working relationship that I developed with Andres might not have been possible had I decided to cover. It was through working with Andres that I first realized that there were payoffs to letting go of covering as a strategy.

Sergio

Sergio, a twenty-year old Filipino-Mexican American, was a student in my gender and sexuality course. In this course, one of my main objectives is to help students deconstruct and denaturalize stereotypes associated with men, women, heterosexuals, and LGBT individuals. A primary strategy for accomplishing this is through journaling—each week, the students in this class write about the way their gender and sexuality has shaped their interactions with parents, friends, romantic partners, teachers, coworkers, and other people they encounter in their everyday lives. In the first few weeks of the course, Sergio's journals focused on the pressure he and his younger brother Kenny felt from their father to prove their masculinity. Sergio identified as straight and said he had been encouraged by his father to pursue sports, act tough, and be popular with women. In his journals, Sergio wrote candidly about being compliant to his father's demands. However, in his reflection papers, he noted that his brother was more resistant. Kenny hated sports (despite being forced to play by his father) and begged his father for permission to join a dance troupe. According to Sergio's journals, his father refused and constantly berated his little brother to forget about dance lessons because they were only for "girls and gays." Sergio admitted that he too was guilty of telling his brother at different moments to "stop acting gay." Sergio said that he and his brother were not particularly close because of their different interests.

As in my statistics course, I decided to come out to my students on the first day of the gender and sexuality class rather than cover. I also shared stories with my students about having been harassed in high school for being gay and the challenges I faced being open about my sexuality with my immigrant parents. The more I opened up about my own experiences, the more Sergio opened up about his experiences in high school where he was a bully toward other young men. After reading about the concept of fag discourse in C. J. Pascoe's book *Dude, You're a Fag*, he confessed in his journals that he regularly used gay epithets but had not realized the deep pain that these words might have had for his targets, including his brother.

After the course ended, Sergio came into my office hours to update me on his relationship with his brother. Though he was not sure if his brother was gay, he said that my openness about my sexuality, coupled with the class discussions, helped him see the importance of creating a space where it would be okay if his brother were to come out as gay. "I always tell Kenny that I have a gay professor and that I'm friends with him," he said, "I always tell him that it's okay if boys like other boys." Sergio said that his brother became intrigued when he found out his older brother had a gay professor he had become friends with. "Really? You're friends with him?" Sergio said his brother would ask, even while vehemently denying he is gay himself. Sergio also said he has become more adamant about policing his friends' use of the fag discourse, especially when they make fun of his younger brother. "Sometimes my friends laugh or say little comments when they see my brother acting feminine," he said, "but I always tell them to shut the fuck up now."

My unwillingness to cover had clear payoffs for how Sergio navigated his relationship with his younger brother. Sergio used his friendship with a gay professor to signal his status as an ally to his younger brother—an important resource for Kenny if he were to ever come out as gay. Rather than be complicit in his brother's experiences with bullying, Sergio also drew on our relationship to deflect the bullying Kenny encountered from other young men in his life.

Conclusion

Implicit within every civil rights movement is the desire for a level playing field. In our history, women and minorities have fought for the right to vote, immigrants have fought for the right to become citizens, and LGBT people most recently have fought for the right to marry. The achievement of suffrage, citizenship, and marriage equality are certainly markers of progress that must be celebrated. Nonetheless, women, racial minorities, and sexual minorities must not see such landmarks as mere mechanisms for individual striving. The beneficiaries of these historically marginalized groups must not lean in to their newly acquired privileges—this would only serve to initiate new systems of inequality within their own communities.

Reflecting back on my friend Gregory's thirtieth birthday party, I secretly reveled at the opportunity to achieve acceptance from a group of men who at one point in their lives dismissed the idea of having a gay friend. However, I knew that I could not lean into their standards of masculinity, despite the fact that I adhered to them on the surface. I could not lean into an ethos of masculinity that distinguished between "good gays" and "bad gays" based on something as arbitrary as gender presentation. While I regret not speaking up in that moment, I have used every opportunity in my current position as a university professor to disarm my desire to engage in covering.

In choosing not to cover, I have witnessed transformation in my students, as exemplified by my rewarding experiences with Andres and Sergio. In disclosing my own sexuality to the class, my hope is that I help to create a safe space for my students to embrace their own vulnerabilities, even if they do not publicly voice these identities in the classroom. My hope is my personal narrative has demonstrated how the decision to let go of covering is also a decision to let go of shame. It has been my experience that letting go of shame can in turn enhance students' intellectual and career development, as well as improve their personal relationships outside the classroom.

Note

1.   I use pseudonyms for friends and students referred to in this chapter.

REFERENCES

Cantú, Lionel, Nancy Naples, and Salvador Vidal-Ortiz. 2009. *The Sexuality of Migration: Border Crossings and Mexican Immigrant Men*. New York: New York University Press.

Connell, Catherine. 2014. *School's Out: Gay and Lesbian Teachers in the Classroom*. Berkeley: University of California Press.

Decena, Carlos. 2011. *Tacit Subjects: Belonging and Same-Sex Desire among Dominican Immigrant Men*. Durham, NC: Duke University Press.

Downs, Alan. 2006. *The Velvet Rage: Overcoming the Pain of Growing Up in a Straight Man's World*. New York: De Capo Press.

Duhigg, Charles. 2014. *The Power of Habit*. New York: Random House.

Goffman, Erving. (1963) 2009. *Stigma: Notes on the Management of Spoiled Identities*. New York: Simon and Schuster.

King, Donna. 2012. "Toward a Feminist Theory of Letting Go." *Frontiers: A Journal of Women Studies* 33 (3): 53–70.

Levine, Martin, and Michael Kimmel. 1998. *Gay Macho: The Life and Death of the Homosexual Clone*. New York: New York University Press.

McBride, Dwight. 2005. *Why I Hate Abercrombie and Fitch: Essays on Race and Sexuality*. New York: New York University Press.

Meyer, Doug. 2012. "An Intersectional Analysis of Lesbian, Gay, Bisexual, and Transgender People's Evaluations of Anti-Queer Violence." *Gender & Society* 26 (6): 849–73.

Ocampo, Anthony C. 2012. "Making Masculinity: Negotiations of Gender Presentation among Latino Gay Men." *Latino Studies* 10 (4): 448–72.

———. 2014. "The Gay Second Generation: Sexual Identity and Family Relations of Filipino and Latino Gay Men." *Journal of Ethnic and Migration Studies.* Forthcoming.

Pascoe, C. J. 2007. *Dude: You're a Fag: Masculinity and Sexuality in High School.* Berkeley: University of California Press.

Schilt, Kristen. 2011. *Just One of the Guys? Transgender Men and the Persistence of Gender Inequality.* Chicago: University of Chicago Press.

Stockdill, Brett, and Mary Danico. 2012. *Transforming the Ivory Tower: Challenging Racism, Sexism, and Homophobia in the Academy.* Manoa, HI: University of Hawaii Press.

Ward, Jane. 2008. "Dude-Sex: White Masculinities and 'Authentic' Heterosexuality Among Dudes Who Have Sex With Dudes." *Sexualities* 11 (4): 415–35.

Yoshino, Kenji. 2006. *Covering: The Hidden Assault on our Civil Rights.* New York: Random House.

6

The Gold Pen

Deborah J. Cohan

I hate yellow gold. I always have. It looks gaudy and cheap to me. My skin is pale, my eyes green, and my hair almost black, and silver looks better on me. I like chunky silver bracelets, cuffs, or bangles, and a few big silver rings with African motifs. I also hate thin pens, the ones that are hard to grip. I prefer thicker pens, the ones that others often seem to dislike because they write more like magic markers. So I am not sure why I am obsessed with my dad's pen. It's gold; it's thin; it's one of those fancy Marc Cross pens that businessmen have used for decades. The powerful kind of pens that close deals, sign contracts, and make things happen. In my dad's case, he made a living wrestling with words, arranging them just right into catchy ad campaigns. With his pen, he scoured others' prose and made relentless revisions of others' ideas, and more privately, he wrote my mom and me love letters and poetry, hate mail, and then apology letters.[1]

On July 12, 2012, the movers were at my home in Boston to box me up and move me to South Carolina. The next day they would load everything onto the moving truck, drive off with it, and on July 15, I would get on a plane with one suitcase, my backpack, and my mother, who had agreed to join me, to help me unpack and get settled in my new home. I had decided it would be wise to pack certain things myself—like the contents of my jewelry box where I have been keeping my dad's pen—but the packers convinced me that the more I let them pack and transport for me, the easier. I tend to over-pack anyway so this made sense. I found an oversized, red silk drawstring jewelry bag, dumped the contents of the jewelry box into it, and handed it to one of the men.

I arrived in Bluffton, and a few days later so did my stuff—all 149 boxes and my Nissan Sentra. As I unpacked, some things surprised me, things Mark, my ex-husband, and I had not used that had been stored in boxes in our basement from my dad's place—boxes of slides from childhood trips to Europe, childhood diaries, letters that my grandmother had written to me, letters that my mother had written to my father, and so many photographs. It was intriguing figuring out how to repurpose furniture and objects in my new home. That spirit of re-invention inspires me. We unpacked my bedroom, but I couldn't find the pen in the jewelry bag. Then I went to unpack my study and set up small colorful pails of pens and pencils on my desk, the same desk my father used years ago, and I still could not find the pen. How could I suddenly have lost the one thing that I have held onto for the more than seven years since my dad has been sick? How could I be that careless and disorganized? How was it possible that I had doubles and triples of some things, that I had every pashmina, every book, and way too many spatulas, and yet I could not find this pen? How have I managed to lose the one thing that seems most my dad, that tethers me to his work and the life of his mind?

I understand my dad lost his mind—after all, that's what the diagnosis of de-mentia is all about—but I have not lost my own memory of my dad's mind with all its crevices of brilliance, darkness, and madness. All I want is this pen. For me, it represents a link to a writing life, a creative life, a juicy life, and a prosper-ous life. It is also a link to my dad's healthier days, an evocative object that helps me recall his vigor and vitality and robustness. I have other objects I know he used or enjoyed when he was living independently, but many of these are objects of leisure. My dad's words are what I remember most, and the pen is the tool to craft and mix and blend the words that I long for. The very one he used.

Pens also remind me of a time less tethered, a time when a machine wasn't the mediating force between the brain and the hand and the words on the page. I intuit that I may never use this pen to actually write. I just want it around to anchor me to creativity, to my dad's and to mine.

I remember how my dad looked hunkered down over the oversized dining table in our house, working on advertising slogans and marketing presentations for prospective clients late into the night with multiple yellow legal pads and his gold pen. I can see the way his right hand gripped the pen, and his left hand gently yet with a sense of firmness held the paper in place, his head cocked slightly to the left; all that was obvious to me was how words looked like they effortlessly flowed out of my father and onto the paper. Occasionally, he made notes on the margins of the papers for his secretary so she would know to flip the paper over and follow the arrows for inserting section A, B, or C. This was the seventies and eighties, before my dad used a computer with the cut and paste functions. But when you would read my dad's work over in its entirety, it was seamless. The whole scene conjures up an intense sense of work, well, actually of procrastination. I relate to this. In college, I often worked on papers until two, three, and four a.m. and have retained something of my topsy-turvy, twenty-something routine even today. In recent years, I have tried writing in the mornings and afternoons, yet there is still something about the night, the way creativity seems to linger more quietly yet swirl around more urgently and magically, that pulls me in, that gives me a surge. My dad was critical of my schedule, thinking I stayed up far too late and slept too much of the day away, and I often internalize that same criticism, wishing in some ways that I was a true morning person. Perhaps he was trying to get me to learn from what he perceived to be his own mistakes.

But the iconic image of my dad propped up with his pen in the middle of the night simultaneously moves me and arrests me. My dad at one with the pen: the relationship is reassuring in its durability and reliability yet unsettling in its relentless quest for perfection.

Two summers before I was to move to my new home in South Carolina, Craig, my dad's therapist, called and asked me to bring slides for my dad to see, so I loaded up the trunk of the car with boxes of slide carousels, rented a projector, and made the drive to Cleveland. I didn't know it then, but that would mark the last visit I would ever have with my father. A talented photographer with a keen eye, my dad had taken all of these pictures through the years, and Craig had decided this would be a good activity to share together. Craig, my dad, and I made our way to the family lounge to go through the slides—some were from childhood trips with my mother to the French Riviera, the English countryside, Scandinavia, Italy, Carmel, Big Sur, and Maine. Others were pictures from concerts, botanical gardens, and museums. I was concerned about what it meant for my dad to be inundated with all these images. As it turned out, the projector didn't work and we were unable to view the slides. So Craig wheeled my dad upstairs while I loaded everything back into the car. When I returned to Dad's room to find them, Craig took me aside and quietly whispered, "Your dad broke down a little."

I asked, "Why? What did he say?"

Craig told me that my dad had said, "You're not gonna leave me, are you?" and then suddenly Craig burst into tears, covered his mouth with his large hand, and ran out of the room and down the hall. I felt compassion for his sense of shame in crying as a therapist, for his need to rush away from me. I imagined there might be unconscious father/son dynamics going on and potential countertransference issues for him in letting go of my dad. There are times in my own work with college students, particularly when teaching about violent trauma and its effects and seeing how it resonates with too many of my students' life experiences, that I cry or hold back tears or speak with a broken voice, and more accurately with a broken heart.

Looking back, I was always caught up in my dad's writing, and especially in its slickness and precision, qualities that went missing upon my dad's diagnosis of dementia. I remember visiting him at the dinner hour on a Sunday night at a different nursing home in Cleveland, probably in 2006 or so. He was seated with a woman named Rose. The other woman assigned to the table was Ann, but she was not there that night; her son Fred and daughter-in-law Joan had come to take her home for dinner. This is something I was unable to do since I was visiting from Boston. After dinner, we were all hanging around the lounge area and Joan approached us; she had just dropped Ann back at her room, and she went into detail about what she had prepared for dinner. They had steaks on the grill, sugar snap peas, sweet potatoes, and sherbet with cantaloupe and berries for dessert. It sounded healthy, colorful, and bountiful. On behalf of my dad, I was thoroughly envious. I longed for him to have this sort of meal, either home-cooked or in a great restaurant; I wished I could regularly afford to take him out for dinner. But I also know that to do that I needed to hire an aide to help us. All of this was prohibitive in the midst of searching for a tenure-track position while juggling crushing student loans and credit card debt. I was faced with a far more limited financial landscape than the one in which I grew up. The whole thing was like a bad sequel to the nineties indie film, *The Slums of Beverly Hills* with this one called something like *Going on Medicaid in Beachwood, Ohio*. A sort of tragicomedy in which I come to understand class privilege as fluid and dynamic, nervously shifting in the course of one's lifetime.

I recall that Joan asked my dad what he had for dinner. He did not respond. I thought to myself, "But Dad, you just had dinner an hour and a half ago. You used to be able to recall meals you had months and years ago in fancy restaurants."

Fred said, "Jim, you don't remember?"

And to compensate for any potential embarrassment, I jumped right in: "Oh yeah, my dad had matzo ball soup, a small salad, pot roast, mixed vegetables, boiled potatoes, and marble cake." I wanted to add, but don't, "On dusty rose-colored plastic plates, the kind used in hospitals around the world." There's something about those dishes that would look dirty and unappetizing even if Ruth's Chris steaks were sizzling on them or Cheesecake Factory cakes were served on them.

As we were all talking, the nursing aide brought my dad neon-orange peanut butter crackers as a snack. My dad's hands shook as he tried to release the plastic surrounding the crackers, just as they had shaken when he ate his dinner. The image was haunting—my dad had trouble stabbing the grape tomatoes on his salad. I recalled how he took his left hand to hold the tomato still and then tried to steady the fork in his right hand to prick the tomato. Yet twenty-five years ago, during an argument at a dinner party with my mom's parents, he had thrown plates in the kitchen with great precision. On better, calmer days, he had grasped his pen with ease, dreaming up sharp, pointed ad campaigns. But the tomato, that small ball of fleshy, juicy red matter, was out of his reach, out of his control. And then even the conversation began to lack precision and self-control as he remarked to me, "I wish I could shower with you again. When you were a baby, you would get naked and I would wear a bathing suit and I would take you in the shower." And then, completely out of context, he turned to Fred and says, "Bananas give me gas."

From about 2000 until 2006, my dad used his pen less and less and started to transition to using an iMac, that now retro-looking machine with the royal blue sides, not exactly the choice of most men in their late seventies, but he possessed an aesthetic all his own. After 2006, steeped in the confusion of dementia, he stopped using both the computer and the pen.

I spent months believing that only if and when I found the pen again would I be able to write. As a result, my creativity felt conditional at best. At some point, I stumbled upon an old favorite book by Carolyn Heilbrun, *Writing a Woman's Life*, in which she is critical of this line of thinking, for it is ultimately self-punishing:

> We women have lived too much with closure: "if he notices me, if I marry him, if I get into college, if I get this work accepted, if I get this job"—there always seems to loom the possibility of something being over, settled, sweeping clear the way for contentment. This is the delusion of a passive life. When the hope for closure is abandoned, when there is an end to fantasy, adventure for women will begin. (1988, 130)

I decided to try to tame my self-expectations about finding this pen. After all, clearly it was gone. Inspired by Buddhist teachings that it is best not to cling, to not be too attached, I tried to live out the mantra, "Not too tight, not too loose."

In late fall 2012, I found myself interested in dating and very reluctantly decided to join Match.com; it felt like the only way to meet anyone. I was sick of being picked up by seventy-something, wealthy, retired golfers at the Starbucks near Hilton Head. I realized this online dating thing was where my dad's craft would really shine. He would have me neatly and crisply packaged with a great photo and tagline and a nifty description of what I seek in a relationship. If nothing else, we'd get a good laugh out of the whole thing, and he would be amused by the terrible self-marketing of others. So I took a chance. And I met Mike. We spent an entire month emailing and calling until our first date on December 1. We arranged to meet for lunch at noon and wound up leaving each other after eleven p.m. Later that same week, I found myself sharing relationship advice with a former student from years ago who has become a friend, and I said, "The real litmus test is if you never want the conversation to end."

An English major, a director of media relations, a music buff, a lover of word play, and an avid reader, Mike is no stranger to the significance of words and the power of voice. Like my dad (and he really isn't), there's a basic similarity: the appreciation for a good story, a good tagline, a catchy, memorable slogan that captures it all. A few days after our first date, we were talking on the phone about aging, dementia, and abuse, and I shared with him a bit about my dad. I briefly made mention of the fact that this is the subject of much of my writing. The next day he emailed me indicating an interest in reading my work if and when I would be up for sharing it. So later that day I sent him my first gritty essay about caregiving for my dad that had just been accepted for publication. I figured the quality of writing was decent enough, and that the content would either make him interested to know me more or be completely off-putting and make him run like hell. Either way, these seemed like good things for me to learn early on. To know if he can sit through that level of discomfort, really be here, talk about it, ask questions, and still want to stay. I hate to admit it but in some ways perhaps I was testing him. His gracious response and curiosity ignited in me a desire to write more, to get my work out; it has made me gutsier about my writing, the way I have longed to be.

Every morning since December first, with the exception of the mornings we are able to wake up together on weekends, Mike has sent me an e-mail. However, I have never received words on paper, neither a card nor a letter. The tiny cards that accompany the flowers he has sent don't count because it's not his writing. Other than seeing him sign his name on a restaurant bill or tally up my losing score when we play Uno, I have no idea what his handwriting even looks like. There seems to be nothing about how we function that relies on a pen. On words, yes, many of them. But not on pens. Perhaps it is indeed possible to write, and live, and love without the pen.

⌒

Long intrigued with silence and solitude but not always making the time for it that I know is nourishing, I decided in August 2012 to finally read Anne LeClaire's *Listening Below the Noise: The Transformative Power of Silence*. A woman minister sitting next to me on an airplane had recommended it. LeClaire talks about her journey in practicing full days of silence, essentially letting go of the surface chatter of the world to venture into the depths of her own being. This resonates with me. I know that in stillness there is greater light and clarity for living a more expansive, profound, creative, and spacious life. What hadn't yet registered with me was how that same stillness and quiet is necessary for dying. LeClaire recalls a story of a friend's husband who said when nearing the end of his life, "I'm dying. Dying requires concentration. It requires quiet" (2009, 149).

Standing at the ticket counter at the Savannah airport on August 13, 2012, ready to check in to race to Cleveland for a visit to have my last goodbye with my dad, I received a call from hospice that he had just died. I fell to the floor sobbing. It was as though my dad had left me mid-sentence. How do we finish the narrative of our lives without our parents? Minutes later I overheard a young boy, about eight years old, ask his mom, "Do you know where Dad is?" I wanted to scoop the kid up and say, "Ya' know, honey, I have the exact same question."

On the last day of my father's life, he stopped speaking, and I have come to believe that with his urgent desire to protect me, he would not let me see him that way, nor would he let me interact with him in the absence of words. The thing is, my dad and I were never really quiet around each other. It was only when my dad lived in nursing homes that we experienced more quiet together than ever before. While he slept or while the nurses assisted him, I got into a habit of always having with me a tote bag of work to do, papers to grade, books to read, and a legal pad to jot down notes about this whole experience of caregiving for an ill and elderly parent who had been abusive. So much confused me, and writing seemed like a way to sort through the muck, to let the grime of the experience fall out of me and away from me. Writing was a way out and a way in.

Alternating between my dad's naps, hallucinations, and jarring moments of lucidity, I sat and stared at him, wept, studied his face and his body and the room, and compulsively wrote, with one of my own thick pens on legal pad paper, never on my laptop, which I did not bring on my trips. Somehow, the words that best captured how I felt revealed themselves in front of him. It was as though, as he continually lost his grasp of language, I was able to more fully come into my own sense of voice about our experience.

In the spring of 2009, I wrote this as my dad took a nap:

I watch you as you sleep, not unlike you probably watched me as I slept as a newborn baby and as a young girl. In wonder, in awe, in calm, and in worry. A parent watches a child sleep with anticipation of a future. An adult child watches a sick parent sleep with a sense of the past. You are finally still and quiet, you a man whom I know as chaotic and loud. We rest in this calm as you fall in and out of slumber and I grade papers. I need to study your face, memorize it, as I know I'll need it one day, yet the you now is not the you I want to remember. In a few days, I'll be back with over a hundred students, giving lectures, attending meetings, going to a concert, a lunch with a friend, a performance of *The Vagina Monologues*, and in my week ahead, I worry about being too busy, about running from one activity to the next, breathless, yet one day, Daddy, you did this, too, right? How would you restructure those days now? What did you hope for? What do you hope for now? With your tongue half out of your mouth, you resemble a little boy with Down Syndrome. You look tired though I can't tell if you're tired of this life. Yesterday I brought you coffee from Caribou with one of their napkins that made a jab at Starbucks that said, "Our coffee is smooth and fresh 'cause burnt and bitter were already taken." Whenever I see great lines and logos, I think of you. Your creativity still shines through as we leaf through *Metropolitan Home* and marvel at minimalist spaces. Your stained maroon sweatpants are pulled up halfway toward your chest and your stomach looks distended. Earlier today, I saw as you put imaginary pills to your mouth with your fingers, something I assumed to be a self-soothing ritual you performed after the nurse told you it was not yet time for more medication. Being in Cleveland, I'm surrounded by childhood friends hanging out with their dads, younger men than you, in their sixties and early seventies, robust, athletic, energetic men vigorously playing tennis and golf, working, traveling, and chasing after their dreams, not figments of their imaginations in thin air. Oh, Daddy. Your eyes open suddenly and you ask, "What are you writing?" I quickly respond, "Oh, nothing really, it's just for school."

However, writing about my dad in front of my dad seemed like a profound act of betrayal. It also felt mean. As I see it now, it helped me grieve and let go. Contained in a tight, unattractive, physical space with my dad, enmeshed in his care in ways I probably should have never been, I was writing to untangle a knotty family narrative, to finally record and understand my experience as my own. By writing in front of him, I think something else happened that was necessary. I came to realize that all we had to give to each other was space. Psychic space. Most importantly, I needed to give him space and quiet to eventually die. My dad's almost eight years of debilitating illness made me grasp his final inability to help and guide me, and that gave me the space I needed to dream of what I wanted to do. Though he helped me and was involved in most major decisions I had made in my life, dementia forced him to check out. It also forced me to check in with how well I was writing my own life.

I remember one day, a little over two years before he died, he asked me, "Deb, what does 'quiet' mean and how do you spell it?" Of all the words to ask about—I was floored. Quiet is a word that small children know. How could my dad be eighty-two years old and unable to process this simple word? But it felt tremendously revealing; this was my dad with a loud voice and a mean bark at times. People remarked that he had a great voice. Even in his eighties, he often sounded much more youthful. His voice was soothing, booming, crazy making, gentle, and loving all at once—and it was always clear.

I value what's involved in cultivating one's voice. Feminist politics and my antiviolence work have always led me back to the power of finding one's voice. I think voice is both the quality of how we speak as well as what we speak about from a gut level of clarity and wholeness. On my fortieth birthday, my dad left me a gorgeous voicemail in which he told me he loved being my father; I obsessively recorded it in various places so I would be sure to always have it. While I am fortunate to have an uncanny memory for voices anyway, his voice is one I want to hear again and not just in my head.

I have heard that it's in the silence that we most come to know another person and ourselves. Six weeks before my dad died, the nursing home called me wanting my signature to get my dad into hospice. All the years of worrying about how and when they would call to tell me he died were replaced in my head with, "He's dying; it's happening now." I asked to speak with him. I really just found myself wanting his advice more than anyone else's, and I said, "I want you to know I love you, Dad." I tried to say it in a way that he wouldn't be fully aware that I knew he was dying.

He replied, "You don't need to worry about that, Deb; I know you do."

I then asked him, "What's your advice for me, Dad, for anything in the world?" I so desperately wanted his input, maybe even his criticisms to weigh against my own perceptions and judgment. Sometimes in the past he would say, "It's your life, Deb, live it." And now, for the first time, he said nothing. There was dead air. Not a word. Just blank space. In my head, I was saying: "Wait, Dad—for decades you wanted to tell me what to do and how to do it and now I actually want and need your advice and you aren't gonna give it?" Then suddenly this silence became oddly reassuring and liberating for me. Finally, there was no dictating, no steering, no telling me what to do more of, what to do less of, criticizing what decisions I made, no shouting or swearing at me at the top of his lungs. His parting gift to me was the absence of all that. There was just quiet space, actually an odd silence of acceptance and connection. And in that was freedom for me. Perhaps the air wasn't dead, but more alive and full of possibility for me to recraft my life than ever before. To write my life into being, into meaning. The legacy he left me with is this.

~

It was a Wednesday in late February 2013, and I was packing up at the end of my Introduction to Sociology class. My student Caitlin approached me to explain to me why she'd had so many absences. I started to put the washable markers away that I had been using on the white board in class. I stuck them in the small pouch that I never seem to use and suddenly found myself touching something thin and familiar. I looked down and saw the gold pen. I don't even recall putting it there, but then it made sense that I must have because the backpack was my carry-on luggage for the plane, where I put all the things I most definitely did not want to risk losing. I smiled at myself in that way where maybe no one could see it on my face, but it was deep within my very being. My dad had always wanted to see me teach a class and never did; he wanted to move to the Carolinas and never did. And suddenly, right there, was my dad. In my classroom in South Carolina. I wanted to either laugh hysterically or cry, but I knew what I had to do in that moment: I had to talk to Caitlin. I had already learned to begin to write a life without the pen: a life full of new love and intense possibility.

Caitlin told me, "I am so sorry I haven't made it to class, See, it's just that my friend shot and killed himself, and this is all on top of my dad dying a few months ago, just like you, Deb." Grief tugged really hard. I was suddenly struck by what students remember of what we tell them, what they relate to, how so much of what's important for them is not the pure academic stuff but the life stuff, the survival skills. During the course of the year, I had become more open about how my dad had died right before school started, how I was divorced, how

I had grown up in an emotionally abusive home. I had been feeling an extraordinary pull to not sugarcoat the realities.

Caitlin began to cry and then told me about her worries in caring for her little sister since her widowed mother had a heart attack within days of the father's death due to the stress of it all. It hit me that Caitlin was just eighteen, that I was forty-three, perhaps about the age of her mother. I had thought I was too young to lose my father, that this man so deeply lodged in the world, in my world, was gone far too soon. I am certain Caitlin was too young to lose a father. Instinctively, I reached out to hug Caitlin, and we exchanged very few words; quiet presence through this pain was all that was necessary. I lightly touched her face as she cried. I completely let go of what is supposedly appropriate in a professional, academic context. I was suddenly reminded of Craig, the therapist at the nursing home.

All that I clung to is what seemed right in that moment of deepened vulnerability—for Caitlin and for me. I have learned that if I throw the whole of myself into teaching, the students learn more and so do I. I have also learned that teaching and learning can heal. Healing only happens from the rawness that's exposed. I told Caitlin I am here if she needs anything. But we were headed into spring break and she soon vanished after that. She'll never know how serendipitous it was for me to share new fatherloss and to find that pen all in the space of that tiny conversation.

I left campus, jumped into my car, and immediately called Mike. "You'll never believe this. I just found the pen," I exclaimed, and then I chuckled. "I even think there's a story in here, something about how I'm glad that I found it but even more glad that I first had to figure out how to let it go."

NOTE

1. I explore my father's abuse in fuller detail in a previously published work titled "Sugar," in a 2014 special issue on *Writing the Father* in the journal, *Life Writing* 11 (1): 127–36. Available online at: *www.tandfonline.com/doi/full/10.1080/14484528.2013.838736#. UuiwkXn0BZg*. "The Gold Pen" and "Sugar" are chapters in a larger memoir I am currently developing.

REFERENCES

Heilbrun, Carolyn G. 1988. *Writing a Woman's Life*. New York: Ballantine Books.
LeClaire, Anne D. 2009. *Listening Below the Noise: The Transformative Power of Silence*. New York: Harper Perennial.

7

Whether Willing or Unwilling

The Personal, the Professional, and Two Years of Too Much

Meghan M. Sweeney

> *Nolens volens, adv.*: Whether willing or not;
> willing or unwilling, willy-nilly.[1]

Pretty much everyone experiences it: a year when (quickly or in excruciating slow motion) everything seems to crumble. My own year turned into two and included a tricky childbirth; a dramatic weight loss, hospitalization, and eventual diagnosis of an autoimmune disease; my father's aggressive brain cancer; and my mother's early and confounding memory loss. There were a few other cancer scares thrown in for good measure as well as a minor car accident, a stolen bike, and, for comic relief, a dramatically flooded basement (perfectly timed to coincide with my father's transfer to Hospice). On top of all this were the (now sidelined) issues that came with being a new mother and a professor.

I imagine the screenplay: middle-class thirty-something girl's got it good . . . until one day when it all begins to unravel. It would never make it to the screen—"Heavy-handed!" "Maudlin!" producers would say and pass it up for a more streamlined, sensible kind of tragedy.

Until all of this started happening, in the fall of 2011, "letting go" seemed to me to be a particularly spurious, self-help-y kind of pursuit. At best, it was something that I did in yoga class every other week. Even when it wasn't the wisest decision, I was someone who held on: to friendships that may have run their course, to piles of notebooks from junior high. I certainly held on to my worries, seeing them not as a negative byproduct of a hectic life, but a sustaining force in my own profession. Without the rigidity of the nine–to-five workweek, a gentle, persistent anxiety was sometimes the only thing that kept me going.

As an English professor, my job follows me everywhere. While I welcome the intrusion of my professional world into my personal life, I have been cautious about going in the other direction. I am not a confessional teacher. Until recently, revealing even small personal details about myself in class left me feeling raw and exposed, as well as irresponsible. I wanted to avoid being either a rigid, taskmaster type or a cuddly, big-sister type. Keep it professional, I told myself, and, in my snarkier moments, I added, "you're not out to make any twenty-year-old friends." The entire semester I was pregnant (and hugely so), I didn't say a word about it to my students until the end of the semester. I was the elephant in the room, but I avoided conversation about it because I didn't want my body to define me. I winced at the thought of my students patting my belly, coming up with names for the creature inside, and generally juvenilizing me the way that some old ladies at the mall did. So I kept my friendly small talk about other things and they, taking a cue from me, did too.

I've sloughed off several old selves since then though—many of them through necessity rather than desire. In this essay, I tackle some questions that have persisted as I navigated my way through the past two years. Most crucially: how can experiencing and acknowledging the frailty of the body change the contours of one's pedagogy and professional life? In what ways do the terms I have used to define myself (and define myself against) as a feminist shape my understanding of what is possible and desirable as a person with a career, a child, and important relationships to maintain?

One other pressing question: how might I explore these issues in a way that is not overly sentimental or naïve? As Ann Jurecic observes, critical writing about illness can "appear reductive to literary scholars who value complexity" (2012, 12). Thus, I acknowledge the wide variety of literary critics, sociologists, philosophers, and medical practitioners who demonstrate that personal narrative and critical reflection / scholarly engagement are not mutually exclusive. I appreciate work by writers such as Jurecic, Eve Kosofsky Sedgwick (1999, 2003), Sandra Gilbert (2006), Jenny Hockey (Hallem, Hockey, and Howarth 1999), and others who have, particularly in the last fifteen years, eloquently demonstrated the many forms that feminist explorations of suffering, loss, and mourning can take. At a time when a wariness that borders on hostility still dominates critical practice, critics need interpretive approaches that balance skepticism with a willing attentiveness to texts as well as an openness to liminal experiences, our own and the accounts of others.[2] Such practices serve as powerful reminders of the frailty of the body, providing not an occasion for mere sympathetic response, but for "the deep embodied knowledge" (Jurecic 2012, 124) of what Eve Sedgwick calls "recognition" and "realization" (2003, 167–68).

Giving birth was the inaugural liminal experience of my own, when I felt the first shock of recognition. In the midst of my hallucinatory state brought on by a complex cocktail of hormones and numbing medications, Henry came into the world, yanked out by his ankle. As with other new parents, I was given complimentary membership to the club of the profoundly sleep deprived. It seemed as if everyone who had been through the new baby wringer was happy to share, unbidden, stories about their own lowest parenting lows.

Thanks to them and to my own reading, I felt as if I knew, as much as any novice could, about what to expect after delivery. I felt an almost constant sense of low-grade panic but attributed it to anxiety about my mother's illness, sleep deprivation, and the gaping (if adorable) maw that was the new baby. My body felt hollowed out, but I chalked it up to complications from my long labor and C-section as well as ceaseless breast-feeding.

One morning, before I learned what was wrong, I read an article by Pico Iyer (2011) called "The Joy of Quiet" as I made my morning oatmeal. In it, he discusses the need to slow down and disconnect in order to connect, quoting the usual suspects (Thoreau and Thomas Merton) as well as unexpected advocates of solitude (designer Philippe Starck). His insights aren't new, as he himself observes, but his questions are relevant: how do we deal with the erosion of private life and the constant bombardment by breaking news (when all news is breaking news)? He discusses his own attempts to ensure that he has the chance to do nothing. By allowing himself this quiet, he experiences what the monk David Steindl-Rast calls "that kind of happiness that doesn't depend on what happens" (qtd. in Iyer). How, I wondered, is this clear happiness even possible? It seemed almost ridiculous.

As I was reading, the oatmeal boiled over and I scraped it off the stove, ate it anyway, and forgot about the article. I thought of it again some weeks later, though, when I was in the hospital, feeling the morphine take effect. Then the doctor informed me, in a tone that was too frank to be condescending, that I was "one sick puppy." He explained that an autoimmune disease was sending me into a catabolic state in which my body, having worked through layers of fat, had begun devouring muscle. Trying to seem competent, I took notes, nodding my head at the dizzying array of new terms as if I knew what they meant: sed rate, Solu-Medral, histoplasmosis screening.

Near the end of my hospital visit (that euphemistic word used to describe being caught up in the medical industrial complex),[3] I took my first, shaky shower and saw how bony I was. I stared at the green person in the mirror (who was about to have her first transfusion) and noticed the scraggly blue patterns of veins along my chest and arms. Cancer patient, I thought over and over and, given the way my white blood cells were behaving, it turns out I wasn't the only one who was thinking that. In just a few days, I had become unrecognizable to myself. Still, that was early spring, and as the months went on, I felt better with my combination of pills and supplements and infusions. Cancer was more or less ruled out, and I began to bring back more foods into my diet just as the baby was starting on smashed avocado and banana. Happiness that doesn't depend on what happens began to seem like a smart idea.

As bad as those months were, they turned out to be the prelude. When I was in the hospital, I felt relatively calm. I was relieved to be somewhere that seemed secure, where my blood and temperature and pain were carefully monitored by someone else. I surrendered to the rhythms of the place, mostly, only occasionally waking up in a panic.

Then, a few months later, my father was diagnosed with metastatic melanoma. I found the interminable periods of waiting and not knowing to be much worse than the physical wear and tear of my own illness. The situation was also exacerbated by the fact that my dad had been caring for my mother and decisions had to be made about her, too.

By December, after his repeated trips to the hospital, brain surgery, rehabilitation, seizures, and hallucinations, my father was transferred to a hospice facility where, despite the grim prognosis, we managed to find some measure of inner quiet. Once we left the hospital, with its tubes and drips and whirrings, he didn't see snakes everywhere. He also didn't have, in Sandra Gilbert's words, that El Greco look (2006, 20); his eyes were bright, his skin as rosy as it had ever been, and it was hard to believe that death would come soon. He was only seventy-two, after all, and he had been, as he reminded us, running up stairs two at a time until a few months earlier.

Yet there were frequent reminders of what was coming. His mind often turned to thoughts of things falling apart; he began to experience his body as a body in pieces. He was fascinated, for example, by "the white lumps at the end of the bed." When we told him they were his feet, covered up by a sheet, he looked skeptical. "It's dough, rising down there."

I found a certain comfort in adopting his way of looking. Dad's rush to a more figurative understanding of his body was surprising, since he had always valued clarity and eschewed fiction in almost all its forms. Now he was being thrust, *nolens volens*, into a world where literal truths were too ruthless and had to be approached sideways. Everything he said seemed symbolic, although, at the same time, it was less mysterious than that. His statements lacked the studied, crafted quality of metaphor, and they were rooted in the body.

Never has the language of psychoanalysis, and in particular of Jacques Lacan, seemed so apt. As a theorist, Lacan can be opaque, even deliberately obfuscating, his language a kind of poetic delirium. Yet his ideas and his mode of delivery fit these circumstances and provided me with a way of conceptualizing the tenuous nature of self. According to Lacan, when we are between six and eighteen months of age, we enter the mirror stage, a key developmental moment when we first "recognize" ourselves in the mirror. This recognition is simultaneously a misrecognition: we perceive an ideal, whole body where there is instead a fragmented, chaotic body: a "corps morcelé." The imaginary (that is, based on an image) relationship continues beyond childhood, because the myth of a unified self depends upon it. Elizabeth Grosz, in discussing Lacan's work, emphasizes the way that the body is "dependent on the acquisition of a psychical image for voluntary behavior": "human subjects need the medium of such a psychical image of the body" she says, "in order to link their wishes and desires to their corporeal capacities, making concerted action and rational thought possible" (1999, 269).[4]

The self is a collection of fragments that glom on to one another, but which will all, nevertheless, eventually disperse. Dad's new way of being spoke vividly to the tenuous quality of the psychical image. "Pieces of my life are disappearing," he said one afternoon as we sat staring at the snow, "I've lost thousands of pieces of my life." He wasn't lamenting this fact, exactly, just stating the truth. He also saw coins dropping from his pockets, rolling on the ground, being scattered on the bed. After a while, I gave up telling him that there were no coins and just gathered them up for him, which seemed to help. I also gathered up memories on a tape recorder and was surprised at how taut their narrative structures were, given the way everything else was falling apart. Dad's grasp of what was happening in the present moment may have been shaky, but he could tell you about the guy he worked with for six months back in 1968 with startling accuracy.

As these "life events," as I'll euphemistically call them, began piling up, the borders between the professional (by January, after the baby turned one, I was back in the classroom) and the personal began to seem more permeable. Maybe I just lost the energy I had had for boundary patrol. It wasn't that I went on and on about my personal life; I simply wasn't afraid to let students know that I had a life outside of the classroom that was having an impact on my life inside the classroom. Still, I felt as if I had to model how to be an Adult in Crisis: keeping my shit at least somewhat together. Grading got done, lessons were planned, wayward students were tracked down. In modeling how to keep it together in front of my students, I kept it together, and they helped me out in numerous little ways. When my dad died in the middle of the semester, my graduate students left a card in my box, with good wishes and a surprising—but endearing—number of hand-drawn hearts at the ends of their names. One undergraduate, who was still dealing with his father's death the semester before, offered quotes from Dickens and Shakespeare that were a comfort to him. Others helped simply by moving the class along when they saw that I was unusually sluggish. And it was, despite everything, a good semester.

As in previous terms, I had a fairly good rapport with my students: they learned something, I learned something; we got along just fine. But now, my various crises led me to think more deeply about teacherly ethos and in particular about the role that grief, loss, and comfort might play in the college classroom. The way that students had comforted me and that I, in turn, comforted some of them wasn't clammy or weepy, "suggestive of complacency"; instead, this kind of comfort seemed to draw on the word's roots, the Latin *confortare*, "to strengthen much."[5]

Although it doesn't deal with loss and comfort specifically, Marshall Gregory's (2001) article "Curriculum, Pedagogy, and Teacherly Ethos" provided a guide for thinking about how to articulate the blend of the personal and the professional. It helped me acknowledge that although the thought of being "assessed by students in deeply personal ways" is unsettling, we don't "have to like it in order to concede that such evaluations both always occur and always play a crucial role in student learning" (78). As Gregory makes clear, good teachers strive for balance, showing "how to work for the humanization of the social order, how to be critical of self without falling into self-loathing, how to be critical of others without being thoughtlessly callous, and how to be compassionate of others without being unduly sentimental" (87). Lofty, but important, goals.

After reading Gregory, I turned to a 2009 issue of *Feminist Teacher*, in which editors ask specifically how teachers might acknowledge the presence of grief in the classroom and how "owning" this grief might be a "transformative pedagogical practice" (Barron 2009, 28). In one essay, Blaise Astra Parker writes about her struggle to decide how much to talk about her own embodied grief in the classroom, even though the course was one that dealt with issues of feminism and the body. "Concerned with my professional identity, I also feared seeming self-indulgent," she admits (2009, 76). In another essay, Rachel Alpha Johnston Hurst writes about the "need to be hyper-vigilant about the students' sexist assumptions that a feminine person will comfort and mother them" through their own losses. Nevertheless, while "this professional distance may steer us away from confessing our emotional lives to each other in the classroom, it does not" she maintains, "mean that we absolve ourselves of the burden of emotion" (2009, 40).

Reading these essays, I thought about my own current experiences and the professors I had when I was an undergraduate who, without veering into self-indulgence, were able to address personal and emotional issues. One in particular stood out. In my sophomore year, my ethics professor shared an article he had written about in vitro fertilization in which he described his experiences with infertility. This was one of many nuanced articles that we read on the topic; he was careful not to hijack our opinions or become maudlin. Instead, his writing and teaching were reminders that we could be critically aware examiners of our personal experiences and that these experiences might serve a pedagogical purpose. I was impressed by the way that he could take an extremely intimate subject—one that dealt with sex organs, even—and frame it in such a way that we saw it as one more piece of information to help us shape our own ethical arguments. It was a sign of tremendous trust.

Like my former professor, gender theorist Eve Kosofsky Sedgwick reveals (1999), in nuanced, careful language, the ways that medical experiences might shape a professional life. In describing her diagnosis with breast cancer that spread to her lymph system, she insists that the experiences, "while draining and scary, have also proven just sheerly interesting with respect to exactly the issues of gender, sexuality, and identity formation that were already on my docket" (153). Sedgwick is addressing a very specific set of incidents that included a mastectomy, chemically induced menopause, and baldness. Yet conceptualizing illness as "sheerly interesting" (as academically and pedagogically illuminating) is itself illuminating. Presumably, "sheerly" in this case means something like "nothing other than." It is richly resonant, though, conjuring up a precipitous drop and (through its homophonic connections) images of sharp blades and the tender skin of sheep. The "sheerly interesting" of liminal medical experiences inspires the vertiginous feeling of being close to the cliff, the knife. It's not a thrill-seeking experience but the recognition/realization of the tenuous nature of existence.

In her book *Touching Feeling*, Sedgwick (2003) more explicitly discusses the transitional realm between diagnosis and death, suggesting that such liminality is a privileged scene of teaching and learning. In particular, she is invested in the Tibetan Buddhist notion of the *bardo*, or space between states of being. In the Tibetan "instructions for dying" she examines, both teaching and learning mean "'opening to' (a person or predicament), 'opening around' or 'softening around' (a site of pain), listening, relaxation, spaciousness" (174). Although these phrases may sound, to her ears, "hardly more than New Age commonplaces"—Buddhist insights are, after all, sometimes used to uphold floppy self-help ideologies— they nonetheless seem to her "able to support a magnetic sense of the real far into the threshold of extinguished identity" (175).

I haven't, just yet, been pushed far into the threshold of extinguished identity: my own diagnosis, for now, is not nearly as dire as Sedgwick's. As I get my bimonthly infusions, monitor my white blood cell count, and, as executor of my parents' affairs, spend hours on the phone with the SSA, tax advisors, and lawyers, in addition to cleaning out forty years of memories from a big house, I understand how much more harrowing it could be. I can't help but think about the economic conditions of my situation and how much they have shaped me. If I am able to reflect on my experiences and ponder how they might have an impact on my pedagogy, it is in no small part because have a partner, friends, and family to help with the emotional heavy lifting—and because I have a job with solid benefits.

Actually, as a state employee in North Carolina, my health insurance policy is, in some respects, worse than the one I had in graduate school, where graduate students were unionized and had a decent dental plan. However, at our university we do have the benefit of a generous FMLA policy that provided me with twelve weeks of paid leave after I gave birth—generous, that is, by US standards. The "International Labor Organization standards state that women should be guaranteed at least 14 weeks of paid maternity leave" (World Policy Forum 2013). Many countries in Europe (Germany, Austria, the Czech Republic, and Sweden, among others), offer fifty-two weeks or more of paid leave. The United States is one of only eight countries, out of 188 that have known policies, without paid leave. To offer some perspective: other countries without paid leave include

Western Samoa, Suriname, and Papua New Guinea (World Policy Forum 2013). What is considered lucky here is taken as a basic right many places in the world.

The US Family Medical Leave Act of 1993 does require certain employers to provide employees unpaid but job-protected leave for qualified medical or family reasons. However, as a recent NPR report (Ludden 2013) observed, "some 40 percent of the workforce is not eligible": "Same-sex partners can't use it to care for each other,[6] and people can't use it to care for a grandparent" (although some states have expanded the definition of eligible family members in their policies), and "businesses with fewer than 50 people are also exempt." It's an embarrassment.

Since I was back in the hospital less than two months after delivery, my time off wasn't just a matter of adjusting to the rhythms of a newborn and recovering from a Caesarean, although that would be reason enough for leave. It also meant learning how to deal with an immune disorder. Without that time, I would have been less likely to recover so (relatively) quickly and go into remission. I think, frequently, of what this experience would have been like if I had a different kind of job, a minimum wage job or a high-pressure corporate job, even one I liked. What if I had been unable (either because of economic necessity or because of precarious notions of ambition) to take the necessary time to recover?

In the months when I returned to my job and was thinking about what it meant to be productive even with a baby and other family issues, the old notion of working women and ambition became a hot topic again. Everyone, from CNN to *The New York Times*, was talking about women "leaning in." *Lean In* is the title of Facebook COO Sheryl Sandberg's (2013) bestselling book, in which she emphasizes that "conditions for all women will improve when there are more women in leadership roles giving strong and powerful voice to their needs and concerns" (7). At a time when many powerful women eschew the term, Sandberg unabashedly calls herself a feminist. Her book's insistence on balanced partnerships and its analysis of some women's unwillingness to "own" their own successes (44) have been transformative for many readers.

Although part of me embraces what she says—she seems, for a COO of an enormous company, surprisingly reasonable—I'm somewhat exhausted by some of her assumptions, and in particular those regarding productivity. She does emphasize that there are times when "leaning back" is more appropriate than "leaning in," but she nonetheless often frames ambition in terms of ceaseless striving (95). In both her 2010 TED Talk and her book, for example, she uses an analogy to think about women who want to start a family. Sandberg, who has two children, tells women to keep their "foot on the gas pedal" until the very last minute (103). She emphasizes the importance of women remaining deeply involved in their careers even when pregnant so that months or even years of productivity are not lost.[7] But the analogy also raises questions that she doesn't ask: Where is the car going that is so important? Is there another way to get there, perhaps one that doesn't involve fossil fuels? That is to say, what is it about this "workplace" that makes it worth pursuing? What are the hidden costs? We don't see much here about life beyond work, if there is one.

In a rebuttal to the book, Kate Losse (2013), who worked for Facebook, argues that *Lean In* should be seen as a "product with strongly corporate and technocratic as well as feminist ambitions." Losse reminds us that "how can I be a more successful worker?" is not the only feminist question we might ask. Instead of putting our feet on the gas pedal or, to use another analogy from Sandberg, angling for a seat on a rocket ship (in her case, a job at Google) we might instead explore other ways of conceptualizing a productive life. The alternative to rockets and fast cars doesn't have to be "inertia" or "stagnation" (Sandberg 2013, 62)—it might be something in between, or something altogether different. What seems a thrilling velocity from one perspective might seem a relentless search for novelty from another; what seems inertia and stagnation from one perspective might seem to be rest and replenishment from a different point of view. Letting go of the need to jump on the rocket does not mean letting go of the idea of a productive self; it means embracing a redefinition of self that has embedded within it a recognition and even a celebration of limitations (King 2012). Letting go also involves releasing oneself from the idea of the "perfect letting go"—one in which the self would be infused with serenity, in which worry would scatter like leaves.

I may attain this serene state at some point, but for now, worry seems to be a constitutive part of my own happiness, and I have to learn to work with it. By that I don't mean holding on to the bone-aching worry that comes with illness and loss; rather, that a certain amount of fretfulness is inevitable and can even be productive. Rooting myself in language (as with Sedgwick's "sheerly interesting") helps me visualize this. As a verb, "fret" means to be peevish; it comes from the Old English *fretan*, "eat up, devour," a reminder that worry can gnaw away at the self. Yet there is another old sense of fret meaning to "adorn with interlaced work" especially in gold or silver embroidery that comes from the Old French *freter*.[8] I am trying to think about the ways that one fretting could lead into another, that, rather than being devoured, I could instead imagine the fragile, eaten-away self as artful, laced patterns. Visualizing fretting becomes a kind of meditation exercise, one that seems more possible for me than a pure, clear letting go of thought. In this view, which resonates with much feminist thought of the last several decades,[9] the falling-apart self then becomes a marker of experience rather than something to be fixed.

There isn't, I know, a clear narrative trajectory that goes directly from illness and loss to realization/recognition. Some days, I'd prefer everything to be fixed—both repaired and unchanging. Since that's not an option, though, I muddle through with metaphors, exploring the language of liminality and loss. For now, I'm happy enough, no matter what happens.

NOTES

1. *Oxford English Dictionary, OED Online.* s.v. "nolens volens."
2. Paul Ricoeur's concept of suspicion is useful for thinking about more productive forms of skepticism, although his term "the hermeneutics of suspicion" has been widely misused. In her careful discussion of the term, Alison Scott-Baumann (2012:4) observes that Ricoeur "describes it as an overly powerful mechanism for suspecting others, which is what we do when we believe we know more than others do." As such, Ricoeur eventually rejected the use of the term, ultimately developing other techniques using suspicion that worked "against the delusion that we are omniscient" (184).
3. Sandra Gilbert (2006) discusses the "absurd" concept of hospitality connected to the hospital. "Doctors, nurses, even clerks in the admission office as 'hosts'? Ill or dying patients as 'guests'?" Nevertheless, she admits, the hospital "can indeed be understood as a sort of temporary refuge, albeit a frequently unpleasant one" (181).
4. An instructive alternative to the myth of the unified self comes from Christine Battersby, who writes, "Not all talk of identity involves thinking of the self as unitary or contained; nor indeed need boundaries be conceived in ways that make the identity closed, autonomous or impermeable" (qtd. in Hallem, Hockey, and Howarth 1999, 121).
5. *Online Etymology Dictionary.* Douglas Harper, historian. s.v. "comfort." *www.etymonline.com/index.php?term=comfort.*
6. This is an issue that is still being fleshed out after the Supreme Court's June 2013 ruling that the Defense of Marriage Act (DOMA) is unconstitutional.
7. As Kate Losse and others have observed, *Lean In's* vision of the workplace is surprisingly homogenous, populated by straight women and men who want children.
8. Oxford English Dictionary, *OED Online,* s.v. "fret," v.1, v.2, v. 4. I've always thought that "fret" must be connected to the French word "frotter," to rub; the *OED* suggests that this is a possible, but uncertain, link (see verb 4).
9. See Sedgwick's work as well as Judith Butler's later work and many others.

REFERENCES

Barron, Monica. 2009. "Introduction: Special Cluster on Grief and Pedagogy." *Feminist Teacher* 20 (1): 28–30.

Gilbert, Sandra. 2006. *Death's Door: Modern Dying and the Ways We Grieve.* New York: Norton.

Gregory, Marshall. 2001. "Curriculum, Pedagogy, and Teacherly Ethos." *Pedagogy* 1 (1): 68–89.

Grosz, Elizabeth. 1999. "Psychoanalysis and the Body." In *Feminist Theory and the Body: A Reader,* edited by Janet Price and Margrit Shildrick, 267–71. New York: Routledge.

Hallem, Elizabeth, Jenny Hockey, and Glennys Howarth. 1999. *Beyond the Body: Death and Social Identity.* New York: Routledge.

Hurst, Rachel Alpha Johnston. 2009. "What Might We Learn from Heartache?: Loss, Loneliness, and Pedagogy." *Feminist Teacher* 20 (1): 31–41.

Iyer, Pico. 2011. "The Joy of Quiet." *New York Times,* December 29. *www.nytimes.com/2012/01/01/opinion/sunday/the-joy-of-quiet.html.*

Jurecic, Ann. 2012. *Illness as Narrative.* Pittsburgh: University of Pittsburgh Press.

King, Donna. 2012. "Toward a Feminist Theory of Letting Go." *Feminist Frontiers* 33 (3): 53–72.

Losse, Kate. 2013. "Feminism's Tipping Point: Who Wins from Leaning In?"

Dissent Magazine, March 26. *www.dissentmagazine.org/online_articles/feminisms-tipping-point-who-wins-from-leaning-in*.

Ludden, Jennifer. 2013. "FMLA Not Really Working for Many Employees." *National Public Radio Morning Edition*, February 5. *www.npr.org/2013/02/05/171078451/fmla-not-really-working-for-many-employees*.

Parker, Blaise Astra. 2009. "Losing Jay: A Meditation on Teaching while Grieving." *Feminist Teacher* 20 (1): 71–80.

Sandberg, Sheryl. 2013. *Lean In: Women, Work, and the Will to Lead*. New York: Knopf.

Scott-Baumann, Alison. 2012. *Ricoeur and the Hermeneutics of Suspicion*. New York: Continuum.

Sedgwick, Eve Kosofsky. 1999. "Breast Cancer: An Adventure in Applied Deconstruction." In *Feminist Theory and the Body: A Reader*, edited by Janet Price and Margrit Shildrick, 153–55. New York: Routledge.

———. 2003. *Touching Feeling: Affect, Pedagogy, Performativity*. Durham: Duke University Press.

World Policy Forum. 2013. "Is Paid Leave Available for Mothers of Infants?" Interactive map. World Policy Analysis Center. *worldpolicyforum.org/global-maps/is-paid-leave-available-for-mothers-of-infants*.

8

Letting Go
How Does a Feminist Retire?

Diane E. Levy

Occasionally on campus, I run into a colleague who has been at our university for as long as I have—over thirty-six years. The greeting is always the same: "Are you still here?" Finally, though, I am indeed approaching retirement. This involves a whole new outlook on work and life and identity. I now find myself a "woman of a certain age" with values evolving from those I have held during the last several decades. As a baby-boomer who lived the struggles of the sixties and embraced the new feminism of the seventies, I wonder how these frameworks serve me as I slide out in the twenty-first century.

Some Reflections on Second-Wave Liberal Feminism

We all owe a tremendous debt to second-wave feminists for their hard work in raising awareness of the pervasive sexism in the United States and other parts of the world and for the dramatic changes they implemented in women's lives, from reproductive rights to the right to equal pay for equal work.[1] Sometimes it's hard to realize how much has changed over the last forty years.

Often when I teach, I share a personal story that shocks my students. I tell them how when I was twenty-two and a newly married grad student, my grad student husband and I each earned $3000 as graduate assistants. In those days, that was good money. We applied for an apartment but were denied for lack of income, even though $6000 was sufficient earnings. The policy was that management only "counted" my husband's income, because as a married woman, my income was not considered to be reliable—I could get pregnant and leave the labor force. In order to be approved, we had to either get a cosigner or a doctor's note saying I was on birth control. Women literally didn't count. We have indeed come a long way since those days, but we have much work yet to do to bring about equality.

Like so many others of my generation, I cut my feminist teeth on the values of the liberal wing of second-wave feminism—women should have rights equal to men in all domains of life.[2] As one of a growing number of women coming out of graduate school, I felt both internal and external pressure to use my newly minted PhD to maximum effect. I got a great job as an assistant professor of sociology and over the years worked hard, made my way to full professor, and held a variety of administrative positions. Along the way, one marriage ended, another began, and a daughter was born and raised. In all this time, there were certainly difficulties—never enough time, conflicting schedules, juggling career priorities of two professional parents, stressful days at both home and work—but I always assumed I would continue with both a career and a family. I felt a responsibility to myself, my daughter, and my students to be a role model, to show how it can be done. The mantras of liberal feminism provided me with encouragement, if not exactly a roadmap.[3]

As second-wave feminist ideas came to public consciousness, the liberal branch of feminism came to dominate US mainstream, mass-mediated popular culture, and the drive to dismantle patriarchal institutions shifted to reforming them. The focus was mainly on achieving equality within jobs, education, and income, and the process involved successful changes in laws and social policies. But there was a downside to the widespread embrace of liberal feminist thought. The liberal feminist emphasis on individual rights and free-market enterprise marginalized much needed analysis of systemic and group-based obstacles to the well-being of women (and men). Here I offer two examples of liberal ideas that seemed to be goals worth pursing but that, in the end, failed most women; the myth of having it all and choice feminism.

Having It All

In the 1970s and 1980s, celebrities and entrepreneurs such as Helen Gurley Brown—who is credited with inventing the phrase "having it all"—became influential in shaping everyday understandings of the feminist movement. The liberal idea of having it all, success at work, marriage, and motherhood, quickly moved to the center of debate among women. For some the notion was progressive, for others it was divisive and confusing. In fact, the features of second-wave liberal feminism may have set up my generation of women for disappointment, unmet expectations, and more than our fair share of guilt. For many of us, striving to have it all resulted in having some of everything and all of nothing.

I was one of those who found striving to have it all problematic largely because it set up unrealistic expectations without institutional changes in the workplace and the family to support them. Even Sheryl Sandberg, the COO of Facebook and author of the best-seller *Lean In* (2013), makes the strong point that having it all and doing it all is a cruel myth that set us up for certain failure. More of a goal than a plan, trying to be the perfect mother, partner, and career woman created "the greatest trap ever set for women" (121). Why a trap? Because the goal of having it all was not supported by structural accommodations in the workplace or at home. Compared to virtually all other modern nations, the United States has the least support for working families in both governmental and corporate worlds. For example, the US Federal Family and Medical Leave Act of 1993 guarantees workers in firms with at least fifty employees twelve weeks of job-protected leave *without pay* for childbirth or for attending to an ill family member. Corporations may do better, but overall, the picture still supports the old-fashioned notion that home and work are separate. Few working families in the United States have the option of the structural benefit of onsite childcare, paid family leave, or support for workers dealing with elderly parents. At home, recent data show that although men are doing a bit more housework, women still perform more than their share of domestic labor (Bianchi et al. 2000). If even Sheryl Sandberg with all her resources admits to feeling guilty when leaving her children on a business trip, how are average women expected to cope?

Choice Feminism

Another mantra of mainstream liberal (and more recently neoliberal) feminism is the idea that the women's movement succeeded in liberating individual women to choose what they want to be and how they want to live. Sandberg's *Lean In* is a perfect example of this neoliberal feminist perspective. Supposedly, women can now choose to attend university or not; when to marry and how many children to have; maintain a career or stay at home with kids; pay attention to housework or let it slide. In reality, many of these "choices" are made by our circumstances. Despite the feminist rhetoric, economic considerations and social pressure constrain our ability to select our own paths. Choice feminism ignores the lived reality of the majority of women (and many men) who lack the resources and social structural supports necessary to live freely autonomous lives.

And even those of us who have more resources at our disposal encounter structural constraints that limit our choices. As a young assistant professor, I felt I had little choice but to work hard, publish, teach many sections and new classes, and forgo a family life in the quest for tenure. Many women like me waited for tenure before having children, and had little or no maternity leave to care for them. I taught class the morning I went into labor, not for some idealistic feminist stance, but because I had no coverage or sick leave.

The language of individual choice not only conceals hidden and subtle forms of sexism; it has divisive consequences for women, as exemplified in the "Mommy Wars" which pit stay-at-home mothers against mothers who also work outside the home. Unfortunately, each group feels they need to justify their choice by sometimes belittling the other's choices. Despite the rhetoric of choice, not many women of my generation could afford to be at home full time, especially those single moms raising children; even those women who could manage a few years at home were viewed negatively by their careerist peers. The real issue is not deciding which group is happier or which approach is better for children, but confronting and changing the social structural constraints that place women in the situation of having to live up to unrealistic expectations within a neoliberal patriarchal system that is organized around individual striving and competition, not social justice or an ethic of compassion and care.

Retirement and the Feminist Theory of Letting Go

As I near retirement and begin to question the wisdom of striving and competing to have it all in a society that is structured so unequally, I find I am turning to alternatives to liberal feminism for some guidelines for this next stage. As we exit our occupational statuses, how can my generation of feminists confront the sexism, classism, racism, and ageism that permeate our culture and still manage to take care of ourselves? What can twenty-first century feminism offer?

In her book, *Lots of Candles, Plenty of Cake*, Anna Quindlen (2012, 41), a woman of my generation, says, "one of the glories of growing older is the willingness to ask why and, getting no good answer, deciding to follow my own inclinations and desires." Quindlen, whose writings over the years have combined feminist ideology with practical common sense, seems to be telling me something. I can begin to question the careerist path I have led over the last forty years: the striving, accumulating, and attention-seeking of the American prescription for success. After forty years of putting myself out there and working to distinguish myself as a "somebody" with the second-wave liberal feminist goal of having it all, I find I would now like to allow myself to be "nobody special," as I move toward a new definition of a meaningful life. In her essay, "Toward a Feminist Theory of Letting Go," Donna King (2012, 53) asks, "Does feminism provide theoretical supports for women who want to (or must) slow down, grow quiet, and let go of striving?" To this I may add, to those who are aging and/or questioning the careerist path of success? These are the questions I've taken up as I move toward retirement.

As I think about questions of aging and letting go, I find myself considering the struggles facing most aging women in the United States. There is the double standard of aging which results in the valuing of older men over older women. There are the pervasive negative stereotypes of older women (and old people in general) that marginalize and denigrate us (Calasanti, Slevin, and King 2006). Older women become "objects of scorn" as they fail to attract the coveted male gaze of youthful sexuality (21). There is the carry-over of gendered work and family expectations into the retirement experience. For example, women's domestic work continues into retirement when their paid work is over; men experience retirement more fully as freedom when their paid work ends, but also as a lack of routine and purpose. On occasion, one hears of women complaining that their retired husbands are following them around the house, offering unsolicited advice about cooking or housework and generally getting in the way. No wonder many married women say, "For better or for worse, but not for lunch!"

Since most occupations no longer enforce mandatory retirement, both men and women of the baby boom generation have timing choices and are staying on longer—for economic and personal reasons. When I asked a sixty-six-year-old colleague if she was planning to retire, she replied, "No way! I've never had it so good!" Her husband is retired and making dinners, the kids are gone, and now she can finally devote all her attention to the work she still loves.

However, not all women have the luxury to decide whether they will stay or leave the labor force. The Great Recession of recent years has caused many of my generation to postpone retirement or wonder whether they can *ever* retire. The economics of retirement are a serious factor that separates women with privilege from those without. I am aware that my education and affluence afford me many more choices as I age and look toward retirement than for most women. Data from the American Association of Retired People (AARP) show women's retirement security as more vulnerable than men's: "Women are more likely to live alone, tend to live longer than men, and are at greater risk of outliving some sources of retirement income, making it more difficult for women to meet their retirement needs" (Waid 2013, 1).

Women are also more likely to depend on Social Security for a higher proportion of their income and have higher medical costs and a higher probability of needed nursing care than men. For people over age sixty-five, men's income from employment and from all sources is about twice that of women (Hayes, Hartmann, and Lee 2010). Overall women are more likely to live in poverty, and this is also true for older women: the poverty rate in 2011 for women over age sixty-five was 4.5 percent higher than for men in the same age range (Waid 2013).

As feminist scholar Toni Calasanti and her colleagues argue, "old age is a political location" that has been ignored by feminist scholars, as have social policies such as Social Security reform that affect older peoples' lives: "To leave age relations unexplored reinforces the inequality old people face, an inequality that shapes other relations of oppression, and one that we reproduce for ourselves. . . . We can envision feminists striving to be empowered and to 'age successfully' while overlooking the contradictory nature of this endeavor, embedded as it is in the denial of age." (Calasanti, Slevin, and King 2006, 25)

But What Will You *Do*?

There is a new expectation of aging and retirement as years when we should continue to be productive and demonstrate success. As I get closer to this benchmark and find myself on "short time," I am receiving no shortage of advice from those who have passed through this stage: "Have a plan." "Don't just lie around." "What will you *do*?" "Will you miss your career?" Magazines such as *MORE*, for women over forty, illustrate example after example of "reinvention" in retirement. One can take advantage of seminars, self-help books, and all manner of friendly advice to prepare for retirement. Of course, we all need financial advice—is retirement even feasible? But the overall message seems to be PLAN. Plan to DO SOMETHING: volunteer, start a business, travel, consult. Isn't this concern with a new plan just the application of careerism to retirement, the competitiveness and attention seeking of the career years replicated in a new stage of life? Is there no support for stepping back, letting go, and making a smaller life? Can we never let go of the cultural demand to strive and succeed?

In her presidential address to the Eastern Sociological Society, Phyllis Moen (2005) observed that the life pattern of education, job, and retirement, in that order, no longer applies to the current cohort of retirees. Many need to continue to earn an income, others search for more meaningful work, while still others are interested in "second acts." In their study of workers in diverse occupations, Donald C. Reitzes and Elizabeth J. Mutran (2006) found that many retirees have "lingering identities" into retirement. They note, "retirees still think of themselves in terms of their former careers" (354) and these ex-roles continue to shape their identity. For some, it is preferable to think of one's self as a *former* professor or carpenter rather than a retired one. Identities are complicated and multidimensional (personal, relational, situational, and structural). But I wonder if the desire to retain a former identity can sometimes be in response to the neoliberal emphasis on extrinsic value, where a person is not worth anything if they are not identified as productive in consumer capitalist terms. In a neoliberal environment, retirement becomes yet another arena for competition and striving, rather than a stage of life to be enjoyed.

Letting Go of Being Mom

Along with many in my cohort, my transition to retirement coincides with my letting go of another important adult role—active parenting. Our daughter is grown, possesses her own graduate degree and career, and is learning to negotiate life's bumpy roads. Letting go of the need to guide, organize, and solve her problems is another challenge. Seeing myself as a mom for twenty-five years is a huge part of my identity. I know that I will always be a mother, but it's time to let go of being a mom. Grown children today are much more connected to their parents than was the case in my generation at their age—cell phones, Facebook, Snapchat, and other social media make contact instant and frequent. I see many students walking around campus using their cell phones, and observe that a very large proportion of them are talking to their mothers! If I talked to my parents once a week back in college, that was about right.

Being so tightly connected to grown kids means hearing their daily problems—and being tempted to manage them. A wise friend told me that there are only two things one should say to a grown child who offers information about her life: "uh-huh" and "really?" To these, I add one of my own: repeat back what they just said. So when our daughter called to tell us that the garbage disposal wasn't working in her rented house, I said, "The garbage disposal isn't working?" It was tempting to give advice—get a plunger, call the landlord—but I held firm. "Really, the garbage disposal is broken?" To which she replied, "I guess I'll call the landlord." Problem solved without Mom's advice. This precious tidbit is only one example of letting go, but it reveals mindful attempts to change the social role of parenting. We may have not been the generation of helicopter parents, but it takes restraint and self-control to give up the need to manage our children's lives, and instead let them make their own mistakes and take credit for their own successes. In mothering, I am letting go the "illusion of control" (King 2012, 12) over my child and stepping to the background as a parent.

Letting Go and Growing Close

Release from liberal and neoliberal social statuses and expectations allow one to interact with others at a more personal and honest level. Without the umbrella of competition for position, prestige, and other social resources, one can let go of the urge to manage impressions and strive for attention. The masks we all wear in social settings can come off, and we can begin to relate to each other at a more human level. Letting go of neoliberal pressures to constantly compete and "prove" ourselves can reshape interpersonal experiences (King 2012, 67).

I discovered this as I reunited with the women of my all-girls high school class of 1967. The Philadelphia High School for Girls was a unique place, a public, academic, all-girls' high school in the inner city that welcomed high achieving young women of all backgrounds. My class of about five hundred women was all college bound and highly goal oriented. Competition was fierce—for grades and class standing, the right clothes, the cutest and smartest boyfriend, getting into the best colleges, and being known at the school. Like any high school, there were cliques and labels. Unlike most comprehensive high schools, there were meaningful opportunities to interact and form friendships with students from very different backgrounds holding the same values for education and achievement. As we women teenagers of 1967 went off to college and then graduate and professional schools, careers, and family, our Girls' High experience made us feel special and prepared for the feminist movements to come. We knew that women could be leaders—we had done it.

My high school graduating class has had several reunions but the most recent one was different. It was only at this fortieth reunion that finally the wall of competition began to crumble and class members came together at a new, intimate level. Conversations and confidences that were not possible in earlier years flowed freely—discussion of expectations met and unmet, amazingly honest reflections of school days and memories, and a willingness to break down barriers of social class and ethnicity to find shared experiences in our life patterns. At the tenth and twentieth reunions, it was all about competition—advanced degrees, marriages and kids, careers, and awards. But after forty years, it was about sharing life stories and supporting long-lost friends. One of the "popular" girls who didn't talk to me back in high school greeted me warmly, and we talked as if we had been BFFs. Secrets were shared in newly formed friendship groups about insecurities and disappointments. Women from different ethnic backgrounds revealed their forty-year-old impressions and perceptions of the high school experience. Our shared reflections opened up some painful topics that could not be broached in high school, for example, the fear experienced every day by those with same-sex desire or those whose ethnic and social class difference made them feel devalued and diminished (Layton and Levy 2012).

Over the decades, feminism had changed the lives of these women—offering seemingly limitless opportunities, yet not releasing them from the competition in their career years. Now, as many of us have retired and are no longer caught up in the seemingly endless mode of striving and competing, we are able to relate at a more truly human level and find commonalities in life's ups and downs. Interestingly, the formal class reunions have led to more frequent informal gatherings of women from the class. Looking at a photo from a recent luncheon gathering, it is interesting that the dozen or so women at the table were not close friends back at Girls High and would have been in totally different friendship groups. But time, age, and life's challenges have united them. They share the experience of living in a particular time in history of many firsts for women and the wisdom of reflection on a half-century of life experiences. They have let go of old labels and are able to live in this moment, moving beyond social divisions that separated them and embracing each other as individuals who shared a moment in their life history.

Conclusion

As I am writing this essay, an email comes in from a new sociology journal looking for reviewers. My first instinct is to sign up—to get my name out there with others, continue to be active in the discipline, and achieve another line on my annual review. But this will be my last annual review, and there has been no money for salary increases for years anyway. Diminishing returns and advancing age have encouraged me to question the liberal feminist myths of having it all and choice feminism. As I step back and consider it, I am no longer compelled to seek the attention of professional recognition. I let go of external sources of validation. I pass.

How does feminism assist us in letting go of individualistic striving and attention seeking? Must we work to have it all in retirement? As I contemplate retirement, I do not want to reinvent myself or play a second act, but rather just be. I look forward to letting go of multitasking, leaving my watch at home, and truly living in the moment. Of course, I am still able to work with the social causes that inspire me and contribute to the community and my family—without any external validation needed. A feminist theory of letting go provides me with the intellectual and emotional grounding to question and reject the attention-seeking, striving, and unreasonable "performance norms" that are endemic to neoliberalism (King 2012).

As I transition to retirement, I feel no need for a second act in which I must continue to prove my worth. I embrace instead the opportunity to nurture relationships and connect in new ways with time and body and community. With the emphasis on technology and social media among young feminists, I can stay involved and informed without necessarily putting myself "out there." I've just logged on to a fourth-wave blog called *Feministing|Young Feminists Blogging, Organizing, Kicking Ass*—great stuff! I love their energy, snark, and self-righteous calling out of the antifeminist world. They inspire me and give me hope for the feminist future.

Sure, I still have stuff on my bucket list—travel, learning to play the cello, jumping out of an airplane (just once)—but I plan to approach these activities as possibilities for pleasure and satisfaction, not as requirements for a productive retirement. As feminists of my generation reach this stage of life, I am looking forward to a community of women—and men—that rejects neoliberal demands for striving and competition and advocates instead to make space and create structures for just being as a more humane way of life that is available to, and beneficial for, all.

NOTES

1. The second wave of the feminist movement is generally associated with consciousness raising and social action occurring in the late 1960s and early 1970s. Inspired by Betty Friedan's (1963) work *The Feminine Mystique* and the civil rights movements, liberal feminist leaders such as Gloria Steinem emerged to work for women's equality within existing social institutions, primarily through legislative change.
2. Far from being a unified movement, the second wave is a conglomeration of movements all striving for their own version of women's equality. Judith Lorber (2005) describes at least twelve varieties of feminism in her work, *Gender Inequality: Feminist Theories and Politics*. Liberal feminism, socialist feminism, radical feminism, and post-colonial feminism all developed at the time of the second wave.
3. In general, feminist movement in the United States is thought to have had three "waves." The first wave, from 1848–1920 involved the fight for suffrage. The second wave began as a reaction to the social movements of the 1960s and involved a push for gender equity awareness and legislative change in social institutions. By the 1990s, the third wave rejected the singular striving of the second, and recognized its white, middle class gaze. It allowed more freedom for individual expression of feminism (think early Madonna) and incorporated women of color, queer theory, and a focus on the intersectionality of gender, class, and ethnicity. Third-wave feminists believe they are less judgmental than the earlier cohorts, and have a broader focus to eliminate all forms of social injustice. While the fourth wave is still evolving, it reflects the goals of young feminists who were energized by the candidacy of Hillary Clinton in 2008. Both third-

and fourth-wave feminists allow for more subjective choices and fewer proscriptive norms than their second-wave predecessors.

REFERENCES

Bianchi, Suzanne, Melissa Milke, Liana Sayer, and John Robinson. 2000. "Is Anyone Doing the Housework: Trends in the Gender Division of Household Labor." *Social Forces* 79:191–228.

Calasanti, Toni, Kathleen Slevin, and Neil King. 2006. "Ageism and Feminism: From 'Et cetera' to Center." *NWSA Journal* 18 (1): 13–30.

Friedan, Betty. 1963. *The Feminine Mystique*. New York: Norton.

Hayes, Jeff, Heidi Hartmann, and Sunhwa Lee. 2010. "Social Security: Vital to Retirement Security for 35 Million Women and Men." *IWPR Publication #D487, March 2010. www.iwpr.org/publications/pubs/ social-security-vital-to-retirement-security-for-35-million-women-and-men.*

King, Donna. 2012. "Toward a Feminist Theory of Letting Go." *Feminist Frontiers* 33 (3): 53–70.

Layton, Lynne, and Diane Levy. 2012. "Re-Union of the Girls' High Girls." Unpublished paper.

Lorber, Judith. 2005. *Gender Inequality: Feminist Theories and Politics*, 3rd edition. Los Angeles: Roxbury.

Moen, Phyllis. 2005. "Beyond the Career Mystique: 'Time In,' 'Time Out,' and 'Second Acts.'" Presidential Address to Eastern Sociological Society, February 2004. *Sociological Forum* 20 (2): 189–208.

Quindlen, Anna. 2012. *Lots of Candles, Plenty of Cake: A Memoir*. New York: Random House.

Reitzes, Donald C., and Elizabeth J. Mutran. 2006. "Lingering Identities in Retirement." *Sociological Quarterly* 47 (2): 333–59.

Sandberg, Sheryl. 2013. *Lean In: Women, Work, and the Will to Lead*. New York: Knopf.

Waid, Mikki D. 2013. "An Uphill Climb: Women Face Greater Obstacles to Retirement Security." *AARP Public Policy Institute Fact Sheet 281* (April). *www.aarp.org/content/ dam/aarp/research/public_policy_institute/econ_sec/2013/uphill-climb-women-face- greater-obstacles-retirement-security-AARP-ppi-econ-sec.pdf.*

9

When Enough Is Enough

African American Women Reclaiming Themselves

Shirley A. Jackson

For the last decade and a half, I have wandered through my professional life aware of the impact of my race and gender but feeling they were neither an impediment nor a benefit to what I had accomplished. It is not that I have been unaware of the significance of being an African American woman on a university campus. Early in my graduate school years, several Black faculty women cautioned me about the potential negative consequences of doing more than my white peers do because of my race and gender. The truth of the matter is that I have always enjoyed being involved in activities that are good for "the team," sometimes at the expense of my best interests, personal and professional. I am the kind of person who, when elected department chair as an assistant professor, agreed to the task because it was something both others and I realized I would be good at. While the experience is not one that I recommend to every relatively new professor (I had only been in my department for three years when elected chair), the experience was one that I enjoyed. I learned a lot about the way I work. I also saw that I got a lot of pleasure being a mentor for the department's students and working in collaboration with the rest of the campus community.

Nonetheless, I have increasingly begun to understand the importance of saving myself from engaging in certain kinds of activities (e.g., agreeing to serve on a multitude of committee assignments at the school-wide level, acquiescing when someone refers a student with whom they are directly working to me for help) I am asked to do because I am an African American woman. If I have given others the impression over the years that I am a "superwoman" (Wallace [1978] 1999), it is now in my best interest, for the purpose of self-preservation, to dispel the myth that I am always available or able to do it all. It is imperative that I carve out space that allows me to do what gives me the care that only I can give myself. African American scholar Brooks-Tatum (2012) asserts there is something subversive about self-care, but it is also a necessity for African American women. Although Brooks-Tatum focuses on young academics, I speak for those African American women who are both tenured and tired. There comes a time when we have to take measures to do what is necessary to save ourselves.

Saving myself involves understanding that what is often mislabeled as selfishness is, in fact, self-preservation—the instinct to survive—and it is necessary. Rachel Griffin (2012), an African American scholar who writes about the pain of gendered racism, frames herself as an "angry Black woman" but I cannot say I am angry. Frustrated, yes. Annoyed, yes. And yet these terms do not fully capture what I am experiencing. A better way to characterize what I am feeling is disappointed and disgusted. Everyone knows that we are for all practical purposes replaceable when it comes to the workplace, but we are irreplaceable when it comes to being ourselves, being in our own skin. As the saying goes, "If you don't take care of yourself, no one else will." Self-care is necessary in order to exist for ourselves. Here, I use the Black feminist autoethnographic (BFA) approach to discuss the "aha" moments that brought me to this place in which I realized that the gendered racism in my professional life was destructive at a deep, personal level (Ellis, Adams, and Bochner 2011; Griffin 2012).

Help Wanted?

African American women in academia are "the outsider within" (Collins 1986). We are often perceived as different because of the credentials we hold by those African Americans who do not share the same credentials. Those who do not look like us, particularly whites, and who may characterize us as "uppity knowit-alls" while at the same time constantly scrutinizing our credentials, also perceive us as different. African American women also find themselves penalized for their hard work rather than rewarded or find that their work is dismissed altogether (Patton 2004; Orelus 2013).

For example, I recall my bewilderment the year prior to going up for promotion to professor when the evaluation committee in my department wrote that my conference attendance and participation had been "adequate." Adequate implies that one has only met the minimum standards. In my case, I had attended and presented at an average of six to eight conferences per year as compared to the one conference per year attended by the individual who chaired the committee. The committee's statement belied the fact that at most of the conferences I had been a presenter, session organizer, presider/moderator, and a chair of a section of one of the largest sociology professional associations. Clearly, the standards held for me were nowhere close to what they were for my white colleagues in the department.

What concerned me about the characterization of my activities as adequate was that I knew my peers were not presenting at or attending the same number of conferences. I knew because as department chair not only did I sign off on their travel paperwork but I also read their yearly activity reports, which I used to compile the department's annual report. I felt it necessary to rebut this account of my activities because if I did not, it would appear that I was agreeing that any faculty member in the department who came up for promotion in the future and attended less than six conferences per year was not doing an adequate job. When I finally submitted my application for promotion the next year, it was successful and without incident. The lesson I learned is that it appeared that regardless of how much work I did, it was either not quite enough, ignored, or superfluously scrutinized.

The pace at which African American women work often results in personal sacrifices so that we can meet the needs of those around us (Beauboeuf-Lafontant 2003). Yet the microaggressions that ever so surreptitiously enter into our work lives render us invisible, unappreciated, and ignored (Orelus 2013). Treated as non-persons, it is no wonder that we keep to ourselves, choosing to suffer in silence rather than share the pain in our souls (Stanley 2006; Hall, Everett, and Hamilton-Mason 2012). In my case, I have determined it is not necessary to do those things that benefit others if they do not also benefit me emotionally, professionally, or financially. I have decided to save myself from myself by becoming more selective in what I choose to do with my time. Resigning from some of the committees and boards on which I previously participated and refraining from being at *every* meeting on my schedule have allowed me to make time to take care of myself. I am someone who is not *just* a professor, researcher, committee member, or board member. I am someone who has chosen to reclaim herself in order to do what makes me feel whole.

But You Do Too Much Already . . .

As I have reflected on the necessity of self-care in my life, I return to another "aha" moment. Several semesters ago, a former colleague chaired a three-person committee tasked with determining who would be our next department chair. The colleague most people thought would move into the position had declined. Ours is a small department and no one else threw his or her hat into the ring, so I volunteered to run. When the faculty in the department cast their preferential poll ballots, I was surprised that even after volunteering when no one else had that I was not in the running. The committee went to our dean and the committee chair advocated for a search for a new department chair from outside the university. The dean told us that we were not going to be able to do an outside search. She sent us back to the drawing board to run the preferential poll again. Again, I expressed my willingness to serve as department chair. Shortly afterwards, when the committee met again with the dean, the chair of the committee announced that the department wanted a chair from outside the department, but it could be an internal hire—someone already on campus. I was surprised that the chair of the committee had made this announcement because it was not something we as a committee had discussed. The dean was equally surprised because it is rare for a department to request that its new chair come from another department.

I had already explained the process of receivership to my colleagues and my belief that we should not give the appearance of needing someone outside the department to run it. I was taken aback that this was considered because it had not been my understanding that the department was incapable of drawing upon its own faculty for department chair. Furthermore, to do so would give the impression to the rest of the campus that we were incapable of "playing nice" and required some form of mediation in the guise of a chair obtained from another department. As I was leaving her office, the dean and I looked at each other with expressions of utter confusion at what had just taken place. She questioned me about what was going on in the department. I told her that I had made it clear to my colleagues that I was willing to run for the position but my colleagues were showing they did not want me to do so. She shook her head in bewilderment. We were probably both recalling that I had been elected department chair during my third year in my department while I was still an assistant professor. During the six years I had been department chair, I was the only African American chair in our school, the largest of the four schools at the university. There has not been another African American chair since, nor was there one before. At that time, I had the support of the department and the administration as well as other entities on campus. What had happened since then?

I thought back to all of the years I had spent trying to raise the profile of the department; watching in dismay as the department's three-hundred-plus majors decreased to half that in the six years since I had been chair. During my tenure as department chair, I had maintained an open-door policy for the department's faculty and students who wanted to meet with me spur of the moment, and I had been the sounding board for my colleagues who often asked me to step in and mediate when they had problems with the outgoing chair. Yet when I did so, they watched in silence on the sidelines as I argued in defense of them. I quickly came to the realization that it did not matter that I was a hard worker or supportive of my colleagues and our department's majors, which I assumed were excellent qualities to have in a chair. It also did not matter that when I first offered to run as chair, the committee chair told me that I "do too much already." For some reason that I did not quite understand, it seemed that I was being penalized for working hard.

The results of the election showed that the third person on the committee who had heretofore expressed no interest in the position had won. I felt let down. If this individual had expressed an interest, I would have supported that decision. The fact that my colleagues dismissed my offer to help was even more painful because no one else had expressed the slightest interest in the position. Up until that point, I had been unaware that doing too much was something for which I could or should pay a penalty. This was ironic because African American women faculty often do more than their fair share, but it is perceived differently in comparison to their white peers. Barnett (2006:4) explains that "the same role expectations, qualities, personality attributes, and standards that are admired, well-liked, accepted, and positively evaluated for white, male, and other majority faculty often are criticized, disliked, unaccepted, and negatively evaluated when exhibited by black, female, and other minority faculty." What was it that made it impossible for my colleagues to accept my offer to step in and do the work no one else offered to do? Could Weitz and Gordon's work on perceptions of black women by white students as "loud, aggressive, argumentative, stubborn and bitchy" (1993, 27) apply to my colleagues and their perceptions of me? After all, just because they are sociologists does not mean they are not susceptible to stereotypes.

The "angry Black woman" stereotype is alive and well in the United States and most certainly in academia (Griffin 2012; Williams 2001). The pervasive label of "angry Black woman" looms even when we are not angry but appear to be so. The stigma it carries makes it almost impossible for us to have a bad day for fear that our sadness, quiet demeanor, or desire to be alone will be perceived as anger. In addition, the physical appearance of African American women—how they wear their hair, what clothes they wear, their jewelry, and even their physique—can have negative repercussions for them if considered threatening (Allport 1954; Ho, Thomsen, and Sidanius 2009). Heaven help African American women like me who are physically imposing in height or build and thus perceived as "threatening" (Carroll 1982). She may find herself characterized as someone who "walks in an aggressive manner" as was the case of an African American woman professor I know. On top of this, African American women have to be careful about what they wear in the workplace. A very thin, blond, white woman supervisor I had many years ago confessed to me that she wore her clingy red knit dress whenever she needed to ask for something from her primarily white male superiors. Her ability to wear her femininity openly in the workplace is in sharp contrast to African American women who are in danger of being perceived as overly sexual Jezebels if they wear very feminine clothing. Thus we engage in acts of hypervigilance with regard to how others see us. The widely held perception of white women, in general, as more intelligent, sensitive, attractive, and kind exists in striking contrast to African American women who are perceived to be aggressive and unattractive (Weitz and Gordon 1993, 26). As Harlow (2003) contends, African American women professors are in the position of constantly managing their emotions in the classroom as well as outside. We also need to minimize our threatening physical appearance in order to appear less intimidating in the workplace. The practice of constantly monitoring our behavior, emotions, and appearance is distressing and exhausting.

Gendered racism has continued to bar advancement for women of color in academia and other professions. The focus by feminists on white middle class women and their woes falls on the deaf ears of many women of color because that focus fails to recognize the barriers and hardships that women of color face (Hall, Everett, and Hamilton-Mason 2012). The feminist critiques against inequality in the workplace (and other domains of life) continue to be exclusive, not inclusive. For instance, Sheryl Sandberg (2013), author of the neoliberal feminist book *Lean In*, barely acknowledges the many and complicated barriers to workplace equality for African American women. The concept of leaning in is problematic for African American women because it is rare for them to be included in the first place. The question that needs to be asked then is how can leaning in take place when you are "left out"?

African American women have learned that they need to do more than what their white counterparts do just to be "equal," but at the same time, going above and beyond and "doing too much" is treated as rate-busting. Wallace, Moore, Wilson, and Hart's (2012) essay asserts that although Black women are in the ivory tower, it does not mean they will be exempt from proving they belong there. It is worth noting that while it is acceptable for African American women to engage in activities that are important but undervalued in the academy, their white peers may believe it is not acceptable for them to engage in activities that are more prestigious. Thus, when it comes to doing service work like mentoring students (especially minority students), attending cultural events (often at the behest of university administrators where they serve as the university's "mascot" and are suddenly "visible") (Orelus 2013), or serving as the speaker for minority student clubs ("because they need role models like *you*"), African American women are expected to do the work. That they might serve on a prestigious university committee such as Faculty Senate is highly improbable.

Somehow or another, I had not realized that the work I had been doing over the years (e.g., not only being elected to but volunteering to serve on committees, mentoring new faculty, writing newsletters, maintaining the department's website) was shaping the perception my colleagues had of me. Yes, I had done a lot over the years, and perhaps they thought I was overstepping some invisible boundary. Could it be that my offers to help would shed a spotlight that they were not doing likewise? Or perhaps they simply were grateful someone was doing the work. I was not clear on what they were thinking, but it was at that point when I decided no more. Enough was enough. I wanted different results in how I was feeling in my interactions with others, and that would mean no longer doing what I had in the past. I decided that even if ready, willing, and eager, I would no longer do for those who dismissed my efforts or ignored my very presence. I had simply had enough. Whatever I did from that point forward was going to be for *me*—whatever either served my best interests or gave me the greatest satisfaction. It was time to engage in the self-care that I had been placing on the back burner for much too long.

Grittiness Is as Grittiness Does

"Grit" is a term used by scholars Duckworth, Peterson and Matthews (2007) when they argue that it is necessary for success. In *Grace and Grit: My Fight for Equal Pay and Fairness at Goodyear and Beyond*, author Lilly Ledbetter (2012) describes how she fought Goodyear for sex discrimination. She had worked hard for many years but received unequal pay and went unrecognized for the work she had done. Ledbetter had had enough. In her subsequent battles in the courts, she shows that she was sick and tired of fighting and then losing, but she was also not going down without a fight. Ledbetter, using both grace and grit, was struggling to obtain financial compensation in recognition of the work she had done for far less pay than her male counterparts had received. I contend that while it may seem important when it comes to professional or academic success, grit is not a necessary quality in all aspects of our lives, because we may have interests that require passion but not grit. In essence, there comes a time when it is not about working hard to obtain some particular goal, but about realizing that goals are not enough if they exclude taking care of one's self. I had been going through my career with grit but have only recently shifted my pattern to accommodate a new transformation where I am engaging in care of self rather than care of others. The passion for self-care provides me with a new outlook on what is important to me spiritually and personally. This requires distancing me from harmful influences that may break me down. It is not about giving me time to participate in some activity because it gives me the energy to go back and fight the good fight. Sandberg's stance on this implies it works for everyone the same way. This is simply not the case. Instead of finding my inner grit and leaning in, I am learning to enjoy what it feels like to do something that is not just good for me but because it is *for* me.

African American professors in the academy hope they are receiving equal treatment in the workplace but most know that they will encounter an "ism" at some point in time (Allison 2008; Griffin 2012; Orelus 2013). The form it takes does not matter as much as the sense of shock and dismay when it occurs. The irony is that expectations of an encounter do not lessen its impact when it actually occurs. Constance Carroll (1982) describes the sense of loneliness African American women in academia face as the result of sexism and racism. Unfortunately, her observations of what was going on in the late 1970s remain no less true today. The various forms of discrimination African American women experience tend to be unrelenting, owing in large part to the tenacity of the interlocking systems of race, class, and gender oppression.

The number of African American women in academia is small, and their support networks in the workplace are lacking. They have few people to turn to who know what they are experiencing. When acts of microaggression occur, many African American women keep to themselves—unwilling to share their pain. This makes it even more difficult for African American women to let loose, let go, and be free of whatever demons they have encountered, not only in the dark but in the light of day as well. After all, something must be wrong with *us* if we show we cannot handle the pain and are not as strong as stereotypes suggest we are.

Ntozake Shange (1975) reflects vividly on the pain and hardships experienced by African American women in *For Colored Girls Who Have Considered Suicide When the Rainbow is Enuf*. In *Colored Girls*, the Woman in Orange, who chastises her lover for almost walking off with all of her stuff, realizes just a bit too late that she "gotta have to give to my choice. So you can't have me unless I give me away." Similarly, Michele Wallace (1978) just a few years later painted a less than pretty portrait of African American men, one that recognizes their sexism while also challenging the notion that African American women should be expected to and could do it all. With the same brushstroke, Wallace criticizes white racism. Both Shange and Wallace concede that African American women are in a less than enviable place in society. They must develop the necessary survival skills if they are ever to save themselves from others and from themselves.

Fortunately, as Hall and her colleagues note, African American women have developed a variety of coping mechanisms to alleviate the stress they experience in the workplace and other arenas. The women they studied "attempted to control their reactions to stress by walking away, shifting, or simply praying" (Hall, Everett, and Hamilton-Mason 2012, 218). Those who could, faced their stress head on or let it go. Regardless, these women found it necessary to find some way to deal with the daily stressors of life in the ways that best suited their situations. While some women drew upon others for relief, others engaged in self-care. These coping mechanisms are acts of resistance and methods of self-preservation.

Looking Backward, Forward, Outward, and Inward

In his 1922 poem, "Mother to Son," Langston Hughes's protagonist advises her son,

> Don't you set down on the steps
> 'Cause you finds it kinder hard.
> Don't you fall now—
> For I'se still goin', honey,
> I'se still climbin',
> And life for me ain't been no crystal stair. ([1922] 1998, 370)

Sitting on the stairs is not an option for African American women in academia. They are not only climbing but they are attempting to lift up others as they continue to climb. African American women are working at a breakneck pace and without recognition from others that they also need a break. When they take a break, they face criticism. The additional stressors placed on African American women can and do have an impact on their physical and emotional health (Hall, Everett, and Hamilton-Mason 2012). One African American professor informed me that when she went up for promotion and tenure a few years ago, her department's evaluation committee noted that the pace of her activities had slowed. She was battling breast cancer for the second time and continued to teach online while receiving cancer treatments during this period; thus neither of us understood where it was evident that she had slowed down. While she received promotion and tenure, the irony of the situation was not lost on us. She was not expected to take a break, thus, her colleagues did not give her a break.

The resulting stress involved in the professional lives of many African American women can result in their not taking a brief break but, instead, making a clean break. Several years ago, a cousin left her tenure track position because of burnout. She was not receiving the support she felt she deserved from her department chair and wanted to have a life that did not include working on the weekends or trying to meet the heavy work demands from her department and university. As a result, she moved into a staff position and then subsequently left academia altogether. While she has ventured back in as a contingent faculty member, she still has concerns about returning on a full-time basis. Another African American colleague at my university left her faculty position explaining that she was simply feeling worn down and unfulfilled. I am looking for ways to either avoid potential burnout or at the very least, slow down the inevitable. Most recently, I made the decision that I would not teach during the summer. This was just one more step in my self-care trajectory.

Each year, most of us make New Year resolutions that we hope will turn us into better people, whether to be smarter, thinner, more fit, healthier, better at our jobs, better in our relationships, and so on. Academics often add to these resolutions, depending on how many semesters or quarters we teach in a given academic year. We will have all of the course readings done *before* classes begin, we will change the way we grade, we will change the way we give assignments, and we will finally learn how to use more of the tools on our course management sites. Those who are wise will also remember to include, in their never-ending array of things on which they will improve, items that include *them*. This is my plan as I continue to shed my old habits. Shanesha Brooks-Tatum's (2012) advice that we do what we love, reevaluate where we are in life, set priorities and boundaries, get new role models, and create a wellness manifesto and community, points us in the direction of how to engage in self-care. My movement toward self-directedness means that less is more if less results in more happiness, greater satisfaction, and increased wellbeing of spirit and mind. The practice of self-care is more than just leaning in and trying to get the attention of others so that we can gain more in the workplace. I choose to take another route to getting more by being more. I am opting to take some me time so that I can draw upon passions that bring me joy and embrace my soul. I am taking back all of my stuff. I am going on strike. I refuse to work on those things that will sap my spirit. I will know when to say "no." There will be no giving me away.

REFERENCES

Allison, Donnetrice C. 2008. "Free to Be Me?: Black Professors, White Institutions." *Journal of Black Studies* 38 (4): 641–62.

Allport, Gordon. 1954. *The Nature of Prejudice.* Oxford, UK: Addison-Wesley.

Barnett, Bernice McNair. 2006. "Gender, Race, and the Academic Experience." Paper presented at the American Sociological Association annual meeting, Montreal, Canada, August.

Beauboeuf-Lafontant, Tamara. 2003. "Keeping Up Appearances, Putting on Weight: Understanding the Role of Strength Among Black Women." Paper presented at the American Sociological Association annual meeting, Atlanta, Georgia, August.

Brooks-Tatum, Shanesha. 2012. "Subversive Self-Care: Centering Black Women's Wellness." *Feminist Wire*, November 9. *thefeministwire.com/2012/11/ subversive-self-care-centering-black-womens-wellness.*

Carroll, Constance. 1982. "Three's a Crowd: The Dilemma of Black Women in Higher Education." In *All the Women Are White, All the Blacks Are Men, But Some of Us Are Brave: Black Women's Studies,* edited by Gloria Hull, Patricia Scott, and Barbara Smith, 115–28. New York: The Feminist Press at the City University of New York.

Collins, Patricia Hill. 1986. "Learning From the Outsider Within: The Sociological Significance of Black Feminist Thought." *Social Problems* 33 (6): S14–S32.

Duckworth, Angela L., Christopher Peterson, and Michael D. Matthews. 2007. "Grit: Perseverance and Passion for Long-Term Goals." *Journal of Personality and Social Psychology* 92 (6): 1087–101.

Ellis, Carolyn, Tony E. Adams, and Arthur P. Bochner. 2011. "Autoethnography: An Overview." *Forum Qualitative Sozialforschung/Forum: Qualitative Social Research* 12 (1). *www.qualitative-research.net.php/fqs/article/view/1589/3095.*

Griffin, Rachel Alison. 2012. "I AM an Angry Black Woman: Black Feminist Autoethnography, Voice, and Resistance." *Women's Studies in Communication* 35:138–57.

Hall, J. Camille, Joyce E. Everett, and Johnnie Hamilton-Mason. 2012. "Black Women Talk about Workplace Stress and How They Cope." *Journal of Black Studies* 43 (2): 207–26.

Harlow, Roxanne. 2003. "'Race Doesn't Matter, But . . . :' The Effect of Race on Professors: Experiences and Emotion Management in the Undergraduate College Classroom." *Social Psychology Quarterly* 66 (4): 348–63.

Ho, Andrew K., Lotte Thomsen, and Jim Sidanius. 2009. "Perceived Academic Competence and Overall Job Evaluations: Students' Evaluations of African American and European American Professors." *Journal of Applied Social Psychology* 39 (2): 389–406.

Hughes, Langston. [1922] 1998. "From Mother to Son." In *An Introduction to Poetry*, 9th edition, edited by X. J. Kennedy and Dana Gioia, 370. New York: Longman.

Ledbetter, Lilly. 2012. *Grace and Grit: My Fight for Equal Pay and Fairness at Goodyear and Beyond.* New York: Crown Archetype.

Orelus, Pierre Wilbert. 2013. "The Institutional Cost of Being a Professor of Color: Unveiling Micro-Aggression, Racial [In]visibility, and Racial Profiling through the Lens of Critical Race Theory." *Current Issues in Education* 16 (2). *cie.asu.edu/ojs/index.php/cieatasu/article/view/1001/485.*

Patton, Tracy Owens. 2004. "Reflections of a Black Woman Professor: Racism and Sexism in Academia." *Howard Journal of Communications* 15:185–200.

Sandberg, Sheryl. 2013. *Lean In: Women, Work, and the Will to Lead.* New York: Knopf

Shange, Ntozake. 1975. *For Colored Girls Who Have Considered Suicide When the Rainbow Is Enuf.* New York: Scribner.

Stanley, Christine. 2006. "Coloring the Academic Landscape: Faculty of Color Breaking the Silence in Predominantly White Colleges and Universities." *American Educational Research Journal* 43 (4): 701–36.

Wallace, Michele. [1978] 1999. *Black Macho and the Myth of the Superwoman.* New York: Verso.

Wallace, Sherri L., Sharon E. Moore, Linda L. Wilson, and Brenda G. Hart. 2012. "African American Women in the Academy: Quelling the Myth of Presumed Incompetence." In *Presumed Incompetent: The Intersections of Race and Class for Women in Academia,* edited by Gabriella Gutierrez y Muhs, Yolanda Flores Niemann, Carmen Gonzalez, and Angela Harris, 421–38. Logan, UT: Utah State University Press.

Weitz, Rose, and Leonard Gordon. 1993. "Images of Black Women among Anglo Students." *Sex Roles* 28 (1-2): 19–34.

Williams, Charmaine C. 2001. "The Angry Black Woman Scholar." *National Women's Studies Journal* 13 (2): 87–97.

Part Three

Ethnographies

10

What to Let Go

Insights from Online Cervical Cancer Narratives

Tracy B. Citeroni

Cervical cancer taxes the entire embodied self. Women with cervical cancer bear tremendous bodily pain from the disease and its treatments. We confront insidious social stigmas against people with sexually transmitted viruses. In the United States, even if we are lucky enough to have adequate health insurance, we must navigate maddening health care bureaucracies. We negotiate power relationships with our biomedical providers as we seek to make informed decisions about our health care. We hope and pray to stave off mortality, at least for the moment. For as long as we "survive" we live with physical reminders of the illness and treatments as well as knowledge that we are always at the edge of health. Through it all we must discern which parts of this experience we can release, to be able to find peace in our body-selves and accept our illness and its consequences.

We must learn to let go. Our survival, whether we will die from our cancer or not, depends on it. Acceptance eases suffering, liberates us. But it does not come readily to people with cancer in the United States. American norms of achievement, competition, ambition, and constant striving also colonize the realm of illness. Patients are meant to "fight" for their health. Cancer patients in particular are expected to suit up commando-style for the battle of their lives. We are cautioned against giving up. And letting go is too often seen as giving up. To achieve some measure of acceptance of our illness is not to give up hope or the will to live. Yet this stance runs counter to normative social expectations.

Our ideas about illness tend to congregate around themes of restitution or recovery. We expect to return to our busy everyday lives after a brief retreat during which we seek (most often) biomedical remedy for what ails us. Frank (1995) has written beautifully about the limits of this narrative trope and our need to confront the reality of chronic illness and disability by bearing witness to others' suffering. We should listen to illness stories, and not just the neat, tidy, heroic tales. Online venues yield a plethora of complicated, messy stories. Bearing witness is a quintessentially feminist exercise. In listening, not only do we acknowledge the meaningful subjective experience of others, but we also gain perspective on how to find our own peace amidst the pain. We learn how to better care for others and ourselves. Most experiences of chronic illness are not fully captured by the dominant restitution narrative.

In this essay I explore the possibilities of grounding a feminist theory of letting go in the embodied subjectivities of women with cervical cancer. From the stories of women coping with this disruptive and deadly illness, we gain insight into what parts of the experience most need to be released to reduce suffering and open a path toward acceptance.

Letting Go as Resistance to Hegemonic Cancer Discourse

King (2012, 57) calls for the development of a feminist theory of letting go and argues that "revitalizing a feminist commitment to a society based not on striving and 'success' but on compassion and care may be just what is called for at this historical moment." I heartily embrace her call and this essay is one contribution to an emerging ethic of care and compassion. I look to the embodied subjectivities of women with cervical cancer for insight, and use illness narratives to highlight the urgent need for such a feminist mission. Embodied subjects suffer the limits of human mortality, but they also suffer the limits of biomedical knowledge and practice and the colonizing impulse of consumer capitalist culture. The latter two leave little room for nonattachment. In fact, they actively discourage it.

Contemporary biomedicine and the US health care industry are not exempt from corporate global capitalism and operate according to its neoliberal dictates. Individuals confront the "enemy" to their health within the context of a health care industry that routinely subordinates care to profit and is oriented toward prohibitively expensive high tech late interventions. A cancer patient is meant to submit unquestioningly to the rigors of biomedical treatments and to believe in the efficacy of medical interventions. At the same time, they are expected to assume fundamental responsibility for their health by maintaining a "good attitude" or positive outlook. In this way, biomedicine colludes with a widespread culture of obstinate hope. This hegemonic discourse cannot mediate the embodied experience of illness and may in fact amplify suffering. Letting go in this context can be construed as an act of resistance.

I use interpretive analyses of women's online narratives of their cervical cancer experience, as well as my own autoethnographic reflections, to suggest what may need to be let go and to illustrate the multifaceted challenges to doing so. I argue that a feminist theory and practice of letting go can significantly alter the illness experience of women with cervical cancer and help to ease suffering.

Off to Battle

Debilitating sickness runs contrary to the dictates of life in the global corporate capitalist system. We have no time to be sick. Cervical cancer anchors us in our sick bodies in a way that contradicts a neoliberal capitalism, whose core precepts include disciplined/controlled bodies and body-self primarily as consumer. Letting go can be construed as failure, cowardly capitulation to the invading forces. Most of us learn this lesson all too well and easily adopt the role of cancer warrior. Listen to the words of Fran upon news that she has terminal cervical cancer:

> I've been eyeing this punching bag at Ross lately, but just didn't feel like I had a reason to buy it, but guess what? Now I do. I need to strengthen my skills as a "fighter." I need to put those gloves on and punch away. I will build my upper arm strength or what I like to refer to as my "guns." This will be good b/c I now know I will need a lot more ammunition to fight and kill this beast! So the track shoes are now retired and the boxing gloves are out with a vengeance!!

Nancy embraces the image of slaying a dragon to explain to her children the family's battle with recurrent cervical cancer:

> I told my kids in addition to seeing this journey as a marathon; I also imagine that the cancer is a fire-breathing, purple dragon. [. . .] Well, it's time to push him back into hiding once and for all (and maybe obliterate him altogether, God-willing!) . . . Now, let's slay the dragon!

The impetus to fight, to do battle with cancer, requires an abundance of energy. It also inhibits the development of other ways to talk about coping with the illness. In reading more than nine journals covering multiple years of the lives of women who have died from cervical cancer, I recognize how severely the rhetoric of constant battle drained them. Most were constantly fighting. The exclusive focus on combat seemed to have left them ill equipped to cope with the progression and pain of terminal cancer. They developed no other way to be with their cancer.

This is not just a problem for people with terminal cancer; their trials are indicative of others with chronic illness and the larger problem of finding peace and acceptance in our contemporary consumer culture. We are never supposed to be content with what is, despite the fact that so much of life is beyond our control. We grasp and yearn in vain. Letting go does not equate to giving up. It simply means relinquishing control and embracing what is. Of course, the process is not so simple, especially when outside forces encourage us to do otherwise.

I could not accept a discourse of health that put me at war with my own body.

As I endured the biomedical procedures that might save my life, the feminist medical sociologist in me resisted assimilation into mainstream cancer culture. I bristled at the notion that I was in a "battle" for my life. I rejected the idea that I needed to "fight" to be cured. I hated the implication that those who had died may not have fought hard enough or had in some sense lost the war. I refused to assume responsibility if the mass of tumors that had taken up residence in my pelvis decided to stay and grow. I wanted no part of a discourse of competition between my cancer and me. I devoted myself to making peace with my unruly body. More than a decade hence, this has proven a difficult and ongoing project.

For people who have been diagnosed with and treated for cancer, as with many chronic illnesses, it remains a challenge to let go of a disease that refuses to let go of you. Even though the illness may be in remission, the specter of recurrence looms large. Toxic treatments leave permanent damage to the body and many physical side effects persist. Radiation harms organs including the bladder, bowel, digestive tract, and vagina. It puts young women into premature menopause. Surgery scars the gut, leaving a spider web of adhesions. Removal of lymph nodes promotes lymphedema. Chemotherapy can linger on in neuropathy. Daily reminders of the cancer that did, and undeniably could once again, threaten your life abound. Even the gracious acceptance of survival can be a challenge.

I found little corporeal peace in mainstream images of valiant cancer warriors and survivors. These images assault the cancer patient who does not feel heroic or find solace in metaphors of battle. They pervade public events, organizations, and support groups. It has been a struggle to survive in this context. I have been disconnected from networks of survivors because of this alienating hegemonic discourse. Trying to come to terms with my irradiated, poisoned, contingent post-treatment body has tended toward a solitary endeavor.

Though my sociological imagination has been in overdrive from the very first moment of my diagnosis, I have been unable to write about the experience. Living it daily for more than thirteen years has kept me from leaving the field, so to speak. Perhaps one never does. It took me more than ten years to begin to study cervical cancer narratives more systematically. Over the past two years, I began participating in Internet discussion forums and reading online cancer journals in order to connect with others and understand their experiences of our shared illness. This essay is my first attempt to put an analytical frame on our narratives, to situate my own account within the larger landscape of stories of women with cervical cancer. The process yielded vital feminist sociological insights about making peace with one's cancer.

Beyond the war imagery, other aspects of the illness experience are ripe for release. In the next four sections I review stories of women in conflict over stigma, beauty, fertility, and the end of treatment.

HPV and Stigma

Cervical cancer is a deeply gendered illness. Recent research confirming the role of HPV in causing cervical cancer has lent it the further stigma of a sexually transmitted infection. The creation and heavy promotion of vaccines to prevent the most dangerous strains of HPV have dramatically increased public understanding of the sexual origins of cervical cancer. Knowledge about HPV affects a woman's experience of the disease. We are left to wonder about the behaviors and relationships that may have led to our life-threatening illness at the same time that we must manage the fractured understanding of others about HPV. We also wrestle with the moral judgments that we have unwittingly internalized.

Here is an excerpt from an online journal in which Anna attributes her getting HPV and then cervical cancer to her own "bad" decisions.

> I continued to make one bad choice after another. I was a party girl! Loved to get drunk! Getting drunk put me in compromising situations that I honestly never wanted to be in . . . Yes if you haven't figured it out . . . I am talking about one awful sexual encounter after another. See all the premarital sex in my past gave me the HPV virus which was discovered at the beginning of this last pregnancy. HPV viruses can lead to Cervical Cancer which is what I was diagnosed with.

She then writes that a turn to Christianity saved her from guilt or regret. She has made a kind of peace with her illness and forgiven herself for her previous sexual behavior through immersion in religion. This seems an incomplete liberation as it leaves intact the sexist notion that some women get cancer due to immoral behavior. As we see in the following quote, women who are desperate to absolve themselves sometimes pass judgment against others. After watching the documentary *Crazy Sexy Cancer* (2007), Carol alludes to moral shortcomings in the main character.

> But, like I said it was neat to watch the things she did . . . like the CT scan. She is right . . . the white drink is gross. She referred to it as something you might find on a peep show floor. I think of it more as the water in a bucket after you have washed a really chalk-filled chalkboard. I guess that shows our differences . . . I am a teacher and she . . . well . . . =)

A feminist ethic of care and compassion can awaken understanding. Through the practice it promotes, we might cease to blame ourselves or anyone else for developing cervical cancer. Without such an ethic, it is very difficult to combat the social stigma.

Nancy clearly wants to sideline the questions from her family, friends and readers about the role of HPV in causing her cancer. After raising lots of doubts about the relationship between HPV and cervical cancer, she falls back on the annual well woman exam as the best preventive:

> What scientists and/or gynecological oncologists don't know is: IF HPV actually causes cancer, or IF it's more of an infection of HPV that causes cancer, or WHY it can be dormant in some for years and one day "wake up" and appear to cause cancer, or IF cervical cancer & HPV are related at all??? There are too many questions and not enough answers to the HVP—Cervical Cancer relationship. There is only thing for sure and that is that an Annual Pap Smear for women at least 21 years and older will almost ALWAYS show an abnormal change in cells, IF that's the case.

It is hard to tell from her journal whether Nancy is letting go of the stigma of HPV or denying it by shifting attention to clinical exams and annual pap smears.

I didn't know enough in 1999 to be ashamed of my HPV-induced cancer. Despite having finished my PhD the year prior and starting my first tenure track job, I was woefully ignorant of the causes of cervical cancer. I had never heard of HPV. While I am still stunned at my own lack of information, I realize that it spared me (for the moment) the agony of guilt or the anguish of perceiving stigma from others. I vividly remember reading a brochure about cervical cancer in the waiting room at the oncology clinic in which "early onset sexual activity" was listed as a common risk factor for development of the disease. At the time, I was incensed. It offended my feminist sensibilities to think that women were being marked unfairly for having sex at a young age and thereby being implicated in our own sickness. But I had no idea what the connection was. It was only with the arrival of the first HPV vaccination that I became cognizant of the connection and began my own complicated dance with guilt, anger, and stigma.

Beauty Norms

Attachment also manifests in the gendered expectation that women "look good" in public even when they are sick. Most women are susceptible to this notion. Nancy had a really hard time coming to grips with the way her body and appearance changed during the course of her illness:

> I'm quite surprised at my emotional reaction to losing my hair. I really thought that it would just make me crazy angry and that once it started falling out, I'd pull a Brittany Spears, just grab the clippers and start shaving

my head with vigorous aggression! Well, instead I'm finding that each handful of hair that falls out is more like my Kryptonite . . . I feel weaker, weepy, nauseous. All day yesterday I was afraid to touch my hair, because when I do at this point, I always have at least 30 or more strands that blow away in the wind . . . yuck.

In addition to the loss of hair, Nancy's cancer and treatment resulted in other changes such as weight gain, chronic swelling, and excess body hair that further disrupted her sense of self. Despite her inability to accept her changed body, Nancy does make an occasional effort to release her attachment to her former body-self. Still, mainstream feminine beauty standards also haunt her "new" body-self and she sees the adjustment as temporary. She never quite accepts it.

> While getting ready, I had an ah-ha moment. [. . .] Instead, I think I need to embrace a whole NEW me! Since I've NEVER worn accessories like this; scarves, hats, wigs, earrings . . . whatever that will look like, will just all be a NEW look! I won't look exactly like myself on the outside for a while, and that's the part I'm having to come to terms with.

Over and over Nancy grapples with the physical changes her body is undergoing and how much they position her counter to prevailing ideals of beauty. A substantial portion of her two-year-long online journal is devoted to her discomfort with her physical appearance, her efforts to mediate what she sees as new flaws, and her fervent desire to get her body back. She agonizes over looking "ugly" and wanting to feel "normal" again, which never happens because she dies from the cancer.

Oppressive beauty standards get in the way of letting go. They keep us anchored in normative expectations of feminine appearance that further alienate us from our ailing bodies. Nancy struggled with changes that she felt made her less attractive. Being told that we look better with cancer also stings. I lost more than twenty pounds when I was going through treatment and my friends and colleagues began to exclaim about how "great" I looked. The last thing I wanted to think about was my weight, and it troubled me to know that my outward appearance belied how profoundly sick I felt. Frankly, I was irked that having a devastating and potentially life-threatening illness could take a back seat to my looks. I recognized that people had difficulty knowing what to say to me at the time, but the retreat to gendered compliments seemed evasive. Being told I looked good did not compensate for having cancer. It amplified my suffering.

Loss of Fertility

Fertility is another realm of attachment that women with cervical cancer often face. Carol was not wedded to the idea of having another biological child. She was ready and willing to let go of her fertility if it might save her life:

> The doctor called me back and re-informed me that the lymph node was positive (already knew that one) and that the treatments he was giving me would make me sterile . . . no biggie . . . we already have a perfect child and if they want to take all of my female organs that is fine with me (he said he did not think we would have to, but in my mind if it keeps this from ever reentering my body than they can try to sell this mess on eBay for all I care).

My thoughts aligned squarely with Carol. My oncologist referred me to a fertility specialist to talk about harvesting eggs before starting my treatment. I was thirty years old and married with no children at the time. I cried when I was told the treatment would render me unable to get pregnant, even though I wasn't sure I would ever want to do so. I lamented the loss of the choice. Sitting in the office of the fertility specialist, listening to him go on about the egg retrieval process, it became crystal clear to me that I was not so invested in reproducing my own genetic material. My husband and I agreed that if we wanted children, we would adopt. I had little trouble letting go of my fertility. I joked about radiation frying my eggs.

For other women, the loss of fertility is a crushing blow. One that shatters their sense of self and compels them to do whatever they can to secure the possibility of having biological children in the future. Even if it means tremendous financial cost, delaying the start of treatment, or choosing a treatment that may be less effective. In this case, Valerie decided to delay the start of her treatment to have eggs harvested so that she and her husband might be able to have another biological child:

> Please pray for my ovaries to kick into overdrive and help us produce some eggs! It is kind of a "one shot" deal and Rick and I would love to have another biological child if possible. I was supposed to start chemotherapy this Thursday, but it looks like that may get delayed until the beginning of the following week due to delays with my fertility treatment. Please keep praying for full speedy recovery and if you are age 11–26, go get your GARDISIL vaccination. It can save you from going through an ordeal like mine. . . . i.e. save your life or fertility!!

The socially accepted idea that all women will (and naturally want to) become mothers must come into play here. Some women indeed feel that they are not fully female if they cannot or do not biologically reproduce. The social expectation of biological motherhood might then impose further hardship on women with cervical cancer by making it harder for us to let go of our fertility, even to the detriment of our own health.

Ending Treatment

Women with advanced disease face specific challenges in letting go. Terminally ill patients struggle to reconcile the reality of their prognosis with the social expectation to keep fighting and remain optimistic. Those with adequate health insurance are offered a seemingly endless stream of technological interventions that may or may not save their lives, may or may not decrease their suffering. The impulse is to consume as much medical care as is available, which makes it even harder to accept when there is nothing left to do. How does one achieve peace and acceptance in this context?

Liz entertained the idea of stopping treatment earlier than any of the other women whose journals I studied. She often weighed concerns about quality of life (as well as health care costs) with her fervent desire to live. In a note about her father's death, she commends hospice:

> Hospice is a tremendous organization and people should make more use of it than they do. Though I must say, I hate the frequent TV commercial that says, "It is never too early for hospice." That makes me cringe; it is too early for me.

While she did not turn to hospice easily, I infer from her journal that the pattern of early contemplation readied Liz to make a conscious decision to stop treatment:

> Sure, everyone wants a cure. And there are probably a few, very few, with my kind of recurrent cancer who get it. Though I don't know of any. You try the most promising treatments and it doesn't cure you, then you can chase after other things. There is always more you can do. But there are diminishing returns. Wouldn't it be better to call in hospice and celebrate the end? Think of it as planning a trip, looking at a map, and deciding what roads to take.

Liz communicates some measure of acceptance in her last post, after which her husband takes over writing her online journal:

> I've decided to stop treatment and am now with hospice. I have had some medical equipment delivered. I'm on oxygen now and I love my new commode. Before the commode I was worried I would get stranded on the

toilet and I almost did. I mostly deny pain, but in the middle of the night
my knees ache and wake me up. I'm going to try Aleve. I'm starting to turn
yellow.

In this journal entry, Valerie reflects on the virtues of continuing with treatment that doesn't seem to be working. She is facing a tough decision:

Although as we know from my last trillion chemos and scans, none of the
shrinkage, if we even get any (happened only once), seems to stick. Chemo,
now, really is just buying time and I have to decide whether that is what I
want to do. It takes such a toll on the body and statistics show it is actually
what normally kills a late stage cancer patient. Pretty sad, eh?

Valerie does not write about the specific moment in which she consciously
made the decision to end treatment. Her husband takes over writing updates
and reports when doctors advise them to engage hospice. No mention of Valerie's reaction to this news. She may or may not have let go of the desire to continue with treatment:

I'll just cut to the chase. The short version is that they do not believe Val
could withstand the rigors of a clinical trial and furthermore they don't
believe that she should receive any additional treatment and strongly
encouraged us to consider Hospice. As weak as she now is, the doctors
unanimously believe that any additional treatments will do more harm than
good.

Other women also had to be told by their doctors that they would offer no
more treatment and were very open about their reluctance to go to hospice:

Dr. Carlisle told me that I had fought this battle harder than anyone he has
ever known and that I had focused all my energy on fighting the tumors for
two years and now it was time to focus strictly on [me]. He also said that
individuals with my kind of cancer don't live as long as I have. [. . .] Tears
spilled down my face as reality began to sit in. Naturally when people hear
the word "hospice" it normally takes on a negative connotation and that is
sure what I was thinking.

Fran was initially angry with her doctor for telling her there would be no
more treatment. But his telling her plainly that treatment would no longer help
did prompt her to face the reality of being in the last days of a terminal disease.
Biomedical personnel as well as family and friends typically encourage
women with cervical cancer, even when it is terminal, to pursue treatment. Un-

relenting hopefulness can be overwhelming. Perhaps even more damaging is the exclusive reliance on hope and fighting up to the point when women are expected to realize the futility of further treatment and suddenly make the shift to hospice. How does one manage such a dramatic turn? The hegemonic discourse of uncompromising optimism appears at its most absurd in the context of terminal disease. Consequently, many women feel alienated from their bodies and encounter multiple obstructions in trying to cope with the disease.

Conclusion

Feminist scholarship and practice have given us some notable models for challenging the hegemonic discourse of cancer treatment and survivorship, but the majority of this work focuses on breast cancer (i.e. Lorde 1980 and Ehrenreich 2001). We need more work specific to cervical cancer. We need to confront the particular constellation of challenges facing women with cervical cancer, some of which are reflected in the online narratives I studied and have presented in this essay.

Individual illness narratives offer alternative understandings of living with disease. The multiplicity of experiences revealed can be empowering to newly diagnosed people as well as those of us who are called "survivors." Online stories of women living with and dying from cervical cancer also reveal persistent suffering that might be diminished if only we could discern what to let go and gave ourselves and others permission to do so.

While feminism has much to offer in addressing this problem, we first need to rise above the tendency for mainstream feminism to collaborate with consumer capitalism. Nancy Fraser (2009) argues that second-wave feminism unwittingly benefitted from the shift from state-organized to neoliberal capitalism. In the new political-economic context, she says, "claims for justice were increasingly couched as claims for the recognition of identity and difference" (108). As feminism embraced identity politics, it turned away from a fundamental critique of capitalism. A feminist theory of letting go can reinvigorate this critical discourse. As Fraser argues, "having watched the neoliberal onslaught instrumentalize our best ideas, we have an opening now in which to reclaim them" (117).

Fraser includes care work in a list of noncommodified activities, largely performed by women, which would be revalued through a feminist critique of capitalism. If we consider illness here, caring for each other and ourselves can be reimagined as resistance to consumer capitalist health care and normative cancer culture. Both offer limited resources with which to make sense of our suffering. Military metaphors of battling cancer suggest a level of control in the illness experience that is at best elusive and at worst oppressive. The faux battle removes us from our embodied experience and delays our coming to acceptance. All that energy might be better directed toward resisting oppressive and alienating forces that can increase our suffering from stigma, beauty standards, fertility expectations, and in some cases biomedical treatment. Too many ill people suffer without getting any respite. Not when they are surviving under hostile conditions, social and corporeal. Not even when they are dying.

King's (2012) proposed theory of letting go is a crucial pursuit. It promises liberation. A feminist ethic of care and compassion gives us insight into what we can let go of to ease our pain and suffering in the embodied illness experience. As a collective project, it offers a radical alternative to stringent notions of how best to live with and sometimes die from cervical cancer. Let us let go together.

Note
The author found each narrative using the Google search engine and assigned pseudonyms to protect the privacy of individual writers.

REFERENCES
Crazy, Sexy, Cancer. 2007. Produced, directed, and starring Kris Carr. Gaiam Entertainment.
Ehrenreich, Barbara. 2001. "Welcome to Cancerland." *Harper's Magazine*, November. *harpers.org/archive/2001/11/welcome-to-cancerland.*
Frank, Arthur W. 1995. *The Wounded Storyteller: Body, Illness, and Ethics.* Chicago: University of Chicago Press.
Fraser, Nancy. 2009. "Feminism, Capitalism and the Cunning of History." *New Left Review* 56 (Mar/Apr): 97–117.
King, Donna. 2012. "Toward a Feminist Theory of Letting Go." *Frontiers* 33 (3): 53–70.
Lorde, Audre. 1980. *The Cancer Journals.* San Francisco, CA: Aunt Lute Books.

11

Stay-at-Home Fathers

Are Domestic Men Bucking Hegemonic Masculinity?

Steven Farough

> I'd say that a lot of it is *letting go* of that—"What do *you* do?"—and masculinity tied up in the role was . . . accepting [that] this is your job [being a stay-at-home father], and being happy to say this is how I spend my time.
> —Tom, stay-at-home father of two children

> Just . . . that *letting go*. Going with the flow and not having to fix a problem like it was a leaky faucet that you need to repair, you know. That's definitely a more male trait that I've had a hard time . . . *letting go*. . . . It's a nurturing, caring thing that you don't get . . . you don't get angry when your child cries because you were frustrated that you can't . . . solve [it].
> —Carl, stay-at-home father of one child

These stay-at-home fathers view the act of primary caregiving as a "letting go" of contemporary hegemonic masculinity. This letting go appears to leave behind the dominant style of American masculinity that constitutes manhood through the rigors of work, competition, and control over situations (Kimmel 2011). Tom, a former journalist, no longer feels uncomfortable explaining to others why caring for children in the domestic sphere is a worthy pursuit for him. He has moved beyond that and has found a place in the at-home community that is meaningful and rewarding. Before becoming a stay-at-home father, Carl, a thirty-two-year-old father of one, worked in the payroll department at a university. He found his work uninspiring, and when he and his wife had their son, they decided Carl would be the one to stay at home. The transition from work to domesticity was challenging for Carl, not the least from the fact that he was leaving behind a typical notion of what men are expected to do—work—and enter a space that is deemed feminine. He found his way by learning to let go of the need to be in control, and instead find value in the here-and-now. The narratives of the many stay-at-home fathers I interviewed tell a story of what happens when men let go of the dominant masculine identity so interwoven with the neoliberal pursuit of wealth and self-interest common to late capitalism.

Tom and Carl are part of a sample of thirty-four stay-at-home fathers across the United States I interviewed to explore their experiences with doing masculinity as a primary caregiver.[1] My sample should be seen as a subset of stay-at-home fathers whose choice to be the primary caregiver was largely voluntary. The Pew Research Center has estimated that there are as many as two million stay-at-home fathers in the United States. However, if we were to factor out job loss, returning to school, and disability or illness, the number would instead be between 214,000 to 400,000 (Livingston, Parker, and Klibanoff 2014; US Census Bureau 2012). Although the number of "voluntary" stay-at-home fathers is still small, it is safe to say that at-home dads now have a toehold in the at-home community in the United States. Stay-at-home fathers appear in films and TV series like *Little Children*, *Daddy Day Care*, *Parenthood*, and *Modern Dads*; we use quips like "Mr. Mom" as part of our popular lexicon; and we are regaled with interesting pieces of journalism on stay-at-home dads such as "Wall Street Mothers, Stay-Home Fathers" (Kantor and Silver-Greenberg 2013), or "Mr. Moms (by Way of Fortune 500)" (Kershaw 2009).

In fact, stay-at-home fathers could be seen as a vanguard in the growth of a contemporary version of domestic manhood;[2] in other words, a trend in the modern economic cosmos where men find a place in the neoliberal world to care for children and maintain a household. This has motivated family studies scholar Scott Coltrane to say, "Fathers are beginning to look more like mothers" as they spend more time caring for their children than previous generations (quoted in Cullen and Grossman 2007:63). Domestic masculinity seems radically different from the self-made man archetype that has been such a longstanding element of the American collective consciousness (Kimmel 2011). Unlike the competitive, work-focused view of American masculinity, the domestic turn of manhood appears focused on the private sphere, the immediacy of caring for others and the myriad of daily things that orient one to the here-and-now, a practice that is inescapably familiar with common sense notions about femininity.

The rise of stay-at-home fathers and domestic masculinity unsurprisingly correlates with the gains made by women over the past forty years, but also is the result of the inability to find work among lower income men (Livingston, Parker, and Klibanoff 2014). Therefore, the growth of stay-at-home fathers is bifurcated along class lines, with wealthier fathers volunteering to stay at home and lower income fathers taking on the role largely because of injury or a lack of economic opportunity.

It is clear that the United States has weak social policy for families, leaving many to find solutions to work/family balance on their own (Senior 2014; King 2012; Gerson 2010). Answers to this problem have typically fallen on women, as they are often faced with the dilemma of taking on the "second shift" or opting out of the workforce entirely (Stone 2007). Facebook COO Sheryl Sandberg (2013) weighs in on this dilemma in her book *Lean In*, noting that if professional women are to stay in the work world (and not opt out), they need spouses who are willing to be a "true partner" in child rearing. Such true partners have recently shown up in *New York Times* articles like "Wall Street Moms, At-Home Fathers" (Kantor and Silver-Greenberg 2013), which describes how at-home fathers have become a crucial part of the growth and success of high-level professional women in Wall Street. Because their husbands are running the household, these Wall Street women are then able to focus more exclusively on work.

As important as it is for men to move into the domestic sphere, both as a move to de-gender the work/family relationship and for men's personal fulfillment, this shift will not become more widespread simply by asking men to become better partners for their wives; there are simply too many structural barriers that make work/family equilibrium difficult in the United States. As a result, I would argue that the growth of stay-at-home fathers can be understood as one of many privatized responses conducted by American families living in an economy and polity that has done little to resolve the tensions brought about by the lack of policy support for work/family life balance. Stay-at-home fathers are indelibly linked to this opt out trend as their spouses then lean in—whether out of choice or lack of options.

The Lived Experience of Stay-at-Home Fathers

Although a significant number of stay-at-home fathers in my research came to their role voluntarily, the transition into the domestic sphere was not without its challenges. Many at-home fathers I interviewed found their move into the at-home world was greeted with suspicion by a significant number of stay-at-home mothers. Other research on stay-at-home fathers has also found that they experienced similar stigma and isolation (Rochlen et al. 2008; Rochlen, McKelley, and Whittaker 2010; Roberts-Holmes 2009; Harrington, Van Deusen, and Mazar 2012), and that at-home dads often attempt to re-gender domesticity as a masculine practice (Doucet 2006). However, in my research I found that at-home fathers were able to overcome their sense of alienation by investing in a largely gender-neutral view of parenting. I call this viewpoint humanist masculinity.

The concept of humanist masculinity is loosely grounded in the political philosophy of liberal humanism, where human preferences and behaviors are explained as acts of individual disposition rather than ascribed gender categories. This has the effect of pushing their sense of manhood into the background of their current identity work, as it becomes something that has been accomplished earlier in their lives. The investment in a largely gender-neutral world view does two things for at-home fathers and their relationship to the broader economic order: it first de-genders the domestic sphere to afford stay-at-home fathers a space that is typically constituted as deeply feminine, and second, it allows them to live in the gendered, economic, and familial climate of neoliberalism as it is currently constituted without challenging its structures.

Liberal Humanism and Rational Economics

The first evidence of liberal humanist ethos in the narratives of stay-at-home fathers comes in their depiction of how they became the primary caregiver. This story is largely narrated through the logic of rational economics: the individual who makes a sober cost/benefit analysis and then proceeds with the most efficient path. For stay-at-home fathers, most highlight that their spouse was either someone who earned more money and/or was a career-minded person. They also note dissatisfaction with their former job or describe their temperament as suited for the at-home world. What is striking about these narratives is the use of rational analysis that breaks down traditional heterosexual family roles to their constituent parts. Practices strongly associated with gender are re-signified into universal human attributes that each member in the couple happens to possess. The narratives follow a similar calculus that leads to men taking on the role of primary caregiver: spouse's career pays more, plus daycare is financially prohibitive or produces low-quality outcomes, plus spouse's personality is suited for work, plus husband's muted income earning potential, plus husband's lack of enthusiasm for work, equals father staying at home with children.

For instance, Ben, a former high school teacher with a PhD in biochemistry notes:

> I guess in the beginning it was an economic reality. I was teaching. Teachers don't make a huge amount of money. She was doing well in her company. We did the numbers and we could be comfortable on her income. A big part of it was that, if I was working, it seems that pretty much all that money would be paid out in daycare anyway. It would just be this complicating factor in our lives where we would have to be at certain places at certain times. You know, dropping the child off and picking the child up. And, it just seemed the logical thing to do because we can afford it. And it was . . . the way to keep our lives really less complicated. And, um, I don't like work that much. [Laughs]

Carl also shares a similar account when their baby arrived and he was unemployed:

> We figured that one of us needed to be working. You know, where she had the benefits and everything to keep it. We weren't going to like switch, with

me finding a job and then her stopping her work. It just seemed to make more sense to continue the way it was sort of set up.

Joe, a former carpenter and veteran, felt a similar relief to Ben's, but also points out that his wife was more geared for the work world.

I went back. And we were just finishing up [school] and . . . my wife had put so much effort into her time and her degree that she really did not want to quit her job. Which I had no problem with because [laughing] I was all for quitting my job.

These narratives demonstrate how at-home fathers and their spouses envisioned the husband staying at home through a gender-neutral ethos embedded in the rationality of liberal humanism.

There is also a philosophical investment in viewing primary caregiving through the gender-neutral noun of "parenting" rather than the gendered term "mothering." Thirty-eight-year-old stay-at-home father Derek sums up being a primary caregiver as:

I just want to be a proud parent. And, you know, I've felt like an ass. Don't judge me because I'm a man. So, [it's] "a woman's job." Because . . . it's a parent's job to raise [children]. It's not a man or a woman's job. It's a parent's job. So, that's a hard one to fully get a grasp on. Don't pigeonhole me into a man role or a female role or whatever. I'm taking that parent role.

Tom acknowledges some gender differences between at-home mothers and at-home fathers but believes that what they do is largely the same thing:

You call it a primary caregiver, it's the same thing. Are we going to experience it differently? Certainly. We have gender differences. [Chuckles] Yeah, so? . . . In my experience the basic, you know . . . rewards, frustrations, and just day-to-day experience are very common, are very similar.

Frank, a stay-at-home father of two, points out, "They've said—You know, 'the mother coddles the child.' You know, they don't realize it's possible for the father to do the same thing." Sam believes parenting has more to do with personality rather than gender:

Like, my sister-in-law, she's in between getting her Master's degree and working part-time; she stays home for the most part, you know? And, um, they'll let their kids watch *Teenage Mutant Ninja Turtles*, *Power Rangers* and stuff like that. Their son walks around shooting people. And, you know, I'm in the Army but my kid watches, you know, *Max and Ruby*. And, and so those kinds of things . . . I think that's just totally personal style rather than gender based.

Both the decision for the men first to stay at home and the way stay-at-home fathers came to know their vocation as a *parent* reflect the investment in a gender-neutral logic of liberal humanism, where personality is placed over sex and gender—and husbands and wives are assessed as potentially interchangeable in their ability to care or work. For at-home fathers, it just happens to be that they were either personally more suited *or* their wives merely earned more.

Re-gendering the Domestic Sphere

While it is fair to say that stay-at-home fathers relied heavily upon gender neutrality, they also still saw elements of what they did as masculine. To make the claim that what one is doing in the domestic sphere is masculine is essentially an act of re-gendering, as modern domesticity is so strongly rooted in stereotyped notions of femininity. Stay-at-home fathers were emphatic that what they did as primary caregivers was the same as at-home mothers, but many could not help but feel they cared in ways that were typically known as masculine behavior. This showed up primarily in what they saw as a more "hands off" style of parenting. It is important to note that the way in which they re-signified parenting as masculine was a matter of degree and not in kind. Therefore, they attribute the signifier "masculine" to behaviors that they acknowledge both at-home mothers and fathers do.

For example, Sam suggests, "I was a lot *more*, 'suck it up and drive along' than I think a lot of the other moms are. If you get hurt that's great. Let's see how bad it is. And if you're okay, let's go. You're good. Come on. Go out and play . . . [But] I don't know how different it is [from mothers] . . . You know?" (Emphasis added). Sam believes he is *more* hardnosed with his children than other mothers, a trait he considers masculine. However, he then backtracks by wondering if being hardnosed is really that different from what other mothers do. For Sam, it seems the consistency and frequency of his hardnosed parenting is masculine, not the style itself.

Bill also suggests that at-home mothers might be quicker to attend to their children than at-home fathers.

> You know, obviously they're a little bit more over the top as [far as] safety is concerned. They're little bit more over the top as far where education is maybe of concern. You know, things along those lines that . . . those things matter more [to them] than to me. . . . [I care about] allowing my daughter to just be an individual and to grow up.

As with Sam, Bill describes a more relaxed degree of concern over safety and education that he re-genders as masculine, in contrast to the "little bit more over the top" worry he sees in the mothers. Michael too expresses the matter of degree when he notes:

> There's more wrestling around. But, you know, not stereotypical male in that it's like punching and rough housing. There's a lot of hugs. A lot of cuddling too. But, it's just—I think it's more physical.

As stay-at-home-fathers ultimately attribute some of the acts of their parenting as masculine, they do so with the open acknowledgement that the behavior is not *uniquely* masculine. It is just matter of degree.

Masculinity as Proven

The other crucial element constituting humanist masculinity is the way in which at-home fathers reorient masculinity into an already proven state that does not need authorization from dominant cultural standards of American manhood. Many of the fathers in the sample noted that they grew tired of their careers or reached a point where they felt comfortable leaving work behind. Still others highlighted their successful enactment of masculinity in the armed services or in their earlier life when they had fewer obligations. In effect, masculinity becomes a fait accompli that is ultimately bound by time and limited to their years as younger men. Because their masculinity has already been proven, they can view masculinity as secondary, enabling them to pursue other interests like raising children.

Thirty-eight-year-old Derek says it well when he notes how he has aged out of proving masculinity:

> You know? Yeah, I'm a man. So what? [Laughs] Who cares? I think another thing . . . that allowed me to grow as a human being was . . . waiting until I was old enough to have children. Kind of getting it out of your system, you know. Doing the twenties, you know, party every day and, you know . . . and craziness or whatever.

As a result, Derek believes that manhood is essentially a time-bound enactment whereby he may leave behind its demands so that he may grow as a person and focus on caring for his children. Ray also shares a similar critique of hegemonic manhood:

> I'm the same kind of guy who I was before when I was in the Navy or when to grad school or whatever. . . . I act the same way . . . I have the same drive.

Now my focus is, I think, something that's more fulfilling and more long lasting. And, I keep thinking . . . I look at Kaitlyn now. I look at her and I know she wants to be around me. And she tells me she loves me all the time. I'm the best dad in the world. I look at her face. I keep thinking, "That's what I want to see on my death bed." Because, you know, that's the kind of person . . . the kind of love I experienced in my life. Not that I made this or I was able to go out to have more freedom with the guys. And stuff like that. So, I think, you know, I think it's a trap a lot of guys get suckered into. To think this is the way we have to act. . . . I don't think that's relevant.

Ray has a secure sense of self, and he does not need validation from dominant masculinity. Ray ultimately views his experience being at home with his daughter as more fulfilling than the days he spent in the Navy.

Micah demonstrates he does not need to prove his sense of manhood to himself or others when he notes:

I guess it's just that machismo that comes on a lot of guys, [mocking] "Oh man. You're a stay-at-home dad. Boy, you know, what do you do, sit on the couch and watch *The View*?" Hey, you know! . . . You're going to accuse me of watching *The View*. I turn it on occasionally. If I see something on there, if I want to watch it, I'll watch it. You know? [Laughs] I'm like, "yeah, believe whatever you want to believe." You know, I'm the guy that, you know, doesn't have to necessarily [work] sixty hours a week. Which, I used to do—to prove myself.

Micah no longer feels the need to demonstrate that his manhood adheres to popular conceptions. But in taking masculinity for granted as an already-achieved status, one they no longer have to "prove," do these men miss a more radical opportunity to question the masculine privilege they still retain within an unexamined neoliberal order?

Interrogating Humanist Masculinity

How should we understand the use of humanist masculinity by stay-at-home fathers in relation to both hegemonic masculinity and the neoliberal order? Do at-home fathers throw a wrench into the system or do they help grease its wheels?

In her now classic monograph *Masculinities*, R. W. Connell (1995, 77) notes that masculinity should not be understood as a type but a "configuration of practice" in the gender order—meaning that masculinity is an identity standpoint in the social system of gender that affords male bodies advantages in the public sphere in general and provides greater status than to women on the whole. Connell's theorization of masculinity forces one to view the locus of manhood in a discursive and structural system rather than a personality typology, situating our understanding of the daily cultural practices of masculinity in relation to power.

Tristan Bridges and C. J. Pascoe (2014) argue that challenges brought about by feminist and queer social movements have created a legitimation crisis for hegemonic masculinity, where privileged men selectively incorporate elements of marginalized and subordinated masculinities and sometimes even femininities. Bridges and Pascoe call this "hybrid masculinities." They note the practice of hybrid masculinities tends to be more stylistic than resistive, and generally operates to obscure the continued advantages of hegemonic masculinity.

From this perspective, stay-at-home fathers might appear to be a prime example of hybrid masculinities. I would argue, however, that by opting out of work to care for their children, stay-at-home fathers are personally forgoing income, career development, and presence in the public sphere—all pathways to power in a neoliberal environment. By incorporating the requisite practices of domesticity, they are indeed moving central aspects of culturally defined markers of femininity onto male bodies in a way that is more material than, say, a metrosexual who adopts a gay aesthetic to seduce women rather than to be in solidarity with the queer community.

The stay-at-home fathers in my research are clearly committed to their children and appear to embody the entire project of domestic life, from maintaining the household, to managing extracurricular activities, to the mental and emotional work involved in anticipating others' needs. They embody domesticity and appear to do it well through their humanist masculine worldview.

As feminists like Francine Deutsch (2007) and Judith Lorber (2005) have pointed out, de-gendering elements of social life can be a radical act, as it destabilizes practices of inequity rooted in a binary gender system. If at-home fathers can find solace in a deeply gendered space of domesticity, then their existential and material existence simply makes it more challenging to suggest women are naturally suited for the domestic world.

That being said, the rise of stay-at-home fathers, absent meaningful social policy support for families, allows for the continuing privatization of caretaking, meaning that it can be an option only for those who can afford to do so, or for those who have no choice. For those who are voluntarily stay-at-home fathers, it should be no surprise that their spouses are often in high-level professional work. For instance, in my sample of thirty-four stay-at-home fathers, sixteen had household incomes above $130,000.[3]

The existence of stay-at-home fathers may indeed make their spouses' work lives less encumbered, but their benefit does not trickle down to the many families that also need a better work/family balance. For the trend of domestic masculinity to become even more disruptive to gender inequity in work and family, it requires broad policy initiatives that help to restructure caretaking as a social good that demands significant social and economic support (see Eisenstein cited in King 2012).

In just one of many examples from other developed nations, Sweden, Norway, and Canada have a paid paternity leave policy that provides a government-sponsored financial incentive for fathers to take a leave of absence from work to care for newborns. If they do not, they lose the financial incentive and the time off. Research demonstrates that when new fathers are able to take paternity leave they are much more involved in maintaining a household and continue to care for children even as their children grow (Rampell 2013). And, as Claire Cain Miller (2014) explains, "Countries like Sweden with more progressive policies, such as incentives for new fathers to also take leave, [also] have a smaller [gender] pay gap."

Contemporary stay-at-home fathers construct a more feminist version of hybrid masculinities that may partially disrupt gender norms but does not knowingly and radically challenge hegemonic masculine privilege, and leaves completely uninterrogated neoliberal structures designed to benefit elites. Social policies, on the other hand, that support fathers' involvement in child care are structural changes that reduce gender inequality in significant ways. The de-gendering worldview of humanist masculinity does, however, allow stay-at-home fathers to exist in the at-home community in a way that is meaningful to them. Humanist masculinity and domestic masculinity can help to radically change the current neoliberal order only when they are paired with robust social policies like paid family leave, flex time, job sharing, and subsidized day care. In this way, mothers and fathers from all economic classes can move between work and family life with less stress, more equity, and greater meaning.

NOTES

1. The fathers I interviewed were contacted through a snowball and convenience sampling technique. The small sample size is by no means random, but the fathers did have enough in common to document a set of shared experiences that point to a broader pattern.

2. I use the phrase "modern version of domestic masculinity" to acknowledge the fact that masculinity was domestic in sixteenth and seventeenth centuries in the American colonies where fathers were more involved in the functioning of the household and care of children (Coontz 1988).

3. Families earning more than $130,000 are in the top 25 percent of the income distribution in the United States, but almost 50 percent of families in my sample have incomes above $130,000. In the remainder of my sample, eleven had incomes ranging between $70,000 and $129,999, and seven had between $35,000 and $69,999. My sample is skewed toward higher incomes.

REFERENCES

Bridges, Tristan, and C. J. Pascoe. 2014. "Hybrid Masculinities: New Directions in the Sociology of Men and Masculinities." *Sociological Compass* 8 (3): 246–58.

Connell, Raewyn W. 1995. *Masculinities*. Berkeley: University of California Press.

Coontz, Stephanie. 1998. *The Social Origins of Private Life: A History of American Families, 1600–1900*. London: Verso.

Cullen, Lisa, and Lev Grossman. 2007. "Fatherhood 2.0." *Time Magazine* 170 (16): 63–66.

Deutsch, Francine. 2007. "Undoing Gender." *Gender and Society* 21 (1): 106–27.

Doucet, Andrea. 2006. *Do Men Mother?: Fathering, Care and Domestic Responsibility*. Toronto: Toronto University Press.

Gerson, Kathleen. 2010. *The Unfinished Revolution: Coming of Age in a New Era of Gender, Work, and Family*. New York: Oxford University Press.

Harrington, Brad, Fred Van Deusen, and Iyar Mazar. 2012. *The New Dad: Right at Home*. Boston: Boston College Center for Work and Family.

Kantor, Jodie, and Jessica Silver-Greenberg. 2013. "Wall Street Mothers, Stay-Home Fathers" *New York Times*, December 7, A1.

Kershaw, Sarah. 2009. "Mr. Moms (by Way of Fortune 500)." *New York Times*, April 22. *www.nytimes.com/2009/04/23/fashion/23dads.html*.

Kimmel, Michael. 2011. *American Manhood: A Cultural History*. New York: Oxford University Press.

King, Donna. 2012. "Toward a Feminist Theory of Letting Go." *Frontiers: A Journal of Women Studies* 33 (3): 53–78.

Livingston, Gretchen, Kim Parker, and Caroline Klibanof. 2014. *Growing Number of Dads Home with the Kids: Biggest Increase among those Caring for Family*. Washington, DC: Pew Research Center's Social and Demographic Trends Project.

Lorber, Judith. 2005. *Breaking to Bowls: Degendering and Feminist Change*. New York: Norton.

Miller, Clara Cain. 2014. "The Motherhood Penalty vs. the Fatherhood Bonus: A Child Helps Your Career, if You're a Man." *The Upshot: Gender Divide* (blog). *New York Times*, September 6. *www.nytimes.com/2014/09/07/upshot/a-child-helps-your-career-if-youre-a-man.html*.

Rampell, Catherine. 2013. "Lean In, Dad." *New York Times Sunday Magazine*, April 7. *www.nytimes.com/2013/04/07/magazine/how-shared-diaper-duty-could-stimulate-the-economy.html*.

Roberts-Holmes, Guy. 2009. "'People Are Suspicious of Us': A Critical Examination of Father Primary Carers and English Early Childhood Services." *Early Years: An International Research Journal* 29 (3): 281–91.

Rochlen, Aaron B., Ryan A. McKelley, and Tiffany A. Whittaker. 2010. "Stay-at-Home Fathers' Reasons for Entering the Role and Stigma Experiences: A Preliminary Report." *Psychology of Men and Masculinity* 11 (4): 7–14.

Rochlen, Aaron B., Marie-Anne Suizzo, Ryan A. McKelley, and Vanessa Scaringi. 2008. "'I'm Just Providing for My Family': A Qualitative Study of Stay-At-Home Fathers." *Psychology of Men and Masculinity* 9 (4): 193–206.

Sandberg, Sheryl. 2013. *Lean In: Women, Work, and the Will to Lead*. New York: Knopf.

Senior, Jennifer. 2014. *All Joy and No Fun: The Paradox of Modern Parenthood*. New York: Harper Collins.

Stone, Pamela. 2007. *Opting Out? Why Women Really Quit Careers and Head Home*. Berkeley: University of California Press.

US Census Bureau. 2012. *America's Families and Living Arrangements*. *www.census.gov/hhes/families/data/cps2012.html*.

12

From Retail Banking to Credit Counseling

Opting Out and Tuning In

Kevin J. Delaney

While conducting research for a book about how people's choice of career influences the way they think about money, I encountered a number of women who had once worked in retail banking but had switched careers to become credit counselors. I was slightly puzzled as to why so many of the women I interviewed had left banking. Many had taken a pay cut when they switched careers. There are two ways to explain this pattern. The first is to say that the consolidation of the banking industry led to women being pushed off the higher paying banking career path and into a lower paying career in credit counseling. This interpretation fits well within a set of social science research (Bielby and Baron 1986; Bielby and Bielby 1992; England et al. 1988; Reskin and Roos 1990; Snyder and Green 2008; Stainback and Kwon 2012) that shows that a large portion of the gender wage gap between men and women is due to women being "sorted" into lower paying occupations in a society that devalues qualities associated historically with women (e.g., empathy, care-taking, emotional intelligence, counseling). Racial segregation in the workplace compounds the effects of gender segregation (Cotter, Hermsen, and Vanneman 2003; McTauge, Stainback, and Tomaskovic-Devey 2009; Tomaskavic-Devey 1996). This occupational segregation process, while almost certainly at work here, can leave one with the impression that women are not active agents in the choices they make (even when those choices are made within a set of neoliberal and patriarchal constraints).

As I listened to the stories of the women I interviewed, however, I heard an alternative explanation; one that does not discount the sorting phenomenon but also suggests that women's agency and desire to "opt out" of banking played a crucial role in their choices to change careers. In fact, many women saw this career change as a liberatory journey in which they rejected the path they were on in the banking world for something more fulfilling. While my original project centered on how people's work shaped the way they thought about money (Delaney 2012), I also became interested in how these women placed their career change into a framework of liberation and letting go of certain expectations about money and their careers in banking. Realizing that their career switch might entail a pay cut or a more truncated career ladder, they still made the change as they sought a more fulfilling work life. They desired to be more directly helpful to their clients than they had been able to be in the changing world of banking.

I interviewed a total of eight credit counselors for this project; five women and three men. The interviews took place at nonprofit credit counseling agencies in Pennsylvania, New Jersey and Florida. The women ranged in age from twenty-nine to sixty, while the men were between the ages of fifty and seventy; all of those I interviewed were white. Each interview lasted between sixty and ninety minutes and followed an open-ended format that explored how they became interested in credit counseling and their work experiences in prior careers and as credit counselors.

All of the female credit counselors that I interviewed described having a childhood interest in money and finance. For example, they told me that "they were always good with money" or that they liked saving their allowance as children. They ended up entering careers in retail banking where they found satisfaction for a while, but then changes in the industry made them increasingly unhappy. For example, this is how two credit counselors, Cynthia and Laura, described their previous work in banking:

> I spent thirty years in the banking world. I was a retail banker in the
> Delaware Valley and also in Washington, DC. My latest job was with Core
> States, that became First Union, and then I left for a while, and decided to do
> something a little different in the nonprofit world. (Cynthia)

> I was an economics major. My sister was working for First Union Bank at the
> time. She was able to get me a temp position. So I went in, worked for two
> weeks, then my job was done and I said I am never going back in banking.
> That is it. They called me back the following Monday and said "We really
> liked you, can you come back." You know, I'm a college student, so I'm like,
> OK. I thought it was the most boring thing, banking, money all that stuff.
> And now fourteen years later, I was still in banking. I enjoyed it, I moved
> around a lot. I was in a two year management program. I worked in the
> branches, I worked with small business. I worked in product development. I
> did as much as I could while I was there. Then, they were going through a big
> restructuring and I kinda' hit the wall. I just felt like my time was done there
> and I was able to get out through one of their severance packages. I took nine
> months off and traveled and did all that kind of stuff and I just gave myself
> the freedom to say that this is what I have done all my life, but I am going to
> open myself up to whatever. . . . (Laura)

If they had been men, these women might have had more opportunities to enter commercial or investment banking. However, they had an interest in working with retail customers and, as they put it, "helping people." It also seemed that the work hours in retail banking were somewhat more flexible and conducive to raising a family, something that their male counterparts probably worried about less often and periodically rather than constantly. To be sure, these women encountered some barriers of sexism as they were encouraged toward the retail banking industry. This striking pattern of "internal sorting" within careers in which women get sorted into the lower paying end of occupations gets repeated across an amazingly diverse array of occupations ranging from waiter/waitress through professor, lawyer, and physician. It is often tied to women's responsibility for the family and what is often called "the second shift"; carrying the primary responsibility for home and family life after completing a paid shift in the workforce (Craig 2007; Hochschild 2003).

The story might have ended here, and these women might have moved up and along the retail banking career ladder. But it didn't. Two major things happened in the banking world that led to significant discontent among this group of talented women. First, banks began merging. Many of these women, when detailing their career history to me would say, "Well, first I worked for [x], then they became [y], and two years later we merged with [z]." After each merger the workplace culture became more hierarchical and centralized. Second, deregulation allowed banks to sell more financial products and this brought significant pressure to sell these products to customers. Several of the women I talked with cited this change as a leading cause of their dissatisfaction with the banking world. They no longer could see themselves as helping people but rather they began to see themselves as trying to satisfy the banks' desire, which sometimes felt insatiable, for higher profits. At times, the pressure to sell certain financial products ran counter to the client's best interests. In order to be successful within the changing bank culture, they saw that they would have to behave in ways that did not feel comfortable to them. As Donna King (2012) has argued, the feminist theory behind the concept of "letting go" can entail the decision to leave behind the imperative to continually increase the company's profits at the expense of tending to human needs. This altered consciousness can be framed as a private or public act of resistance (57). As one credit counselor told me,

> When you are in retail banking world, you are sitting there with clients and trying, for example, to sell them a home equity loan and you are trying to up-sell the home equity loan by incorporating all their credit card debt. Well, here [at the credit counseling agency] we don't teach clients to substitute unsecured credit for secured credit just for the sake of getting a better rate, or something like that, because they could put their home at risk. And when you are talking to a low- to middle-income person who might not be the

wisest with their use of credit cards, that is not what you want to do, give them a clean slate and allow them to start over again. (Evelyn)

This ever increasing sales pressure meant they were given less time to train new employees and were able to spend less time with each customer. Seeking a refuge from the pressure to up-sell, these women sought a way to continue to use their financial acumen and their desire to help clients without the pressure to sell financial products that might be inappropriate for a customer. Each had discovered debt and credit counseling services as a way to do that. One woman found this career through the help of a career counselor, another through her reading of books about alternative careers. Several found the career through networking with individuals they knew in banking who had already made the switch.

I spent several days at four different agencies talking with and observing people who worked as credit counselors. Most were women. The few men I interviewed had more varied backgrounds, coming from a variety of sales jobs and one from retail banking; whereas the majority of the women started in banking and switched to credit counseling. The men's stories focused more on their being downsized in prior jobs and less of a sense of liberation or opting out because of career dissatisfaction.

The median yearly salary in 2010 for credit counselors was $38,000 with starting salaries often in the low $20,000 range. While the median salary is higher than the median annual salary for a bank teller, it is about $18,000 less than the median pay for a bank loan officer and about $26,000 less than the median pay for a personal financial adviser (all salary figures are based on 2010 Bureau of Labor Statistics data). It is worth noting that at three of the four agencies where I spent time interviewing and observing, women were the founders and/or directors of the nonprofit. So this career did give women the opportunity to be in positions of power and autonomy and some increased salary.

What this particular case study shows is that people can find options when they become dissatisfied with a changing industry. They not only can choose to let go by opting out of something they find increasingly distasteful or that even goes against their core values, they can choose to opt in to a career that provides more fulfillment, if less pay. As these women developed a critical stance toward changes in the banking industry, they sought an opportunity that would allow them to be more directly centered on their clients' needs rather than the mandates of increasing profit sought by banks. A career change of this sort, then, can represent not only a personal career choice but also an action of social resistance and social change. Not only had these women changed careers, they were also attempting to help their clients out of poverty and debt and were providing advice that could run counter to the larger culture and its imperatives to spend, borrow, and consume. In tandem with the career change came personal transformation. While the career change typically represented a lower salary (at least initially), it also came with much higher job satisfaction. In fact, all of the women I talked with reported increased job satisfaction (of course, this may not be surprising since these women had become dissatisfied with prior careers).

The higher job satisfaction, however, did come in the face of a new set of challenges. No longer was bank management the obstacle to serving clients' needs; now the main obstacles were the challenges of a difficult economy and the structural limitations inherent in the occupation of credit counselor. Credit counselors become deeply entrenched in the problems their clients face. Here is how one credit counselor described her job:

> I feel like I am helping more people. I mean I was helping people in banking—it depended, because my job changed—in my last job, I was behind the scenes and not out there as much—so if I compare my last job there to this, I like the people contact, I like helping people. A lot of people might think I am in the financial business, but from my perspective, I am in the "hope" business. When someone comes in here, yeah I want to teach them about finances, blah, blah, but from my perspective, I just want to give them hope to know there is a way out of this. There is a light at the end of the tunnel. So, if anything that is my calling, you know. (Cynthia)

This idea of providing "hope and help" continued to engage the women I interviewed, but their work also politicized them in important ways, making them more aware and interested in issues of income and wealth inequality, low wage work, minimum wage laws, and the lack of health insurance in many jobs. Every credit counselor I interviewed told me that their job had made them more, rather than less, sympathetic toward their clients and provided them with a much greater understanding of how people get into debt. For example:

> You become more compassionate, because most instances that we see, and we can't be judgmental—but a lot of what is going on is not something the client could control—medical is a big piece of it, job loss is another big piece of it—and then it deteriorates from there. (Evelyn)

> I have a greater appreciation for the fact that your life can change in a minute, you know. How things are just so . . . not permanent, and how quickly your life can turn around. Unfortunately, for a lot of people I see, not in the best way. But it is also a very rewarding job, and I like more the helping people. I helped people in a different way at my old job, so I like that. I like more the hands on kind of stuff. (Laura)

Despite their increased understanding and compassion, credit counselors can help clients only in limited and circumscribed ways owing to the nature of the job. In their day-to-day work lives, credit counselors are mainly limited to offering short term, individualized advice while knowing that their clients often had long term problems rooted in larger structural issues (e.g., low wages; part-time, temporary or contingent work; no health insurance). The very term "counselor" in their job title was a bit of a misnomer. In one sense, they provided financial counseling to their clients. However, they also verged toward a kind of psychological counseling, even in their use of terms like "spending triggers" or "shopaholics" to describe some of their clients (and even themselves when they talked of their own shopping practices). Despite the individualized tools at their disposal, they knew that some of their clients' problems were rooted in the problems of low wage work or overwhelming medical bills rather than psychological dysfunction.

For example, one of the main tools at the disposal of credit counselors is a budget diary that requires clients to record all of their spending for a week or a month. This diary focuses the client and counselor on individual spending patterns. When a client returns with the budget diary, the counselor looks for ways the client overspends or ways that the client might cut back and save money. Counselors also look to short term revenue enhancements like "renting out a room in your house" or "selling off some of your possessions." While these are all somewhat helpful, these tend to be Band-Aid solutions to a much larger set of problems. It sometimes felt like they were sending their clients back into a hurricane armed only with a small umbrella. One of their more useful tools was the ability to consolidate many debts into one payment made to the counseling center, which then disbursed payments out to various creditors. However, this could turn the counseling center into another creditor demanding payment in the eyes of the client, threatening the supportive counseling relationship.

With increased awareness and politicization often came a frustration among counselors at the inability to get at the root of some of their clients' problems. As one counselor put it:

> I think the majority of the people we see have gotten to us either because of a loss of a job, we see a lot of seniors, who have high prescription costs, high medical expenses, and high real estate taxes, and they are on a fixed income. We do see people who overspend, but there is usually some other thing that has trigged them to come to us. . . . The people who come to us, they usually want to pay it back, so usually it is something that has caused them to get to that position. (Laura)

Another frustration I heard expressed centered on the large percentage of clients that came in just once for a counseling session and never returned. Whether this was due to the transient nature of the clients' lives or a frustration at what the agency could—and could not—offer remained a mystery to the counselors. They took solace in the notion that they would be there for anyone that sought their help and they hoped that even a single session provided the client with some practical ideas:

> We try to keep in touch with them but when the collectors start calling, we are a collector to them too. So, it is very difficult to stay in touch with somebody who is not in touch with us. But we do try to get in touch with them, you know invite them back. We do try to keep the client on track. We don't just let a client go by the wayside. If they miss a payment, we call them, we try to encourage them. We try not to be the collector, we try to be the mentor, you know. What can we do to help you? Let's take a look at your budget again. Let's see what we can do to squeeze that payment out, or maybe you shouldn't make any more payments, you are wasting your time. (Dana)

While somewhat limited in their ability to help clients, many of the counselors told me that their jobs had indeed changed their own outlook on money and their lives. These counselors had altered their stance on consumption, becoming more critical of forms of hyper-consumption. As one put it:

> EVELYN: I think from a budgeting perspective, we do now look at money differently. I think we look at it as a commodity and we have more of an emphasis on saving. You know we will go out and talk to people about things you just didn't think about when you were making a lot of money. You know, take the $20 out of the ATM machine in the morning, you go to Starbucks get a cup of coffee, the newspaper, and maybe a bagel, and then halfway through the morning you go get another cup of coffee and after lunch, your money is gone. And I think that we individually even, look at money differently than where we did before, because we see how much waste we were causing.
>
> KD: Do you still get your coffee at Starbucks?
>
> EVELYN: No! I bring my coffee [laughs]. [When I was in banking], I never brought my own coffee. I mean, very rarely, it was something else to carry. I went out to lunch every day. I just never thought about those things. And now it is the opposite.

The majority of the credit counselors I interviewed said they visited an ATM machine less often and withdrew less money than when they worked in banking. Partly this was due to having a reduction in salary, but it also was owing to their increased awareness of their daily spending patterns as a result of their job, as they reviewed clients' spending diaries to illustrate how spending $5 or $6 each day on lunch and $3 on coffee adds up to a large monthly or annual expense.

While not perfect, the switch from retail banking to credit counseling allowed counselors to feel freer to help their clients, and they could think in terms of their clients' interests rather than the banks' interests. Their new occupation made them more aware of the causes of indebtedness and more sympathetic to their clients. Paradoxically, perhaps, their new frustrations came from this deeper understanding as well as the transitory nature of their client's lives which meant that they were often unable to work with clients reliably over extended periods of time. Additionally, as credit counselors learned more about the causes of their clients' problems, they came to recognize the limitations of the individualistic approach to those problems. Using spending diaries and suggesting short-term, emergency solutions to problems could only go so far. It appeared that this increasingly nuanced and detailed understanding of clients' problems was leading toward a more structural view of poverty (e.g., poverty caused by the prevalence of part-time, low-wage work or by the lack of employer provided health insurance). Their job changed their own view of themselves—they reported becoming more politicized, more socially aware, and more concerned with issues of hyper-consumption and inequality. Despite their current job limitations, they seemed determined to continue helping clients in any way they were able to do so:

> KD: Now in the counseling session, are you trying to reform behavior to some degree?
>
> CYNTHIA: Without a doubt. In other words, when we go through the budget with the client, we go through a thirty-two-line budget. And in each area, we may be able to offer them tips on how they might be able to cut back in certain area. We also have a resource directory that we have built up over the years that are available to people that might help them get breaks on their insurance, or breaks with the utility company, or food banks, or different ways like that. We may talk to people about their telephone usage, or other places or ways they might get a better deal.
>
> EVELYN: [We may recommend counseling sometimes] for the higher income, the shopaholics—we have people who buy things who never take the tags off things, they are in their trunk. So, we tell them to take them back [laughs].
>
> KD: Partly you are swimming upstream against the culture; the commercials to spend and consume?
>
> EVELYN: Oh, absolutely, we recognize that the United States is like that, all of us are like that. We want it, and we want it now, and we have been given a vehicle now so we can have it now—credit cards. I mean, what, forty

years ago, there weren't credit cards; maybe a store card or a Diner's club. You didn't have the availability of credit that you have today and we didn't have the level of consumerism that we have today.

DANA: We have some standard lines, particularly for people who have a home: Do you have an extra room in your house, could you rent out a room? Maybe you could get a second job. We do look at those things. Unfortunately, it is just something sometimes that just doesn't fit into the game plan. And a lot of the people that I see, in particular, are single parents—low income women—and they are really struggling. The idea of another job with children to take care of [is impossible]. Some of them have jobs that are low-paying jobs to begin with and they don't have benefits. So, they don't even have health care for themselves, they have to get CHIP [Children's Health Insurance Program] for their children, maybe, and they just pray they don't get sick. It is really difficult, really difficult. I don't see how they manage.

Changing careers can be a means for transforming the self (Delaney 2012; Sher, 2010). Credit counselors present an interesting case study in the concept of "letting go" by opting out of one career for another (King 2012, 67–68). The individuals who have chosen this profession took themselves off the career track of retail banking because they disagreed with some of the corporate practices of banks and had grown tired of the constant merging of banks and the changes in workplace culture that often followed. These women desired to help clients as their primary priority and found that credit counseling allowed them to feel more focused on their clients' issues. However, there continued to be constraints on their ability to truly help as their clients' problems were often beyond the individualistic and psychological tools at their disposal. Despite the limitations, they had found increased fulfillment in their jobs. Perhaps unexpectedly, they gained an increased awareness of the causes of debt, poverty, and inequality. By opting out they had also tuned in to a much deeper and more intimate understanding of the structural problems associated with low-wage work, the lack of affordable health insurance, and societal pressures toward hyper-consumption. This not only deepened their compassion for their clients, it also altered the ways they thought about themselves and their own consumption patterns. It appears that this career change from banking to credit counseling had as much of an impact on them as they were having on the clients they served. One possible avenue forward for these credit counselors is to move from their increasingly detailed understanding of poverty toward a social movement aimed at the root causes of poverty and the feminization of poverty that they were witness to on a daily basis.

REFERENCES

Bielby, William, and James Baron. 1986. "Men and Women at Work: Sex Segregation and Statistical Discrimination." *American Journal of Sociology* 91:759–99.

Bielby, William, and Denise Bielby. 1992. "Cumulative Versus Continuous Disadvantage in an Unstructured Labor Market: Gender Differences in the Career of Television Writers." *Work and Occupations* 19:366–86. doi: 10.1177/0730888492019004003.

Cotter, David A., Joan M. Hermsen, and Reeve Vanneman. 2003. "The Effects Of Occupational Gender Segregation Across Race. *The Sociological Quarterly* 44:17–36.

Craig, Lyn. 2007. "Is There Really a Second Shift, and If So, Who Does It? A Time-Diary Investigation." *Feminist Review* 86:149–70

Delaney, Kevin J. 2012. *Money at Work: On the Job with Priests, Poker Players, and Hedge Fund Traders.* New York: New York University Press.

England, Paula, George Farkas, Barbara Stanek Kilbourne, and Thomas Dou. 1988. "Explaining Occupational Sex Segregation and Wages: Findings from a Model with Fixed Effects." *American Sociological Review* 53:544–58.

Hochschild, Arlie. 2003. *The Second Shift.* New York: Penguin Books.

King, Donna. 2012. "Toward a Feminist Theory of Letting Go." *Feminist Frontiers* 33 (3): 53–70. doi: 10.1353/fr0.2012.0040.

McTauge, Tricia, Kevin Stainback, and Donald Tomaskovic-Devey. 2009. "An Organizational Approach to Understanding Sex and Race Segregation in US Workplaces." *Social Forces* 87 (3): 1499–527.

Reskin, Barbara, and Patricia Roos. 1990. *Job Queues, Gender Queues: Explaining Women's Inroads into Male Occupations.* Philadelphia: Temple University Press.

Sher, Barbara. 2010. *I Could Do Anything If I Only Knew What It Was.* New York: Dell.

Snyder, Karrie Ann, and Adam Isaiah Green. 2008. "Revisiting The Glass Escalator: The Case of Gender Segregation in a Female Dominated Occupation." *Social Problems* 55:271–99.

Stainback, Kevin, and Soyoung Kwon. 2012. "Female Leaders, Organizational Power, and Sex Segregation." *Annals of the American Academy of Political and Social Science* 639:217–35.

Tomaskavic-Devey, Donald. 1996. *Gender and Racial Inequality at Work: The Sources and Consequences of Job Segregation.* Ithaca, NY: Cornell University Press.

13

Keeping Up Appearances
Working Class Feminists Speak Out
about the Success Model in Academia

Roxanne Gerbrandt and Liza Kurtz

Feminists have made huge strides for equality: electoral reform, reproductive rights, and protections against employment discrimination, to name a few. However in recent decades the feminist movement has been strongly influenced by neoliberalism's emphasis on individualism, economic deregulation, and global capitalism. Gender equality has increasingly come to be defined in market terms as equality of accumulation, competition, and consumption in a society that is driven by the constant appetite for more (Eisenstein cited in King 2012).

Feminism in the academy has not been immune to this neoliberal shift. Academic feminism began as a community of renegade intellectuals who worked together to bring feminist voices to universities and colleges. But as feminist academics built credibility within the larger scholarly community, many began to emulate the very power structures they were attempting to transform and transcend. Much of the world of academic feminism became professionalized and institutionalized, dominated by privileged white women (and men). One of the negative consequences has been the marginalizing of working class and poverty class feminists and the silencing of their voices. On the difficult road to acceptance, this brand of academic feminism has left a core concept behind: that of class inequality.

This omission of class may be an attempt at elitism on the part of academic feminism to ensure that it is perceived as worthy of scholarly attention, or it may be a defensive reaction that resists a clear-eyed examination of the class bias endemic in higher education. As Wiegman (2002, 19) notes, academic feminism has become more "bureaucratic, hierarchical, and careerist than ever before." Whatever the motivation, it is a refusal by privileged feminists to dialogue seriously about class differences and inequalities. Acker explains that:

Socialist and Marxist feminists, in particular, had intense debates on women, patriarchy, class, and gender from the late 1960s into the 1980s, criticizing concepts of class that made women invisible and proposing new approaches. However, as solutions to conceptual and theoretical problems proved to be elusive, feminist debates about class almost disappeared. (2006, 3)

Those feminists who have made their careers in the institutions of higher learning are often like the great and powerful Oz when perpetuating the ideology of meritocracy. Some may not like to expose what is behind the curtain of that ideology; they mistakenly see working class attributes as an obstacle that should be left behind on the yellow brick road. This reluctance to include class within the context of academic feminism means that class interests are frequently ignored, which can be toxic for academics from working class backgrounds, many of whom are not interested in restricting their scholarly inquiries to "classless" feminism, and yet may need to rely on feminist networks for mentoring and support.

There have been a small number of feminist scholars that have written about class and middle class privilege with remarkable clarity. Bunch and Reid discuss their own realization of class struggles within feminism:

Of course, I did not imagine that I was a class supremacist. Only after months of struggle (or should I say, fights, hostility, withdrawal, trauma) did I begin to understand that much of my behavior stemmed from being middle class and was oppressive to working class women. . . . No one in our [feminist] movement would say that she believes that she is better than our working class sisters, yet her behavior says it over and over again. (1974, 70–71)

Although there is a lack of critical scholarship in this area, those few published works that address the issue of social class in the academy provide evidence that indicates working class students experience graduate school in a fundamentally different way than their middle and upper class counterparts (see Jones 2001; Long, Jenkins, and Bracken 2000; Grimes and Morris 1997; Mahony and Zmroczek 1997; Dews and Law 1995; Tokarczyk and Fay 1993; Ryan and Sackrey 1984).

This stifling of class concerns in universities and colleges has had a devastating effect on two groups within the academy. As working class and poverty class students attempt to reach their academic goals, they often find an inhospitable environment. As we discuss here, they are frequently denied mentoring, experience both direct and indirect criticisms of their class positions, and are marginalized within the academic community of feminists.

Middle class academic feminists also suffer. They have turned their focus toward protecting individual status and the middle class status quo within academia. The embrace of class privilege, along with the seeming distaste for anything that relates to the working class or poverty class, insulates academic feminism from the solidarity needed to critique neoliberalism and to change the current political-economic model, which is predicated on increased work and alienation.

We argue that a return to feminist roots that embrace class consciousness and critique is crucial to the revitalization of the feminist community as a whole. To accomplish this change, academic feminists must disengage from acritically embracing a privileged middle class ethos in which the only voice considered legitimate is the one that looks and sounds just like them. As Donna King (2012) points out in her feminist theory of "letting go," capitalist values can create deep feelings of alienation and distress when we are confronted with our own or another's failure to embody impossible neoliberal standards of success. As King says, "there are contradictions in our culture, and within feminism, about how women should live our lives, particularly in terms of economic and cultural demands for high productivity, a fast pace, pushing past limits, and denying the body" (54). When academic feminism demands a constant struggle toward accumulation, prestige, and social approval, it leaves no room for those who cannot or will not play the game.

We believe that academic feminism can't afford a business-as-usual mentality. The backlash against feminism's accomplishments has been increasingly hostile in recent decades. Powerful forces within the United States seem hellbent on turning the clock back to the 1950s. In the context of a backlash against women's reproductive rights, comedian Kristen Schaal highlights this with her accurate but jarring joke: "What's the difference between a fertilized egg, a corporation, and a woman? One of them isn't considered a person in Oklahoma" (Schaal 2012).

Equality in the workplace is not faring much better. In 2012 Iowa's State Supreme Court ruled that an employer's dismissal of a female associate for being "too attractive" was not discrimination (Foley 2013). While according to the Institute for Women's Policy Research, "the annual gender earnings gap narrowed by only about one percentage point" from 2001 to 2012 (Hegewisch, Williams, and Edwards 2012, 2). Men also suffer from these regressive gender ideas: Rudman and Mescher (2013) have shown that men who requested family leave time were stigmatized as weak, unable to make it in a "real man's world." It has become clear that regressive voices have become powerful and their actions are fortifying an antifeminist agenda. Meanwhile, much of academic feminism has disenfranchised working class and poverty class people who combined represent the largest percentage of the population in the United States, many of whom share in feminist concerns.

For years many disenfranchised feminists kept their critiques silent: there was no need to add gasoline to the firestorm of antifeminist rhetoric. We believe that now is the time to challenge the status quo, to call again for the inclusion of working class intellectuals and activists within feminism, and to reconsider feminism's unreflexive alliance with neoliberalism.

Our insights into the negative consequences of suppressing working class and poverty class voices in the academy come from our analysis of nineteen in-depth interviews of working class doctoral students from a Research One university, all of whom were in the post-master's phase of their PhD process (Gerbrandt 2007), as well as from our own personal experiences.[1] The research participants, from eight different fields of study, were chosen by rigorous methodologies.[2] Of the participants, eleven were women, eight were men, and six identified themselves as persons of color. Their ages ranged from twenty-six to forty-one at the time of the interviews. I (Roxanne) collected the data and analyzed it as part of a larger research project focusing on working class and poverty class students and their experiences in negotiating the higher education credentialing process.

Finding these working class and poverty class graduate students proved to be quite daunting. At first, I contacted the chairs from each department within the university; this proved to be unhelpful in finding graduate students for the study, but an eye-opening experience nevertheless. Some of the comments from the department chairs revealed much about their unfounded beliefs about social class. When asked about working class or poverty class students in their department, one terse, white-haired professor replied, "We don't have any underprivileged graduate students in our department; we are highly competitive!"

Nevertheless, I eventually located working class and poverty class students in those highly competitive departments. As a requirement for determining working class and poverty class status for this study, all participants were first-generation college students, and their family income was ranked in the lowest thirty percent in the United States at the time of the interviews. These interviews form the basis for the themes we consider in this chapter.[3]

During the interviews, all but two participants began to spontaneously talk about academic feminism. All of the participants identified themselves as feminists during the interview process, while twelve of the nineteen described themselves as "active" feminists. Two themes emerged from the interview sessions: the historical change in academic feminism as critical examination of class and capitalism fell out of favor, and the poor treatment of working class feminists when they became advanced graduate students.[4]

Participants in our study discussed the evolution of feminism away from critical examinations of class as a social force. Many of them once held up the feminist movement as one of their best hopes for enacting equality on both a personal and political level. However, instead of finding an alternative, cooperative feminist model for persons without class leverage, these working class participants experienced exclusions. Theirs are salient commentaries about the move away from class concerns toward a success-at-any-cost ideology, an ideology that has been extremely successful in recasting working class status as personal failure—even among fellow feminists. Julie, a graceful woman who spoke in the monotone voice of someone who has been beaten down for far too long, explains,

> I am a strong feminist. It used to be a strong community. It was definitely my niche where I felt at home. There has been something happening to feminism the last few years however that class has gone to the shadows. I don't know how to describe it. Class seems to be an interesting theoretical kind of thing, but as far as a lived experience, not so much. Of all the women I have met, there have been very, very few who have any knowledge of what it means to come from a working class background. You are expected to get out there and work, not thinking with them!

Both of us (Roxanne and Liza) have had similar experiences to Julie's. We both encountered negative reactions from feminist professors when bringing up class issues. We have been defensively asked by feminists in power positions whether we expected them to feel sorry for us. Of course it was not pity that either of us was looking for but an understanding of a lived reality that we had (wrongly) assumed they would be interested in. It is incredibly frustrating to be shamed and silenced about one's lived inequality. As feminists we can talk about frustration regarding gender inequality, but we are silenced or ignored when acknowledging our experiences of injustices regarding class. As Nicky notes:

> They [middle class academic feminists] want all the women to be exactly like them. You can only think and write one way. Class never comes up. I've tried to bring up class and I get a "What are you talking about?" kind of thing. That was the one time I tried to bring up class there [feminist gathering] and it didn't go well, and it doesn't come up much otherwise. We don't talk about class. The daily traumas of class are just ignored. It is a constant source of frustration that those things can't be breached. It leads to a meltdown, two or three times a year. I mean it is a big part of my life that won't be acknowledged. I expected loyalty with them.

Nicky expresses what Patricia Hill Collins asserts, "Oppressed groups are frequently placed in the situation of being listened to only if we frame our ideas in the language that is familiar to and comfortable for a dominant group" (2000, vii). The problem is that Nicky, like other participants in our study, had previously not experienced the academic feminist community as the dominant group. Before approaching credentialing through a PhD, they had experienced that community as a refuge from the perils of class domination.

In fact, participants in our study reported that the feminist community had once been one of their most valued social spaces. Beyond finding a common perspective regarding gender issues, some working class graduate students had experienced feminism as a place to share their personal insights and feel at home. Many had been happily involved in women's studies or campus feminist groups earlier in their academic careers. As Abbey explained through tears, "We truly cared about each other, and I felt like part of a community." Our research participants commented that in these feminist communities everyone gave and received energy and support. This reciprocal arrangement changed, however, once they reached the post-master's phase of their higher education. They felt professors in the academic feminist support network become hostile to them, and they were deeply impacted by this adversarial attitude occurring within a once welcoming community suddenly divided along class lines.

At this pivotal point in the participants' graduate study experience, the shift from support to hostility and from inclusion to exclusion was painful and bewildering. While a full discussion and analysis of this shift is beyond the scope of this chapter, we believe that there are some clear factors to be considered. First, as graduate students transition from a master's phase to a post-master's phase, the primary classroom activities are largely completed. There are no longer any publicly objective criteria for advancement. There are no tests or papers for the students to use as a direct comparison with their peers. In the post-master's phase of study, the student must rely on social connections to advance any further. In effect, this puts the graduate student at the complete mercy of the professors' judgment of their potential success.

Abbey explains this best:

When I came here to graduate school, I thought I would have a sense of belonging with the feminist community again. I thought I would get that camaraderie and that validation . . . I was certainly looking for it, but I didn't find that anywhere here. If you talk about class, you get jumped on right away, like you are trying to prioritize it over gender or race. They don't want to hear it. So we can't talk about class, and the most blatant wounds that people feel are silenced. To me, that was most disappointing. I had a higher expectation, so it hurt more.

Whether the class bias our participants experienced was consciously directed at them or not, the result was the same: they inhabited a damaging social environment that was counterproductive to their well-being. This working class disadvantage was reported by all the participants regardless of their self-identified status as feminists. But those with the strongest commitment to feminism reported feeling betrayed and abandoned when they experienced hostility to class issues. They noted, too, that their middle class feminist peers were not treated as outsiders, but were welcomed into the academic feminist community at every level of their study. Participants repeatedly mentioned that the most difficult part of their graduate program was not the academic work itself, but their negotiation of the cultural and social conditions related to being class outcasts. As Katrina explains with a defiant tone:

> We have a big problem with race in that we don't intersect it with class. And we don't get class at all. But, BUT! . . . If you confront things that people don't want to look at, well, you're in big trouble, especially with the feminist powers-that-be. It is hard for working class women to work with them because they refuse to look at class outside of abstract theory. They become very hostile and that hurts because they are supposed to be a sisterly refuge and it's more like going to the front lines. The people that ask the hard questions to them will run up against roadblocks.

The reader might be inclined to ask, "How does all this hostility and exclusion really work?" They can be big incidents, such as a refusal to commit to being on a student's dissertation committee, or worse yet, sabotaging a student's work by providing misinformation. Most of the time however, it is a constant bombardment of small rejections. For example, I (Roxanne) received a compliment on my skirt from a feminist professor. I replied, "Thank you; they have some nice things at the West End Goodwill this month." My intention was to share inclusive information; however, I did not receive a thank you in return. Instead, I was loudly asked (as she was backing away from me with her nose wrinkling), "Did you wash it?!" I wanted to say, "Of course I washed it. I'm poor, not dirty." But I didn't. I went away, hurt and embarrassed in front of the other graduate students. It was a cut to my self-esteem, and sometimes self-esteem can die by a thousand cuts.

Another participant, Hailey, also saw the support she had received vanish once she reached the final stages of her doctoral program. Previously her mentors within academic feminism had assisted her, but she found no one to connect with when she moved to the next stage:

> Well, I don't think they would come right out and say this, but you can tell that they think that working class students have NO business being here. You can tell this by the way they interact and some of the questions they ask. The way we communicate is also very different. That's all. We are just not legitimate at this level. It's very hard to talk about. Feminism used to be a place where I was at home. Now, in reality, they discriminate based on class both institutionally and mostly socially. Sometimes I feel just so disconnected.

This disconnectedness is a common experience among many of those who come from a working class environment as they enter the later stages of their quest for credentials. Visano notes that she, ". . . like many from working class backgrounds, encountered the combined forces of isolation and alienation with an alarming frequency" (2006, 254). The differences between classes become highlighted at this stage of study.

Communication, which reveals much about a speaker's ethos, is strained. One of the most striking differences between working class and middle class communication are the relational aspects of speech. Working class communications tend to focus on the collective, using words and phrases that invite and encourage connectivity over competition. As an example, I (Roxanne) noticed a dramatic difference in language use and communication during work on a feminist conference some years ago. Those of us who identified as working class feminists used the term "we" when talking about the efforts of hosting a conference. After the conference, we noted our participation in collective terms, highlighting the fact that we participated as a group to facilitate a successful conference.

However, I was taken aback by the language of some feminists from middle class backgrounds. They parceled aspects of the work to take individual credit for the project, highlighting some imagined competitive aspect of the conference. Some even went as far as to invent titles for themselves and their role in the organization and participation of the conference. Their language focused on the "I": highlighting individual efforts and taking personal credit for group endeavors.

While individualizing efforts create good entries on a curriculum vita, this sort of cutthroat one-upmanship is antithetical to a working class feminist consciousness. We argue that working class feminist consciousness is a good and necessary thing. We ask what has all of the relentless striving within a "free-market feminism" gotten us except stress, division, and inequality? Can we "let go" and re-imagine a new feminist community? Might we all be more satisfied with feminism if it were a place of trust and much needed support?

To achieve this re-imagined feminism, we should first realize that there is no community without trust. How can there be trust when working class people in a middle class environment must at all times strive to be "keeping up appearances" and be someone they are not? For those who come from working class or poverty class backgrounds, it is more than just cross-dressing a part to act middle class. It is also changing speech from relational to individualistic. It is changing one's sense of humor (no more dark sarcasm), it is changing one's food tastes, and it is changing activities of pleasure to other, more "acceptable" ones (even when those activities are not personally pleasurable or affordable). It is not a community when some must live in fear that when the real self is exposed, it will then be ridiculed. It is not a community when gatekeeping tactics are employed so that only "authentic" people from the middle class or higher can be embraced as members of the professional feminist elite.

The fact that working class or poverty class graduate students might not *want* to relate to others in a middle class way is an understanding that seems to be missing from the academic feminist perspective. Marcy, a strong and brilliant academic, explains:

> I have been active in feminism for years, but there is this tendency to privilege gender. And my class background means more to me than my gender. It has more of an impact on me; not that gender hasn't had any impact, but class has been really a big factor. The feminists were not understanding the class element AT ALL and why a working class woman might not WANT to present themselves as a privileged dominant person and losing relational aspects to one's speech.

When our participants insisted on retaining their working class identity after moving to a PhD course of study, they received a painful rejection from a previously welcoming community. Penny echoes the comments of many, noting that professors and students in the feminist community suddenly seemed to change their attitude toward her after she was advanced to candidacy. It seemed to her that it was time to viciously compete or get out:

> I used to have a place in the feminist community. But most of them do not know what it is like to be poor and how it is a REALLY formative state. It's not like, "Oh you were poor; that sucks," NO! It's like a whole system of reality. It's not like something that I will have erased one day, even if I wanted to. I will be working class all of my life, materially and socially. I wish I would have had a safe place to speak my words and experiences here without it being so alien to everybody else.

We should note participants voiced some exceptions in their encounters with middle class academic feminists. There are wonderful middle class feminists, and I, (Roxanne) am particularly grateful for them. However, these rare feminists are just that, rare. Themes revealed in these interviews give us a way to start thinking and talking about issues of class within the broader feminist community. Mahoney and Zmroczek warn, however, "The difficulties of exploring class within feminism should not be underestimated. Debates around class seem to sometimes provoke reactions of guilt, defensiveness, or even hostility from middle class colleagues and friends" (1997, 5). We argue that the outcast status many of us report here is a result of our culture's deeply held notions of what it means to be a member of the working class or poverty class. Elizabeth exposes one of these assumptions, explaining:

> There is a lot we could learn from one another, um, but it's too bad that they [middle class feminists] don't want to even dialogue. It is their assumption

here that if you don't know how to speak like them, then you don't know how to think. What kind of discussion can you have with somebody if they don't believe you know how to think?

Assumptions about people who are members of lower classes abound. The typical stereotype is that no matter our race or sex, we are lazy, stupid, and morally inferior; the only thing we have to offer is our physical labor. These unfounded but pervasive notions shape toxic interactions in much the same way as sexism and racism do. To give a personal example, I (Liza) have fewer class markers than some others from working class backgrounds, and I can sometimes "pass" or appear middle class even though I am not. I remember speaking with a feminist professor in her office one day, concerned that she was oversimplifying an idea to the point of misrepresenting it. The situation was already difficult to navigate, since I (as a lowly undergraduate) was trying to encourage her to include more nuances in our class discussion of a difficult topic. As I was circling gingerly around my point, she stopped, looked directly at me, and said, "You have to understand. These are students from poor families. We can't give them too much at once. They won't understand."

The entire interaction put me in a momentary state of shock: how could someone say such an insulting thing about people's class positions? But she didn't know I was a working class student; she thought that I was from her class. I was suddenly cast as a member of a group of middle class feminists who were superior holders of knowledge, tasked with parceling that knowledge out to those less fortunate, like some generous benefactors in a Dickens novel ladling out the gruel.

Feminists at practically every university and college are engaged in a battle for positions within the larger academic community (Smith 1987). However, we find the continued pursuit of the "personal success at all costs" model of academic feminism to be counterproductive. By excluding and belittling working class feminists, academic feminism risks turning into a further isolated endeavor. This point is made clear by bell hooks (2000) who frankly warns that classism is undermining the whole of feminism. Feminism has always been an uphill battle against a capitalist status quo that relies on hierarchy and inequality to properly function. How much more difficult will the struggle for equality be if middle class academic feminists continue to alienate working class feminists rather than stand in solidarity with them?

We would like to make clear that the working class narratives included in these pages are personal brushstrokes that point to a much bigger picture. At this point in history, academic feminism has opportunities to remake itself by reaching out beyond the borders of current discourse. This expansion, however, requires us to confront the fact that free-market feminism reproduces social barriers that are as effective as the physical barriers of a gated community. We reinforce these obstacles for ourselves and our peers constantly, through the internal and external forces that demand a constant and unrelenting stream of individual accomplishments as a signifier of importance. These barriers only serve to reinforce our doubts about what feminism can achieve as a movement as well as deep personal fears about ourselves and our role in feminism.

This is not to say that we do not need feminists within powerful institutions—we do—but elite feminism founded on competition and exclusion cannot be the only path. Instead, we can practice mindfulness at every turn and recast ourselves from the holders of knowledge into a community that seeks knowledge from many standpoints. The need for such communities is increasingly clear. The stakes are too high; rights that seemed locked into place are under assault from powerful groups that are simultaneously racist, antifeminist, and antagonistic to class concerns.

To become inclusive of class issues and respectful of diverse voices, we need to let go of our own self-image of feminism as the select province of "successful," powerful women and men. This idea, the representation of feminism that is most commonly seen in the media, is seductive precisely because it is egoist and singular, valuing the power of one person over another as the highest possible expression of equality: an equality of oppressors rather than an equality of all. What if we let go of the idea that success looks the same for everyone? By creating space for ourselves to pursue our true desires, we open our movement to those we have traditionally left behind simply because they did not fit the mold. We can allow those who have previously been marginalized to be their authentic selves without being compelled to keep up appearances. Perhaps it is time to rethink the criteria for feminist membership, to open our movement to the guidance of voices that have long been ignored.

NOTES

1. Our definition of class derives from a relational and historically specific context and intersects with other inequalities: *The degree of empowerment to live free of economic, political, embodied, and social oppression.* Working class corresponds with a low degree of empowerment, middle class with an intermediate level of empowerment, and poverty class with negligible empowerment.
2. For a description of our methodology, see "Exposing the Unmentionable Class Barriers in Graduate Education," Gerbrandt 2007.
3. To protect our subjects' anonymity, all names have been changed.
4. Academic feminism is not monolithic, and there are many different interpretations of feminism within the field. It is important to note that the experiences we report are not critical of any particular theoretical camp within feminism.

REFERENCES
Acker, Joan. 2006. *Class Questions: Feminist Answers.* Gender Lens Series. Lantham, MD: Rowman & Littlefield.
Bunch, Charlotte, and Coletta Reid. 1974. "Revolution Begins at Home." *Class and*

Feminism: A Collection of Essays from the Furies, edited by Charlotte Bunch and Nancy Myron, 70–81. Baltimore, MD: Diana Press.

Collins, Patricia Hill. 2000. *Black Feminist Thought: Knowledge, Consciousness, and the Politics of Empowerment*, 2nd edition. New York: Routledge

Dews, C. L. Barney, and Carolyn Leste Law, editors. 1995. *This Fine Place So Far From Home: Voices of Academics from the Working Class*. Philadelphia: Temple University Press.

Foley, Ryan. 2013. "Iowa Supreme Court: Perfectly Legal to Fire Woman for Being Too Attractive." *Salon.com*, July 12. *www.salon.com/2013/07/12/ iowa_supreme_court_perfectly_legal_to_fire_woman_for_being_too_attractive_ap*.

Gerbrandt, Roxanne. 2007. "Exposing the Unmentionable Class Barriers in Graduate Education." PhD dissertation. Department of Sociology, University of Oregon, Eugene, OR. *gradworks.umi.com/32/76/3276050.html*.

Grimes, Michael D., and Joan M. Morris. 1997. *Caught in the Middle: Contradictions in the Lives of Sociologists from Working-Class Backgrounds*. Westport, CT: Praeger Publishers.

Hegewisch, Ariane, Claudia Williams, and Angela Edwards. 2013. *The Gender Wage Gap: 2012*. Institute for Women's Policy Research. IWPR #C350. *www.iwpr.org/publications/ recent-publications*.

hooks, bell. 2000. *Where We Stand: Class Matters*. New York: Routledge.

Jones, Sandra J. 2001. "Becoming an 'Educated Person': Narratives of Female Professors from the Working Class." *Wellesley Centers for Women Working Paper*, 1–37. Wellesley, MA: Wellesley Centers for Women Working.

King, Donna. 2012. "Toward a Feminist Theory of Letting Go." *Frontiers: A Journal of Women's Studies* 33 (3): 53–70.

Long, Melanie L., Ranck Jenkins, and Susan Bracken. 2000. "Imposters in the Sacred Grove: Working Class Women in the Academe." *Qualitative Report* 5:1–13.

Mahoney, Pat, and Christine Zmroczek. 1997. *Class Matters: "Working-Class" Women's Perspectives on Social Class*. London: Taylor and Francis.

Rudman, L. A., and K. Mescher. 2013. "Penalizing Men Who Request a Family Leave: Is Flexibility Stigma a Femininity Stigma?" *Journal of Social Issues* 69 (2): 322–40.

Ryan, Jake, and Charles Sackrey. 1984. *Strangers in Paradise: Academics From the Working Class*. Boston: South End Press.

Schaal, Kristen. 2012. "The Vulgar Games: Republican Policy Routine." *The Daily Show with Jon Stewart*. Aired March 12. *www.thedailyshow.com/watch/tue-march-13-2012/ the-vulgar-games—republican-policy-routine*.

Smith, Dorothy E. 1987. *The Everyday World As Problematic: A Feminist Sociology*. Northeastern Series on Feminist Theory. Boston: Northeastern University Press.

Tokarczyk, Michelle M., and Elizabeth A. Fay, editors. 1993. *Working-Class Women in the Academy: Laborers in the Knowledge Factory*. Amherst: The University of Massachusetts Press.

Visano, Livy A. 2006. "Class Enriching the Classroom: The 'Radical' as Rooted Pedagogic Strengths." In *Reflections from the Wrong Side of the Tracks: Class, Identity, and the Working Class Experience in Academe*, edited by Stephen L. Muzzatti and C. Vincent Samarco, 241–60. Oxford: Rowman & Littlefield.

Wiegman, Robyn. 2002. "Academic Feminism Against Itself." *NWSA Journal* 14 (2): 18–37.

14

Letting Go and Having Fun

Redefining Aging in America

Deana A. Rohlinger and Haley Gentile

American women are told that they can "have it all"—a successful career, a strong body, a beautiful family, shiny hair, and a flawless complexion—if only they strive hard enough. Having it all is the female variant of a Horatio Alger story. Personal and professional achievement is within the reach of women who use the right products and stay vigilantly focused on their goals. In reality, having it all is a capitalist-driven chimera infused with a commercialized distortion of feminism. The notion that women can achieve equality by succeeding in male-dominated corporations and demanding partnerships at home (or simply hiring others to do undesirable tasks such as cooking and cleaning), while looking fit and fresh at the same time, can be exacting, particularly since most women lack access to the tremendous resources necessary to make having it all a reality. That, of course, is the point. Dissatisfaction with the self fuels America's economy, as those who stand to profit both nurture women's insecurities and offer a panacea—for a price. There is always another wrinkle to be filled, a new fashion trend to acquire, or another rung to climb on the occupational ladder.

With the aging of the baby boomers, corporate logic informing who is a worthwhile target for goods and services has expanded to include the "grey market," which prior to the Great Recession was brimming with millions of older Americans with disposable income. Given corporate capitalism's success in courting young consumers by creating dissatisfaction with the self, advertisers are using the same strategy to sell products and services to older people. The double standard of aging in the United States has provided marketers with the fodder to engage older women, in particular, in buying a wide array of products and services touted as age-reversing. In the context of contemporary marketing campaigns to capture the Silver Dollar, one group comprised of women over fifty, the Red Hat Society, was ideally positioned to capitalize on corporate desire to profit from women's anxiety about aging.

The Red Hat Society (RHS) was founded in 1998 by Sue Ellen Cooper. Having read the poem "Warning" by Jenny Joseph ([1961] 1992, 1999),[1] which depicts a woman anticipating making choices when she grows older that violate behavioral expectations, such as wearing "purple / with a red hat which doesn't go, and doesn't suit me," Cooper decided to form a "red hat" society of her own in an effort to change how older women are regarded in American society. The RHS does so by stressing the importance of having fun. The RHS website explains:

> Our main responsibility is to have fun! We see this group as an opportunity for those who have shouldered various responsibilities at home and in the community their whole lives to say goodbye to burdensome responsibilities and obligations for a little while. . . . We feel like we have all been so dutiful and so "busy" for so long that we deserve a break. . . . We are all helping to develop an enormous nurturing network . . . by joining red-gloved hands and spreading the joy and companionship we are finding within and among the chapters. (The Red Hat Society, Inc., "About Us")

For the organization's inaugural event Cooper and several friends went out for tea in "full regalia," which included a red hat with purple clothing. The organization quickly doubled in size as word of the group spread through friendship networks. The RHS has grown dramatically over the last fifteen years and currently claims thirty-five thousand chapters and more than one million members, or "Red Hatters," around the world.

Cooper quickly discerned that she was in a position of power. Corporations saw the RHS as a way to reach prime life consumers between the ages of fifty and sixty-five without big budget advertising campaigns—word about products would travel through the group's social networks. However, Cooper, who formed a corporation and made the RHS name and symbols registered trademarks shortly after founding the organization, controls all licensing agreements. Since she is interested in changing stereotypes about older women, she has been extraordinarily selective about the kinds of products that bear the RHS trademark. Cooper, who often notes that she did not start the RHS to make money, has turned away dozens of licensing proposals for products that are "not consistent" with the RHS message and image. This includes offers from credit card issuers, medical companies, and the maker of Depends, an adult incontinence product. Cooper, in short, found that she could exert some control over the market insofar as she could promote a vision of aging that focuses on connections among women, self-discovery, and self-expression.

While Cooper's story is an interesting one, the relevance of the RHS extends well beyond product endorsements. By founding the RHS Cooper created a "free space" (Evans and Boyte 1986) for older women—a space where women could challenge dominant gender ideologies and craft new understandings of gender and aging (Brown and Rohlinger 2015). Red Hatters used this space to flip the script on dominant cultural narratives and challenge consumer-capitalist mandates that regard aging as a condition that must be delayed by women at (literally) all costs. Cooper's emphasis on having fun plays a particularly important role in the re-imagining of aging. At the group level, the focus on fun creates a collaborative leisure space in which women are free to be themselves. Red Hatters explicitly reject cultural notions that women should judge and compete with one another. Instead, they cultivate a sisterhood that emphasizes connection and consensus. At the individual level, the emphasis on having fun empowers women to cast off the little old lady stereotype and explore their interests. Red Hatters see aging as diverse and regard this moment in their lives as one that should be embraced.

Here we draw on fifty-two in-depth interviews we conducted with Red Hatters representing thirteen different RHS chapters in the Tallahassee, Florida, area, and on our observations of local meetings and events. We illustrate the transformative potential of having fun and discuss how having fun can be a form of letting go of dominant gender ideologies that allows women to craft new understandings of gender and aging.

Sisters Having Fun

Scholars and activists alike grapple with the problem of dissension within groups. Diverging interests, strong personalities, and friendship networks can create conflict within an organization and undermine its ability to accomplish its goals. One benefit of leisure groups is that they can have no explicit purpose other than having fun. This, however, does not mean they lack political potential. Leisure groups provide a space in which women can resist gender stereotypes (Green 1998), cultivate collective identities that directly challenge the status quo (Hunt and Benford 1994), and develop new standards for social and self approval (Brown and Rohlinger 2015; Kaplan and Liu 2000). Organizations that emphasize having fun, in other words, can provide a space in which women can share stories, reflect on their lives, and revision the future.

This, of course, is not an easy task even in groups like the RHS. Red Hatters are diverse in terms of their age (respondents ranged from fifty to eighty-six years old with a median age of sixty-five), employment status (65.4 percent work part- or full-time, while the remaining 34.6 percent were either retired or homemakers), race and ethnicity (75 percent identified as white, 13 percent as Latina or Hispanic, and 12 percent as African American), and politics (our respondents were almost equally split, with half identifying as politically or socially conservative, the other half as politically or socially progressive). Absent a framework for understanding participation, diversity can lead to conflicts that disrupt (or even destroy) an organization (Lichterman 1996).

Red Hatters avoid dissension (political and otherwise) by viewing their participation through the lens of sisterhood. Cooper introduced this language shortly after establishing a website for the group. How she discusses sisterhood, however, is unique. She does not position the RHS as a sorority or a feminist movement, but as a combination of the two. Descriptions of "sisterly kindness" and "sisterly love" are interspersed with more feminist conceptualizations of political sisterhood, in which women collectively challenge social inequality. For example, in her book, Cooper ([1998] 2004) writes:

> We find ourselves irresistibly drawn, first to the spirit of the Red Hat Society and then to one another. Rather than each of us wandering off by herself, we have begun to gather together at every opportunity to celebrate sisterhood and demonstrate solidarity. I believe that the Red Hat Society arose first and foremost from women's love and need for one another. Originally, we gathered together to play and kick up our heels, but we soon found that we were developing friends who would also stay around and hold our hands when our laughter turned, as it sometimes will, to tears. (112)

Similarly, the website describes a movement of sisters united despite their diversity:

> [The RHS] evolved into a women's movement of sorts—a movement consisting of women committed to supporting each other through fun and friendship, allowing each individual the empowering permission to play.... No matter what a woman's face, socio-economic status, or religion, we are there to support each other. We value being a woman and understand the importance of promoting the next phase of our lives! After all, we defined that movement. We are that movement. We have a responsibility to our legacy. (The Red Hat Society, Inc., "The Story Behind Our Legacy")

As a result, while Red Hatters did not always imbue sisterhood with political meaning, respondents noted that sisters supported and respected one another regardless of their differences.

Talk played an important role in creating sisterhood. By engaging in respectful disagreement and avoiding politically divisive issues like abortion, gay marriage, and immigration, women were able to emphasize their similarities. Red Hatters admitted that self-expression was easier because the focus on fun undercut competitive dynamics among women. As Sharon (a fifty-six-year-old CPA) noted, "There is no pressure" to being a part of the RHS. Women can express their ideas without fear of reprisal or rejection. Dolores (a seventy-one-year-old housewife) added, "I can express my own opinions. I can call my own shots. I'll cooperate and do anything anyone wants me to, but if I have a suggestion to make, the other Red Hats, they'll accept me the way I am. I like that." Gwen (a sixty-one-year-old housewife) elaborated:

Almost any other women's club, I don't care what it is or what age you are when you're in it, there's dissension. There always is. In the five years I've been in the Red Hats, we've never had any dissension. We can disagree on something and do it in a positive manner. Nobody gets mad; no one gets their feelings hurt. We can express ourselves civilly. "Well gee, I don't think that's such a good idea, how about such and such." Offer something instead, and it's discussed and everything comes to a consensus, and nobody gets upset. I think because by now, and in this group, none of us has anything to prove to anyone else. We're not trying to one-upmanship one another. It's collaboration, it's a sisterhood, we're all in this together, and it's for fun, it's not serious. Hey, we don't sweat the small stuff. And it's all small stuff! [Laughs]

This does not mean disagreements never emerged. For instance, at the monthly meeting of the local RHS Queen Mothers (or chapter leaders) at a Mexican restaurant, one attendee bemoaned that her tax dollars supported "welfare programs." Her neighbor quickly chimed that while she didn't agree with this opinion, it was "Queen Mother margarita time" rather than "political debate time." The point here is that conflict regarded as unproductive or unhealthy was immediately diffused with a gentle reminder political comments did not serve the group or its purpose of having fun.

Talk allowed women to develop norms regarding (in)appropriate interactions and create a space in which they could discuss aging openly. In this way, the RHS became a consciousness-raising group, where women could break the silence about aging. Gina (a sixty-one-year-old corrections officer) explained:

You really have to cope with life and the changes that are taking place in you physically, mentally, and economically. For me, it's been a real awakening to understand what aging is. And the Red Hat Society helps with that. You find that you can do things that you maybe didn't think you could or want to do. It's socializing with people who are dealing with the same obstacles you're dealing with. I think it helps you to know that you're okay. You're normal. You're just like everybody else. Other people cope with these issues and you can cope with them too.

Pam (a fifty-three-year-old homemaker) agreed, noting that her RHS sisters helped demystify the aging process. She gave the example of menopause, highlighting how RHS members challenge the cultural silence around the physical changes associated with aging:

Some of us have already gone through "the change," and some are still in the process of doing it and there's still some that haven't quite even gotten started yet. So there's a lot of support as far as what we've gone through and what worked for us, and understanding. And we joke about it, so it's kind of a support group. Like I said, it's not one of these terrible things you used to hear whispered when you were growing up, and you'd hear adults talking, "Oh, she's gone through the change." We're all comfortable enough with it where we can support one another. We make allowances—like we'll get some really cold air-conditioned rooms [laughter]. . . . And, who gets to sit closest to the air condition vent in the car [laughter]. Things like that. You can talk about it. I mean that stuff was taboo back when we were growing up.

The RHS focus on fun and sisterhood created a free-space for members to discuss aging openly. Red Hatters share their hard-earned wisdom and experience in an environment where they are greeted with commiseration and empathy. Suddenly, their individual trials and tribulations are collectively affirmed and useful to those beyond themselves. Deborah (a fifty-two-year-old office worker) confided, "It gives me comfort that there are women I can talk about aging issues with." Cheryl (a fifty-eight-year-old retired government employee) agreed, "It makes me feel very proud of myself, of my age, my knowledge, my experience." When aging women are able to share their feelings and lived experiences with each other in an open and welcoming environment, they continue to defy cultural mandates that would silence them and render their lives invisible.

Empowering Women

"Having fun" empowers Red Hatters. At the group level, the Red Hat costume, which consists of an eye-catching clash of colors, challenges older women's invisibility in public spaces. In her book, Cooper jokes, "How do you ignore anywhere from ten to fifty women decked out in red and purple and sporting such accessories as red feather boas and rhinestone pins that spell out 'QUEEN'? Answer: You don't!" (2004, 9) The Red Hat uniform is not simply a way to get attention. It is a collective means of resistance. Red Hatters provide younger women (and men) an alternative framework for understanding aging. Rather than fight aging, women can embrace it and enjoy themselves (and one another) in the process. Lynette (a sixty-five-year-old receptionist) explained:

Every time we go to a restaurant we attract attention. . . . People stop us and ask, "Now, what is the Red Hat Club?" It draws interest. They see older people are out having fun—as much fun as somebody in their twenties. 'Cause when you're in your twenties, you go out all the time. When people get older, especially if they're married, they tend just to stay at home. I think it's a way of showing people that even though you are sixty or seventy or eighty or even older, you can get out and still have a good time.

Christine (a seventy-year-old teacher) agreed:

[The costume] makes us stand out a little bit. It's kind of a good feeling. It brings attention to us, but I think it's positive attention. Instead of somebody looking and thinking, "Oh, look at this poor old lady" and feeling sorry for her, we [portray] a sense of living and enjoyment. We portray something different. Some [of our members] are slightly handicapped and they move very slowly, but they have a spirit of enjoying life. I think that's what comes out to people when they see Red Hats having fun. . . . I think it even makes younger people think, "Hey, they're still having a good time."

The vast majority of Red Hatters (88 percent) argued that their increased visibility in public spaces had at least some positive influence on American culture insofar as it turned stereotypes of aging women on their head. Older women are not confined to rocking chairs or filling their days with knitting. Carol (a seventy-two-year-old retiree) explained that the RHS "gives a different image of women. It just shows people that older women want to have fun just like young women do." Pam added, "I think it's put a more positive spin on aging. Not that you have to be homebound or in a nursing home or anything—that you can get out there and enjoy life. I think that's a real positive thing." Jane (a sixty-nine-year-old retiree) agreed:

I don't feel like I have to sit in a corner and be quiet. . . . Little by little we are changing society. When we go somewhere, for instance, to eat lunch, like we did today, people smile and wave and it's almost like they are saying, "They are having fun. They are not fuddy-duddies. Maybe it's not too bad to be getting a little older." . . . [The RHS shows them] that we are just part of society [and we are not] stuck in the house and ashamed to go out because we are aging. . . . Again, it's saying that ladies of a certain age are not relegated to sitting in a rocking chair on the front porch. We are vibrant members of society.

In short, Red Hatters feel empowered by their participation in the RHS. They see their outings as having fun and collectively challenging cultural constructions regarding older women, their interests, and their capabilities while they do so. The RHS celebrates diverse aging experiences and creates new social standards for self-approval.

Having fun disguises the fact that the RHS is an agent for change. Every time Red Hatters take to public spaces and have fun they challenge (and potentially change) how people view older women and aging more generally. Red Hatters, however, are not just collectively empowered. All of the women we interviewed reported that they felt either "liberated," "free," or "empowered" personally by their involvement in the RHS. Shirley (a sixty-five-year-old secretary) noted, "It's freedom and it's like, I can just flaunt myself and that is just fine. . . . [The RHS] gives you the freedom to express yourself." Similarly, Elize (a sixty-five-year-old part-time worker) said, "I think it's giving me a license to be a little freer." Karen (a fifty-eight-year-old nurse) agreed, "[The RHS] just gave me permission to be myself. . . . I feel a lot more positive. [I have] the freedom to be me. There are no rules, so I can do whatever I want to do. I like that philosophy. It gives me permission to be me." Gwen added, "It's freedom. We're free at last to be who we are and what we are inside. No more masks, we can just be the people that we are." Cheryl explained:

> [It's] Freedom. Freedom from all of the stereotypes. You know, that you're old and decrepit. . . . [The RHS] makes me feel very proud of myself, of my age, my knowledge, my experience that I can share with other women. . . . There are a lot of changes in your body and your mind, but it's for the better. It's the freedom of old age. You don't have to impress anybody. You don't have to live your life for others. You live for you. What a beautiful freedom it is.

In short, the focus on fun frees older women from cultural norms that cast them as weak, mild-mannered little old ladies who must fight to remain socially visible. In doing so, the RHS broadens the kinds of activities in which women over fifty can engage, particularly those oriented toward self-expression and fulfillment. Indeed, Red Hatters pursue everything from flower-arranging to motorcycle riding. As Sandy (a sixty-three-year-old administrative assistant) put it, the RHS gives members "The freedom to act. To be able to say and be anything you want to be. To do the things you want to do." Jane concluded, "I like myself better than I ever have in my life and I wish I could've said that at twenty-five instead of sixty-two."

Having Fun as a Form of Letting Go

Leisure contexts provide important free spaces for women to evaluate their lives and resist cultural and capitalist mandates, individually and collectively. The focus on having fun challenges the notion that women should compete with one another about their lives and instead emphasizes connection and friendship. The RHS shows women that aging need not be an isolating or invisible process. Trials and tribulations can (and should) be shared with other women, and pursing one's bliss is the order of the day. Red Hatters re-imagine aging as a time for self-care, self-exploration, and self-expression. More importantly, fun is both a collective and individual enterprise. Fun provides the foundation for the creation of a sisterhood that transcends political and social divisions, while allowing women to empower themselves and each other. They project new standards of aging into the world, transforming themselves, and potentially American culture, in the process.

The RHS focus on having fun coalesces with the notion of letting go. Women do not have to fight off aging with expensive surgeries and creams or engage in back-breaking service to be useful to their community. They can let go of capitalist mandates and cultural expectations that focus on striving, consuming, and competing, and explore instead their interests and desires. As a group, they go out and have fun with other Red Hatters in ways that challenge norms regarding women's relationships and behavior. Red Hatters demonstrate, in a very public way, that aging is not the end of the world. In fact, it can provide new opportunities to connect with a community and nurture the self. In this context, Red Hatters are not trying to have it all, but to re-imagine aging for themselves and other women. And their efforts may help to promote cultural change.

Groups like the RHS, however, are unlikely to foment broader political engagement or even convince some women to embrace more feminist ideals. There is an even split between the women we interviewed who do not view the RHS as an extension of the women's movement and those who do, and many more women who gave equivocal responses to this question. The latter group of women often initially said no, but when further probed described tenuous or philosophical connections between the women's movement and the RHS. The biggest hurdle in making this connection was that many Red Hatters viewed the women's movement and feminism as having distinct attributes and philosophies and ascribed unflattering stereotypes to one or the other. Gloria, for example, explained, "When I think of the women's movement I think more of Betty Friedan and some of the other ones, and to me they were the aggressive but negative ones. The feminist movement I think is women just moving along, doing their thing and getting ahead just by proving that they can do it . . . not even proving it, just by doing it." Cindy (a sixty-two-year-old state employee) agreed with this interpretation noting, "In my mind, a feminist is a soft female [pause], and the women's movement was hard, single minded. They didn't fit the image we see of the fashion model or whatever. They were females but they were just [pause] more mannish, and that's not a good word for it either, they were just more single minded determined. And feminists to me are more open-minded. And seem more, and are more, flexible than the women's movement was." Rose (a seventy-four-year-old retiree) attributed negative characteristics to feminism noting, "Honestly, I think feminism was a little bit more extreme." Linda (a fifty-five-year-old nurse) was more to the point, "I've heard . . . feminists described as strident bitches."

Organizing women around having fun, in short, is a double-edged sword. On the one hand, the focus on fun allows women, who may have little in common other than their age, to transform their lives and challenge cultural mores.

On the other hand, groups like the RHS introduce fundamentally feminist ideas without naming them as such. Joyce (a sixty-two-year-old housewife) illustrates this point well as she struggles to answer our question about whether the RHS is a feminist organization:

> I don't think it is really. If you read the story in [Cooper's] book, it started out so innocently. Two girlfriends shopping together and one finding a red hat and liking [it] and then, buying another one for her girlfriend. The next thing they know this mushroomed into a group of them wearing red hats and going out with purple and so whether it's promoting feminism [pause]. I think it does without even knowing it. I don't think it meant to. It's not political. It's not going to campaign for anything but having fun. But sure, it sort of says, without really saying, "Look at me. I'm mature and I'm a woman and I'm here and you're not going to not notice me dressed this way. I'm in the company of sisters." If that's what feminism is about well, yeah [the RHS is a feminist organization]. But, it wasn't the reason it got started.

Unless a Red Hatter is familiar with feminism or has experience with activism, she may not connect the RHS to a broader feminist philosophy or movement.

Of course, we cannot expect one group to serve as a hub for feminism. While stereotypes of liberal and radical feminism are dominant in American media and politics, feminism on the ground has always been quite diverse. Criticizing the RHS for not explicitly recognizing its feminism ignores what Cooper and the Red Hatters have accomplished. The RHS transforms women's lives and offers new social standards for evaluating aging. The power of their vision is its diversity—there is no single way to have fun and, consequently, no one way to age. Corporations have taken notice of this new vision of aging and have tried to capture it in their marketing. While still rare (and sometimes problematic), advertising now shows us older faces beyond the confines of the AARP magazine.[2] Likewise, Red Hatters have infiltrated broader culture, appearing on shows like *The Simpsons* and *Rules for Engagement* as well as in comics like *Pickles*. The RHS isn't a curiosity anymore. It is a culturally recognized organization with the potential to change how both women and men view aging. As Cindy notes, "Maybe it's the current women's movement for older people. You don't have to stay home and vegetate and die and get buried. You can go out and have a life, and that's what these ladies are doing."

NOTES

1. A full version of the poem is available online at *www.poemhunter.com/poem/warning*.
2. American Association of Retired People.

REFERENCES

Brown, Robyn Lewis, and Deana Rohlinger. 2015. "Cohort Consequences: The Effect of Political Generation on Identity and Social Change." *Journal of Women & Aging* 27, forthcoming.

Cooper, Sue Ellen. (1998) 2004. *The Red Hat Society: Fun and Friendship After Fifty*. New York: Hachette.

Evans, Sara, and Harry Boyte. 1986. *Free Spaces: The Sources of Democratic Change in America*. New York: Harper & Row.

Green, Eileen. 1998. "'Women Doing Friendship': An Analysis of Women's Leisure as a Site of Identity Construction, Empowerment, and Resistance." *Leisure Studies* 17:171–85.

Hunt, Scott, and Robert Benford. 1994. "Identity Talk in the Peace and Justice Movement." *Journal of Contemporary Ethnography* 22:488–517.

Joseph, Jenny. (1961) 1992. *Selected Poems*. Northumberland, UK: Bloodaxe.

———. 1999. "Jenny Joseph on the Popularity of her Poem, 'Warning.'" *Lancet*, 354 (9190): 30–32.

Kaplan, Howard, and Xiaoru Liu. 2000. "Social Movements as Collective Coping with Spoiled Personal Identities: Intimations from a Panel Study of Changes in the Life Course between Adolescence and Adulthood." In *Self, Identity, and Social Movements*, edited by Sheldon Stryker, Timothy J. Owens, and Robert W. White, 215–38. Minneapolis: University of Minnesota Press.

Lichterman, Paul. 1996. *The Search for Political Community: American Activists Reinventing Commitment*. Cambridge Cultural Social Studies. New York: Cambridge University Press.

The Red Hat Society, Inc. "The Story Behind Our Legacy." Red Hat Society. *redhatsociety.com/about/legacy* (accessed July 9, 2012).

———. "About Us." Red Hat Society. *redhatsociety.com/about* (accessed July 9, 2012).

Part Four

Ecological Perspectives

15

Letting Go and Getting Real

Applying Buddhist Principles
to Address Environmental Crisis

Janine Schipper

We are on the verge of global environmental crisis. By this I refer to the series of ecological changes that, taken together, threaten the integrity of physical systems and the species that depend on them to live, including our own human species. It is no longer a question of whether or not global warming and climate change are real, nor is there any question that global emissions due to human activities are the primary cause of climate change.[1] The question that stands before us now is: can we as a human species avert global ecological holocaust? (See Bernstein et al. 2007, IPCC 2013, Müller, Höhne, and Ellermann 2007, Rifkin 2009). A radical transformation in Western ways of living is critical to building sustainable societies and avoiding global ecological disaster. Our conventional approaches to addressing environmental issues—focusing on structural change (such as developing bureaucratic arms of government, passing legislative acts, political protest, developing land trusts)—will not be enough. In order to avert ecological collapse we will need to develop entirely new worldviews, or in Rifkin's terms a "biospheric consciousness"—a global empathic sensitivity to the entire planet (2009, 616). Such a shift in consciousness is necessary because, echoing the opening quote and in words attributed to Albert Einstein, "The significant problems we face cannot be solved at the same level of thinking we were at when we created them" (Calaprice, Dyson, and Einstein 2005). Thus I maintain that shifts in our worldviews must accompany any efforts we make to shift our institutions and social structures.

However, social scientists have not placed much attention on collective forms of consciousness with the exceptions of psychological interest in the collective *un*conscious (Jung [1959] 1990), how social symbols embody collective sentiments (Durkheim 1965), and oppositional or critical consciousness by subordinate groups (Mansbridge and Morris 2001, Collins 2008, Friere [1974] 2008). Rifkin's call for a biospheric consciousness (akin to Aldo Leopold's 1949 call for a Land Ethic whereby we extend our sense of community to include all living beings and the ecology that sustains life) requires a shift in cultural perceptions of nature and the development of empathic relationships with the more-than-human world. Yet how do we develop such a consciousness?

The nascent field of Buddhist sociology may provide some interesting insights and possibilities. Buddhist sociology, among other things, applies the insights of Buddhism to collective societal issues (Bell 1979, Loy 2008, McGrane 1994, Schipper 2012). In this collection and elsewhere, David Loy makes a powerful case for applying Buddhist principles to social transformation, maintaining, "we cannot expect social transformation to work without personal transformation as well" (2010, 78) Yet Loy notes that without challenging oppressive social hierarchies, Buddhism has had limited success. In this essay I examine how we have and may continue to draw on Buddhist ideas and practices to challenge oppressive social hierarchies that have brought us to the current collective predicament we now face. Specifically, I explore how the Buddhist "three marks of reality" described below, (in Pāli, *tilakkhana*), may help us address environmental crisis in novel ways, pointing us in directions that are critical for developing a biospheric consciousness. The Buddhist three marks of reality are impermanence (*anicca*), suffering or unsatisfactoriness (*dukkha*), and nonself (*anatta*). While the three marks of reality are intimately interwoven, exploring them separately and as they interconnect reveals some intriguing possibilities.

First, let's look at impermanence (*annica*). The perception of impermanence is considered the insight that surpasses all other insights (*Anguttara Nikaya Sutta*) that leads to full liberation from suffering. When we contemplate reality we see that everything we think of as "real" is impermanent. Even this "present moment" when carefully looked at appears as an ever-changing, dynamic flow of forms, feelings and sensations, perceptions, thoughts or mental habits, and consciousness.[2] Buddhism calls these five characteristics of human experience the five aggregates (*skandas*).

What does contemplating the impermanent nature of reality imply for addressing environmental crisis? Perhaps recognizing that everything is subject to change invites us to let go. If there is nothing substantive to hold onto, then trying to hold on to a perceived reality only leads to, in Kornfield's words, "rope burn" (2009, 247)—or suffering. But what specifically could we consider letting go of in response to environmental crisis?

A Buddhist sensibility might encourage us to let go of core Western values that, in their extreme and when institutionalized, are at the root of our ecological crisis: materialism, consumerism, militarization, and individualism (Foster 2000; King and McCarthy 2005; Shiva 2008). Loy connects these destructive values and the behaviors associated with them with the Buddhist "three poisons": greed, ill will, and delusion. "Today our economic system has institutionalized greed, our militarism institutionalizes ill will, and our corporate media institutionalizes delusion" (2010, 78). Social justice advocates challenge such institutionalized greed, aggression, and delusion; however, a Buddhist approach might simply let go. Letting go does not mean sitting back and doing nothing. Rather, it may be thought of as a way of relating to the present moment, loosening our grip, and orienting and at times re-orienting our individual and group energy. As Michel Foucault ([1977] 1991, [1979] 1998) has demonstrated, challenging systems of domination often reinforces those very systems. When we let go, however, we align with the nature of impermanence, or the Tao, the ever-flowing transformation of reality.

Thich Nhat Hanh (2001) explains that to be effective we may first need to let go of our self concepts and recognize our own impermanent nature. In doing so we can also let go of our concepts of others. Rather than reifying "the other" as the enemy, we recognize our common humanity and the impermanence that underlies all of our lives. In his classic text, *Strategies of Social Protest*, Gamson (1975) found that effective social movement organizations (SMOs) maintained, among other characteristics, an adversarial "us versus them" mentality. In other words, "enemy making" seems to work, or at least coincides with successful SMOs. However, I wonder if this can be said for the long-term success of a social movement, particularly an effort as far-reaching as transforming our ways of relating to and living on the planet. Nhat Hanh takes a radically different approach to social change by bridging social action with contemplative practices that break down us-versus-them dichotomies.

Born in central Vietnam in 1926 and becoming a monk at age 16, Nhat Hanh questioned traditional Vietnamese Buddhism with its emphasis on silent insular contemplation even amidst social upheaval and mass suffering. He coined the term "Engaged Buddhism" and helped found the Engaged Buddhist Movement, dedicating his life to cultivating inner transformation to benefit both self and society.

Some of Engaged Buddhists' main strategies include walking mindfully and sitting in meditation amidst frenetic surroundings (as meditation flash mobs do, for example) to demonstrate there is no need to demonize anyone and through slowing down and waking up, peace is possible. This looks quite different from what we see in traditional protest actions, even in acts of nonviolent civil disobedience. The difference is in both the means and the goal. Collective public mindfulness practices focus not on changing a particular social institution or system but rather on collectively waking up and helping others to awaken to the disturbing realities that our contemporary ways of living create. The methods are nonviolent and disruptive, and perhaps the ultimate form of disobedience. While these actions do not break laws per se, they do break the very values that shape our consumer-driven aggressive militaristic society. These actions also engage in the perhaps millennial-long debate, can we really stop violence with violence? Are traditional nonviolent protest actions enough? Perhaps the most radical thing we can do is let go, sit down, and wake up, and in so doing, help others awaken to the suffering inflicted by our ways of living in modern society.

This brings us to the second mark of reality: suffering, or in Pāli, *dukkha*. Dukkha is a nuanced term that can also mean distress, anguish, and frustration. If we look at the environmental crisis we can see a wide range of suffering—from the difficulties created by rising food prices, to grief over ecological destruction and extreme weather conditions, to anguish over vast species extinction, to the pain and suffering associated with bodily harm and death from environmentally destructive practices. However, the historic Buddha (Buddha means "Awakened One") is said to have taught only one thing: suffering and the cessation of suffering. In fact, the Buddha has also been called the Great Physician because his teachings can help us identify root causes and cures for what physically and mentally ails us. So what is the cause of suffering? In one word: craving. We want that which we don't have, and we don't want that which we do have. We may crave pleasure or crave to eliminate displeasure (aversion). At the level of being, we crave existence or extermination. The Buddha's prognosis for this condition was nothing less than freedom from suffering. Just as any great physician, the Buddha developed powerful healing steps for ending suffering, also known as the Noble Eightfold Path.

Division/Theme	Eightfold Path Factors
Wisdom (Sanskrit: *prajñā*, Pāli: *paññā*)	1. Wise view
	2. Wise intention
Ethical conduct (Sanskrit: *śīla*, Pāli: *sīla*)	3. Wise speech
	4. Wise action
	5. Wise livelihood
Concentration (Sanskrit and Pāli: *samādhi*)	6. Wise effort
	7. Wise mindfulness
	8. Wise concentration

The Noble Eightfold Path is nonlinear. While each of the factors creates a foundation for the ones to come, they also interconnect and support each other, and practitioners are encouraged to develop all concurrently. The facets of the Noble Eightfold Path are sometimes divided into three themes or divisions: wisdom, ethical conduct, and concentration. The eight factors on the path have been conventionally translated as "right," however, they are not moral dictums as in right versus wrong, but rather may be thought of as "wise" or, in Weberian terms, as "ideal types." Here I refer to each of the factors along the Eightfold Path with the prefix "wise." Exploring each of the themes and the factors within each theme provides us with some novel considerations for addressing environmental crisis.

In Buddhism *wisdom* means to see reality as it really is. In this case, we see environmental problems as they are and establish wise views and wise intentions around reality. Wise view recognizes that every action has a reaction (Pāli: *kamma*; Sanskrit: *karma*). So any action that we take to alleviate suffering around environmental problems reflects back upon us. If we wish to alleviate suffering we must act in ways that do not create additional suffering. How can we stand up for and contribute to the well-being of the planet and its inhabitants without adding more suffering to those who we believe participate in actions that we think are harmful? Wise intention supports wise view: it is a commitment to nonharming. Taken together the wisdom factors point to the importance of nonviolent actions. Most environmental actions are nonviolent. Paul Hawken (2008) identifies millions of environmental groups worldwide whose members act nonviolently to address environmental crisis. Yet wise views and intentions are not enough. We must behave in ways that support our understanding of reality.

Buddhist approaches to ethical conduct focus on practical behavior that sets the foundation for raising our consciousness (undergoing a shift in our understanding of reality). Buddhist ethics consist of wise speech, wise action, and wise livelihood. Wise speech means refraining from lying, and from divisive, abusive, and idle speech. Wise action means abstaining from taking life, stealing, and sexual misconduct, and reinforces the nonviolent approach to social change. Wise livelihood calls on individuals to consider their own paths toward generating and maintaining livelihood without harming others.

Taken together, a Buddhist approach to environmental crisis might place ethical conduct (not adversarialism) as central to successful organizing. This is precisely what we have seen in some of the world's most successful and impactful social movements. Mahatma Gandhi led a nonviolent revolution based in *Satyagraha*—holding to the truth—which to Gandhi meant being fearless and trusting his opponent, "for an implicit trust in human nature is the very essence of his (*Satyagraha*) creed" ([1928] 1950, 159). By holding to the truth and loving his enemies as himself Gandhi shined a mirror on British brutality—a country believing itself the pillar of civilization—and ultimately helped liberate India from imperial tyranny. Martin Luther King Jr. (who was influenced by both Gandhi and Thich Nhat Hanh) and the civil rights activists marched with dignity and an ethics centered on respecting the "enemy," not only as a means to express their own humanity but also to evoke and help their oppressors remember their own humanity. The civil rights movement ultimately led to the 1964 Civil Rights Act that outlawed discrimination based on race, ethnicity, and minority status. The world bore witness to a dignified Nelson Mandela, emerging from twenty-seven years of imprisonment, calling for reconciliation with his white oppressors rooted in an ethics of forgiveness, ultimately leading South Africa toward a peaceful transference of power. More recently Aung San Suu Kyi's re-emergence as the leader of the National League for Democracy in the face of fifteen years of house arrest over a twenty-one-year period and consequent election into the Burmese parliament illustrates the power of maintaining an unfaltering commitment to nonviolent democracy and human rights. In each of these cases, people decried the uneven playing field, the way that power was amassed, and the "impossibility" of change. In each case these leaders mirrored wisdom and ethical conduct in the face of brutality and not only influenced major structural changes but also instigated the transformation of deeply entrenched cultural attitudes that maintained brutal tyrants and oppressive power structures.

The environmental movement does not have one wise and charismatic leader maintaining an ethical stand for all to emulate, nor one defining agenda, nor one clear adversary. What makes approaches to environmental crisis so different from these other liberation movements is the scale of the problem—nothing less than looming global ecological collapse—and the need for dramatic changes in the way we live on this planet. A Buddhist ethic calls on the many millions of participants within environmental groups (identified by Hawken) to implement ethical conduct on all levels as a critical foundation for creating positive social change. We might think of this as radical nonviolence—recognizing that it is not enough to simply refrain from taking up arms in response to oppressive circumstances, but that our very life practices must support a nonviolent reality. This requires contemplation and evaluation of the consequences of all our words and actions. If we wish to live on a healthy planet, we ourselves must be healthy. Or in Gandhi's words:

> We but mirror the world. All the tendencies present in the outer world are
> to be found in the world of our body. If we could change ourselves, the
> tendencies in the world would also change. As a man changes his own nature,
> so does the attitude of the world change towards him. This is the divine
> mystery supreme. (1913, 241)

Buddhist activist Joanna Macy's workshop "The Work that Reconnects" (2013) engages in this healing process. Grounded in Buddhist wisdom and ethics, Macy's workshops for personal and social change offer a unique approach to addressing social and ecological crisis and have been implemented in schools, places of worship, and grassroots organizations worldwide. In order to heal, the Work involves facing our pain for the world, which Macy explains is:

> the most subversive thing you can do. This is what the industrial growth society and the corporate military empire wants us to not do. They want us to numbly follow orders and just see what next we need to buy to feel good . . . or to get some place fast. But we are going to pause and honor our pain for the world because this is a jewel we carry inside us. This is your Bodhisattva Heart. This is essential to our waking up to our true nature. This is like a doorway we can go through to see the immensity of who we really are. We are so much bigger than the industrial growth society can imagine, trying to turn us into robots and consumers, when our true nature is this [points to an image of the Earth].

Through the Work, participants "see with new eyes" and "go forth" bringing with them loving attention, compassion, and fearlessness, as they engage in transformative action.

Cultivating wisdom and living an ethical life are considered necessary conditions for developing the third division of the Noble Eightfold Path: concentration. Through cultivating wise concentration and mindfulness we can ultimately raise our consciousness. In Buddhism, this means that through concentration and mindfulness we come to see reality as it is (wisdom), and with such clear seeing emerge humanist qualities such as patience, kindness, empathy, compassion, truthfulness, and forgiveness (Jankowski and Sandage 2011, Kabat-Zinn 1994, Neff and Tirch 2013).

Rifkin foresees the development of biospheric consciousness arising from the development of global empathy whereby most peoples' worldviews are rooted in "the ability to read and respond to another person 'as if' he or she were oneself" (2009, 143). While the development of global empathy may be critical toward the emergence of a biospheric consciousness that fosters new approaches to living on the planet, Rifkin assumes empathic bonds are a natural byproduct of an increasingly connected world. A Buddhist approach, however, views empathy as only one seed in a garden of possibilities (including destructive seeds like greed, despair, and hatred) that in order to germinate and grow must be cultivated. Mindfulness and concentration practices are one way that we can water the seeds of empathy (see Appendix A).

We turn now to the third mark of reality: *anatta*.[3] Westerners commonly misunderstand the Buddhist doctrine of *anatta*, translated as nonself or emptiness, to mean that Buddhists believe that nothing exists. However, Buddhism does not teach that nothing exists, but rather teaches that nothing exists independently and permanently. Put positively, Buddhism views all existence as interdependent. Thich Nhat Hanh explains:

> If you are a poet, you will see clearly that there is a cloud floating in this sheet of paper. Without a cloud, there will be no rain; without rain, the trees cannot grow; and without trees, we cannot make paper. The cloud is essential for the paper to exist. . . . Without "non-paper elements," like mind, logger, sunshine and so on, there will be no paper. As thin as this sheet of paper is, it contains everything in the universe in it. (2001, 55)

When we no longer identify as separate individuals, uniquely designed to meet our own individual needs, when we stop viewing reality through the lens of a separate self and begin to understand the impermanent, ever-changing, dynamically interconnected nature of all that is, we begin to relate to the suffering that goes on in the world quite differently. The us/them dichotomies break down and certain ideas no longer make sense. There is no longer a need to save the world from corporate greed. We realize that we are the world and we are also the corporate greed, for it is through our participation in the world—from eating food shipped from other places, to wearing clothing made in other countries, to engaging in the consumer culture, to using transportation that relies on fossil fuels—that creates the dependence on corporations and feeds the systemic greed at their foundation. We recognize that we are coparticipants in a dance of emergence or, in Buddhist terms, we all co-arise. And so the question becomes, how do we arise in ways that foster well-being and health versus greed, destruction, and violence?

The classic metaphor of Indra's net helps explain not only the dynamic, intimate, interconnected nature of all phenomena, but may also help us understand new possibilities for social change. A multifaceted jewel sits at each vertex of Indra's net, reflecting all other jewels in the net and symbolizing how all members of the universe are infinitely connected and reflected in one another. If this is the case, then as I change, everything else in the universe changes. Sociologists have begun to identify this phenomenon through their work on social contagion—finding that the influences of our lifestyles extend far beyond the circle of people with whom we have direct contact (Christakis and Fowler 2008, 2012). This suggests that our behaviors and actions really do make a difference in the world. The irony of course is that through recognizing that I am not a separate self, I come to understand the depth of the power that "I" have. However, this is not a power rooted in notions of an individual self (and thus played out as "power over" other individuals), this is a power rooted in understanding that we are so deeply and intimately interconnected that the choices each of us make affect everyone around us and beyond. A collective biospheric consciousness emerges as together we awaken to reality as it is: impermanent, filled with suffering, and intimately interconnected. As we develop this consciousness, new ways of living in the world emerge, new choices are made, new social realities become possible.

I would like to end this essay with a personal example. Coming of age in the eighties, a member of the me generation and a child of parents who both fled from the ravages of generations of Jewish immigrant poverty, I grew up in a yuppie, nouveau-riche suburb of New York City and embodied its materialist consumer ethic. As a teenager, my idea of fun was to go to the mall with a friend and purchase at least four items. I chose to go to a college that had a strong economics department because my life plan was to become rich. This mirrored my fellow high school classmates who did continue on this path and are now owners of hedge funds, members of country clubs, financial managers, and so forth. Something different happened to me however. In 1990 I took a college class entitled The Social Psychology of Consciousness and learned how to meditate. Through meditation practice I began to unravel many of the assumptions that drove my emotions, attitudes, and behaviors. Without having the language for it at the time, I began to see reality as impermanent, filled with suffering, and highly interconnected. Making money no longer held much interest. Alleviating suffering seemed far more important and meaningful. Sociology was the only place at the university that seemed to address not just personal suffering but widespread, collective suffering. I became a sociologist who, on the side, maintained a meditation practice. Over the years it became stunningly obvious to me that the thousands-years-old Buddhist philosophies and practices could complement social theory and methodologies and I began writing on Buddhist sociology (Schipper 2012) and teaching a class entitled Consciousness and Social Change. Taking one meditation class changed the trajectory of my life. As the world changes me, so too it changes with me. As with Indra's net, we reflect each other, and the little changes in my life have unimaginable consequences on the lives of those around me and beyond (social contagion). And so I continue to practice concentration and mindfulness. This is not simply a practice for my own peace of mind (although that seems to be another byproduct of this practice) but is a practice into seeing clearly—seeing reality as it is—and in the process becoming more peaceful, forgiving, and empathic and contributing these qualities to a world in crisis.

A student in my Consciousness and Social Change class shared that prior to meditating, he perceived flies as annoyances, pests to be swatted and eliminated. After a month of meditating (as part of the class, I ask students to meditate daily for a minimum of five minutes a day), he experienced flies quite differently and now even feels affection for them when they visit him during practice. He feels concern for their well-being, and certainly does not kill them anymore. Attention to his inner experiences and ultimately a sense of empathy for the fly's plight has begun to develop in my student. He has begun to take deep interest in the more-than-human world and is developing a biospheric consciousness.

Concluding Thoughts

In this essay I have applied some of the insights of Buddhism to our collective social problems—specifically using insights into the three marks of reality to address environmental crisis. Addressing ecological crisis begins right here, right now, with each of us devoting ourselves to understanding and awakening to reality; embodying an understanding of impermanence, suffering, and interconnectedness; and developing a biospheric awareness rooted in empathy for all living beings.

> May all beings be free from suffering.
> May all beings have peace and well-being.
> May we all heal together,
>   and in so doing, play our part in the unfolding
>   of a healthy vibrant planet Earth.

Appendix A

VIPASSANA MEDITATION PRACTICE

Here I describe the basics of Vipassana Meditation Practice. I have been engaged in this daily practice since 1990. My usual daily practice ranges between twenty minutes and two hours. For those new to meditation, I recommend starting with a five-minute daily practice.

INSIGHT MEDITATION INSTRUCTION

Find a comfortable upright position. You may sit on the floor with crossed legs or sit on a chair. If you choose to sit cross-legged, it is recommended that you sit on a pillow (or zafu cushion) and elevate your body slightly above your legs. Adjust yourself to find a comfortable position.

Begin by placing your attention on the breath. Your breath is considered your anchor into the present moment. Whenever you find yourself drifting away from awareness of breath, gently return to your breathing and to awareness of the present moment. You can watch the rise and fall of your abdomen as you breathe in and out, or watch the air as it enters and leaves your nostrils. Choose one place in which to focus attention. The initial part of this practice involves developing concentration. As sensations, emotions, and thoughts distract your attention away from the breath, gently return to observing the rise and fall of your abdomen or the air as it moves in and out of your nose. The word "gentle" is critical here as there is a tendency to berate oneself for becoming, sometimes quite easily, distracted.

As concentration on the breath develops, notice bodily sensations, emotions, thoughts, and other experiences that enter into your awareness. Maintain some amount of awareness on the breath, while noticing other experiences that enter consciousness. The key here is simply to observe what arises in awareness. If a thought, for example, arises, watch it as if you are the sky and the thought is a cloud. The cloud takes form, changes, and dissipates while the sky (awareness) is the medium upon which the cloud floats. Notice the way thoughts, emotions, and sensations take form, how they arise and how they pass. Return again and again to the breath.

This practice is called "insight meditation" because as you observe the way that sensations, thoughts, and emotions arise into being and pass on, and as you anchor yourself in the breath, insights emerge into the nature of reality.

NOTES

1. "Warming of the climate system is unequivocal, as is now evident from observations of increases in global average air and ocean temperatures, widespread melting of snow and ice and rising global average sea level." IPCC, *Climate Change 2007: Synthesis Report*, p. 30. Same conclusions found in IPCC 2013. Also see Nuccitelli 2013.
2. Consciousness is nebulously defined in Buddhism but is possible to experience. Perhaps consciousness is most easily thought of as the ability to inquire into and discern the nature of reality.
3. See Immergut and Kaufman's (2014) "A Sociology of No-Self" for a Buddhist sociological analysis of rethinking the concept of "self" within sociology.

REFERENCES

Anguttara Nikaya Sutta 9:20, abridged; IV 393–96. *www.urbandharma.org/udharma14/angnik.html*.

Bell, Inge. 1979. "Buddhist Sociology: Some Thoughts on the Convergence of Sociology and the Eastern Paths of Liberation." In *Theoretical Perspectives in Sociology*, edited by Scott G. McNall, 53–68. New York: St. Martins.

Calaprice, Alice, Freeman Dyson, and Albert Einstein. 2005. *The New Quotable Einstein*. Princeton, NJ: Princeton University Press.

Christakis, Nicholas, and James Fowler. 2008. "The Collective Dynamics of Smoking in a Large Social Network." *New England Journal of Medicine* 358 (21): 2249–58. *www.nejm.org/doi/full/10.1056/NEJMsa0706154*.

———. 2012. "Social Contagion Theory: Examining Dynamic Social Networks and Human Behavior." *Statistics in Medicine* 32:556–77.

Collins, Patricia Hill. 2008. *Black Feminist Thought: Knowledge, Consciousness, and the Politics of Empowerment*. New York: Routledge.

Durkheim, Emile. 1965. *The Elementary Forms of the Religious Life*. New York: The Free Press.

Foster, Jeremy. 2000. *Marx's Ecology: Materialism and Nature*. New York: Monthly Review Press.

Foucault, Michel. (1977) 1991. *Discipline and Punish: The Birth of a Prison*. London: Penguin.

———. (1979) 1998. *The History of Sexuality: The Will to Knowledge*. London: Penguin.

Freire, Paulo. (1974) 2008. *Education for Critical Consciousness*. London: Continuum.

Gamson, William. 1975. *The Strategy of Social Protest*. Belmont, CA: Dorsey.

Gandhi, M. K. 1913. *The Collected Works of M. K. Gandhi*. New Delhi: The Publications Division.

———. (1928) 1950. *Satyagraha in South Africa*. Ahmedabad, India: Navajivan.

Hawken, Paul. 2008. *Blessed Unrest: How the Largest Social Movement in History Is Restoring Grace, Justice, and Beauty to the World*. New York, NY: Penguin Books.

Immergut, Mathew, and Peter Kaufman. 2014. "A Sociology of No-Self: Applying Buddhist Social Theory to Symbolic Interaction." *Symbolic Interaction* 37 (2): 264–82.

IPCC. 2007. *Climate Change 2007: Synthesis Report. Contribution of Working Groups I, II and III to the Fourth Assessment Report of the Intergovernmental Panel on Climate Change*. Pachauri, R. K and Reisinger, A., eds. Geneva, Switzerland: IPCC. *ipcc.ch/publications_and_data/ar4/syr/en/contents.html*.

———. 2013. "Summary for Policymakers." In *Climate Change 2013: The Physical Science Basis. Contribution of Working Group I to the Fifth Assessment Report of the Intergovernmental Panel on Climate Change*, T. F. Stocker, D. Qin, G. K. Plattner, M. Tignor, S. K. Allen, J. Boschung, A. Nauels, Y. Xia, V. Bex, and P. M. Midgley, eds. New York: Cambridge University Press. *ipcc.ch/report/ar5/wg1*.

Jankowski, Peter J., and Steven J. Sandage. 2011. "Meditative Prayer, Hope, Adult Attachment, and Forgiveness: A Proposed Model." *Psychology of Religion and Spirituality* 3 (2): 115–31.

Jung, C. G. [1959] 1990. *The Archetypes and the Collective Unconscious*. Princeton, NJ: Princeton University Press/Bollingen Foundation.

Kabat-Zinn, Jon. 1994. *Wherever You Go There You Are: Mindfulness Meditation in Everyday Life*. New York: Hyperion.

King, Leslie, and Deborah McCarthy. 2005. "Environmental Problems Require Social Solutions." In *Environmental Sociology: From Analysis to Action*, edited by Leslie King and Deborah McCarthy, xi—xxx. Lanham, MD: Rowman & Littlefield.

Kornfield, Jack. 2009. *The Wise Heart: A Guide to the Universal Teachings of Buddhist Psychology*. New York: Bantam.

Leopold, Aldo. [1949] 1966. *A Sand County Almanac*. New York: Ballantine Books.

Loy, David R. 2008. *Money, Sex, War, Karma: Notes for a Buddhist Revolution*. Somerville, MA: Wisdom.

———. 2010. "Self Transformation, Social Transformation." *Tikkun* 25 (5): 54–57, 76–78.

Macy, Joanna. 2013. "Joanna Macy: The Work that Reconnects—Chapter 3: The Spiral of the Work." Video recording. *www.turntowardlife.tv/joanna_macy_workshop_video*.

Mansbridge, Jane, and Aldon Morris. 2001. *Oppositional Consciousness: The Subjective Roots of Social Protest*. Chicago: The University of Chicago Press.

McGrane, Bernard. 1994. *The Un-TV and the 10 MPH Car: Experiments in Personal Freedom and Everyday Life*. Fort Bragg, CA: Small Press.

Müller, Benito, Niklas Höhne, and Christian Ellermann. 2007. *Differing (Historic)*

Responsibilities for Climate Change. Oxford Climate Policy. *www.oxfordclimatepolicy.org/publications/documents/DifferentiatingResponsibility.pdf.*

Neff, Kristen, and Dennis Tirch. 2013. "Self-Compassion and ACT." In *Mindfulness, Acceptance, and Positive Psychology: The Seven Foundations of Well-Being*, edited by Todd B. Kashdan, and Joseph Ciarrochi, 78–106. Oakland, CA: Context Press/New Harbinger.

Nhat Hanh, Thich. 2001. *Thich Nhat Hanh: Essential Writings.* Maryknoll, NY: Orbis Books.

Nuccitelli, Dana. 2013. "Survey finds 97% of climate science papers agree warming is man-made" *Guardian*, May 16, 2013. *www.theguardian.com/environment/climate-consensus-97-per-cent/2013/may/16/climate-change-scienceofclimatechange.*

Rifkin, Jeremy. 2009. *The Empathic Civilization.* New York: Tarcher/Penguin.

Schipper, Janine. 2012. "Toward a Buddhist Sociology: Theories, Methods, and Possibilities." *American Sociologist* 43:203–22.

Shiva, Vandana. 2008. *Soil Not Oil.* Cambridge, MA: South End Press.

16

Consuming Violence

Oil and Food in Everyday Life

Patricia Widener

Oil and food are consumed routinely by the majority of us—sometimes with great thought and sometimes with little reflection. Here I explore how this consumption may lead to the suffering of others. This suffering, or violence, arises from a range of multiple and cumulative experiences, including extreme and global disparities, inequalities, and physical and social separations between the producing and consuming communities. These forces—singly and collectively— then constrain an individual or community's ability to live safely and with dignity (Farmer 2003; Rees and Westra 2003). In other words, the experiences of privilege, profit, or pleasure of the consumer are intimately linked with the potential misery of the producers, though these two remain alienated from each other socially, culturally, and economically.

Among products that are routinely consumed, oil and food are particularly germane points of comparisons because of what they mean to so many people. The users of both, for example, may view themselves and be viewed by others primarily as consumers, rather than as global citizens who think and act with a sense of connectedness to other people and environments. Oil and food also have under-supported alternatives (non-toxic renewable energy, and fair sustainable farming for example). Moreover, both offer pleasure. Food offers physical pleasure (such as taste, satiation, and gratification) and social pleasure (celebrating important cultural occasions and nurturing family and friends). As for oil (that is, until alternatives have been adopted), it enables us to travel to visit the places and people we enjoy, while many of the material goods we covet are made and transported using petroleum. With these points in mind, I draw upon a few case studies, some based on my research and some based on my teaching, to demonstrate some of the global linkages in the everyday activities of producing and consuming oil and food.

The Violence of Oil

Generations of people across many parts of the world have been raised in an atmosphere of conflict and contamination due to the production and consumption of oil. Whether large or small, leaks, breaks, spills, explosions, contamination, and conflict are accumulating worldwide, impairing ecological and societal well-being and human health among affected communities and workers. In the United States alone, each generation since the 1960s has experienced a major oil disaster: the 1969 oil spill at an offshore oil rig near Santa Barbara; the 1989 *Exxon Valdez* oil spill along the Alaskan coastline; and the 2010 British Petroleum (BP) *Deepwater Horizon* disaster that killed eleven workers and dumped oil into the Gulf of Mexico for eighty-seven days. Each served as a wake-up call and national reminder of the irreparable impacts of oil, of the need to better regulate and monitor each aspect of the industry including protection of workers, local communities, and local economies, and also of the need to reduce oil use and to commit to less toxic and more renewable energy sources. But while the Santa Barbara disaster helped to launch the environmental movement of the 1970s, and the other disasters reenergized existing environmental campaigns, each disaster has ultimately failed to alter mainstream consumer habits or lessen the industry's political and economic power and influence.

In addition to these major American disasters, there are other large-scale disasters worldwide, and smaller leaks and spills that are less visible, underreported, or unreported. Except for those people who are most directly impacted, many of these disasters are not reflected upon during the course of our day or year, or even when we put gasoline into our cars. The United States is expanding oil production into new areas (such as North Dakota), in new ways (such as oil fracking), and through new means of transportation (the Keystone pipeline system for example). I have referred to this current period as a protracted age of oil—despite the potential and realized risks, despite the known disasters, and despite our knowledge of the link between fossil fuels and climate change (Widener 2013).

For a global perspective on the violence that oil consumption entails, let's consider a few noteworthy examples: the 1995 state-military hanging of Ken Saro-Wiwa, a Nigerian Ogoni activist who organized his community to resist the international oil operations on or near their land; China's oil operations and oil pipeline project in Burma (Myanmar) which has led to protests, arrests, land seizures, and polluted waterways (Arakan Oil Watch 2008); the Sarayacu indigenous community of the Ecuadorian Amazon who have been resisting oil exploration in their territories and subsistence hunting and gathering grounds since the late 1980s; Russia's more recent oil operations near the Arctic, described by Greenpeace as a remote and "forgotten disaster" of oil ponds and polluted waterways (Burgwald 2012); the 1990 Iraqi invasion of Kuwait and the subsequent Kuwaiti oil fires; and the American occupation of Iraq (possibly for oil) in 2003.

These cases are worth remembering. Across time and place, oil conflict and contamination are accumulating.

In an effort to capture both the anger and compassion for the world's affected people and ecosystems, Oil Watch (1999), an international activist group, depicted an image of the world as an oil rig penetrating a bleeding Mother Earth held up, embraced, and embodied by a woman who is releasing breast milk that is potentially contaminated or life-sustaining. In this work, entitled *The Oil Flows, The Earth Bleeds*, there is destruction on the one hand and care, support, and nurturing on the other. Letting go of oil as an energy source may first require us to recognize who benefits from and who is harmed by its production and consumption, and then to cultivate globally minded actions that prevent those injuries.

Based on my work in Ecuador (Widener 2011), I argue that one type of oil injustice occurs when some communities experience the burden or curse of oil, while others experience the benefits. One community or ecosystem is sacrificed for the privilege or protection of another. The connections and separations between these communities maintain this destructive arrangement. Even committed activists have failed to overhaul the political economy of oil or to convert oil-committed political leaders and consumers into global leaders and citizens who act for the welfare of everyone. Those burdened by oil (workers and nearby residents, wildlife, and the larger ecosystem) have few options and little power to alter these conditions, while the political, economic, and consuming beneficiaries advocate too rarely for socially just and environmentally safe alternatives. As Harvey Molotch explains "Evil is both banal and complicated; both of these attributes contribute to its durability" (1970, 141). Banal, complicated, and durable—these attributes help to explain why consumers refuse to let go of, or even think critically about, the routine uses of petroleum and petroleum-based products. Meanwhile the power, wealth, and influence of the oil industry are likely explanations for why political leaders fail to support nontoxic and more sustainable alternatives.

Donna King's (2012) concept of letting go offers a framework for understanding and relinquishing human attachments to oil. The benefits of a letting go perspective are threefold. Letting go of certain consumption patterns may allow individuals and communities more time, energy, passion, and compassion to become critically engaged in global environmental justice, health, and human safety concerns, and to promote renewable, nontoxic energy sources. Letting go of oil consumption can also lessen our individual, national, and global dependencies on toxic substances and may encourage political leaders to resist permitting corporate access to risky fossil fuels. By personally letting go, one may then demand that political leaders do likewise. To be sure, until we learn to let go of our oil addiction, we will continue to depend on oil and petroleum-based products, thus enabling government agencies to accept industry actions without regulation, oversight, or penalty and to marginalize alternative energy sources. This continued commitment to oil also emboldens the oil industry to decrease safety standards so as to maintain the flow of oil—in the belief that no one is watching and no one cares how oil is obtained—leading to oil profits for corporations and oil risk for others. Lessening our attachment to oil, monitoring the industry, and demanding alternative energy sources have the potential to free others to have a life without oil conflict or contamination, while reducing the world's greenhouse gas emissions.

The Violence of Food

Much like oil, food is also routinely consumed often without thought or reflection. The comparison may seem counterintuitive, but oil and food are intertwined in many ways: petroleum facilitates food production in terms of chemicals and equipment used and in long distance transportation; both contribute to greenhouse gases and climate change that will be borne unequally by communities and future generations; and both have consumers who may be unaware of, and political leaders and economic interests who appear unconcerned about, the harmful practices of both industries. To demonstrate some of the multiple meanings in the production and supply of routinely consumed foods, as a teacher I offer two cases in my sociology classes: North American tomato and citrus farmworkers and African cocoa harvesters.

The case of farmworkers in the United States is a demoralizing but important one to understand. According to a Department of Agriculture report, the poverty of farmworkers "is more than double that of all wage and salary employees," while farmworkers also "face exposure to pesticides, risk of heat exhaustion and heat stroke, inadequate sanitary facilities, and obstacles in obtaining health care" (Kandel 2008, 1). Migrant farmworkers have been beaten, enslaved, and overcharged for transportation and housing, including housing that is dilapidated and too small for the number of people forced to reside there. Birth defects associated with chemical exposure have also been linked, though not confirmed, with women who were pregnant while working in the fields.

Like oil-related disasters, these problems are not new: they have been documented over a long period of time. The 1960 television documentary *Harvest of Shame*, for example, captured migrant farmworker experiences in Florida. That was followed by the 1992 documentary *No Grapes* that exposed the field experience and dangers of pesticide exposure for farmworkers in California, and then in 2005, the documentary *Dreams Die Hard* depicted modern day slavery in Florida's fields. Every so often a report appears on the appalling conditions in the fields; yet too little has been achieved in stopping these types of exploitative practices despite the public knowledge of them. The point is that there are farmworkers in the United States who have been unpaid or underpaid, exposed to chemicals in the field, who may themselves go hungry, in order to provide fresh or processed food for American households.

In Florida alone, the Coalition of Immokalee Workers (CIW) has documented exploitation in the tomato and citrus fields in terms of wages, workplace treatment, and living conditions. In collaboration with food activist student and faith-based groups nationwide, CIW has confronted well-known fast food restaurants and grocery store chains for better wages and worksite conditions. For the tomato harvest, their campaigns have demanded a penny more per pound. It is also worth noting that it is not the physical distance, but the social and economic distance between the farmworker and the consumer that is so vast. The rural farming community of Immokalee, where CIW is based, is less than an hour drive northeast of Naples, less than two hours west of Fort Lauderdale, and less than three hours south of Tampa. These are three well-known tourist destinations that residents and visitors frequently crisscross by road, yet the physical proximity between these travelers and the farm working communities cannot overcome the social and economic chasms between them in terms of awareness and supporting action (Giagnoni 2011; Bales and Soodalter 2010).

This discussion of farming in Florida, where I teach, makes some of my students uncomfortable. But it is the discussion of chocolate, a profoundly unjust pleasure in some cases, which has the majority of students reflecting on what they know and do not know about what they casually consume. Though this may be commonly known, it bears repeating: children, teens, and young adults work for little or no pay and may experience severe beatings in the cocoa fields of the Ivory Coast where the majority of the world's cocoa supply originates. Many of them have been forced into labor that they cannot leave and for which they are not paid. It is probably an understatement to say that those who are paid are not paid well or treated fairly, while their labor serves as just one link in the production of chocolate, a chocolate that they have not tasted (Bales [1999] 2004).

This is not to say that all chocolate is produced under these conditions; nonetheless, these conditions have been reported in the Ivory Coast by the organization Free the Slaves. The documentary film *Slavery: A Global Investigation* (2000), based in part on the book *Disposable People* by Kevin Bales ([1999] 2004), reveals the knowledge and tolerance of modern day slavery in the cocoa fields among plantation managers, corporations, and government representatives where it occurs and in the nations where cocoa is converted into chocolate and consumed. In this way, chocolate embodies and reminds us of the history and legacy of colonialism. Not identified in the film, but perhaps found in your local grocery store, one European manufacturer—unknowingly perhaps—depicts the historical experience of colonial cultivation and European chocolate consumption in its packaging: a gold embossed imperial image of a sailing ship framed by cocoa nuts.

The case of chocolate highlights the extreme suffering of some workers coupled with the extreme pleasure of consumers. In my sociology class, after we review the labels of a range of chocolate products and sample the chocolate, we then watch *Slavery*. Before passing out the chocolate, I ask if there is anyone who has never tried chocolate, and in six years, no one has self-identified as having never tried chocolate. After the film, a few students have been frustrated with the exercise. Even though we have been reading and discussing inequality along the chains of production and consumption for weeks, the story of chocolate is too unflatteringly close. Most American holidays, religious and secular, are celebrated with chocolate, which shows how ingrained chocolate is in our everyday lives and customs, though cocoa is not grown in Europe or the United States (excluding a small amount in Hawaii). Students are also disturbed to know that, for the most part, all of us will continue eating chocolate without being able to verify that everyone along the supply chain (including the production of sugar) has been treated humanely, fairly, and paid a just wage.[1]

As of 2014, the US government has failed to pass legislation requiring that chocolate manufacturers demonstrate and provide labels attesting that the cocoa used has been produced without child, forced, or unpaid labor, while the largest manufacturers have failed to verify such conditions or to voluntarily provide such labels, though some have proposed phasing in a line of certifiable slave-free, fair trade chocolate. Only a few organizations, such as Fair Trade, Fair for Life, and Rainforest Alliance, certify when farmers and farmworkers are paid—ideally a living wage—for their work.[2] Yet these groups do not represent the bulk of mass-produced and consumed chocolate.

Letting Go So Others May Live

The practice of letting go may enable others to begin to live decent, more dignified lives. In the United States, empathy for workers exposed to a range of economic and social hardships has been obviated by an emphasis on the immediate gratification of consumers' shortsighted tastes and desires—desires that are orchestrated, in part, by corporate interests and political indifference or support. Indeed, the industrial practice of farming and food processing has conveniently removed consumers from understanding food and the processing of food and food-like items, and from knowing personally the farmers, farmworkers, or processors.

The same can be said in the case of oil. William Rees and Laura Westra argue that, "Not acting to reduce or prevent eco-injustice would convert erstwhile blameless consumer choices into acts of aggression" (2003, 116). This is a strong statement, but it supports one of the main points of letting go: live, act, and consume with the intent not to harm. Yet will we? The necessity of food and the routine of grocery shopping (and filling the car's gas tank) dilute the urgency of these concerns, while the many communal and individual pleasures we find in food (and travel) promote public and household denial of suffering along some food and oil chains.

Letting Go of Harmful Consumption

The depth and breadth of oil- and food-system injuries are so long-standing, so complex, and so full of suffering (and pleasure) that we may resist identifying ourselves in their procurement. As in the cases I've noted, the production, distribution, and consumption of food are at times experienced violently: unpaid and underpaid workers, brutal working conditions, chemical poisoning, malnutrition and hunger—to name a few—due to political, economic, and social arrangements imposed by some people on too many others. Oil production and oil disasters also take human life, destroy communities, ruin ecosystems, and disrupt small local economies. Yet many consumers and attendant corporate interests fail to make these connections or reject or deny them. Indeed, the political economy of oil and food has structured a globally integrated supply chain that is so distal and so complex as to ensure—almost—its own invisibility. (For significant works on some of the multiple meanings of global consumption, see Dauvergne 2008, 2010; Rees and Westra 2003; Schor 2010; Speth 2008; Urry 2010). This arrangement promotes and rewards consumers while minimizing connections between consumers, workers, and environments and diluting notions of global citizenship.

The perspective of letting go supports this understanding in its encouragement of nonattachment–to tangible, material items and to intangible ideas of striving, privilege, and possession—in order to enhance the lives of more people. It is a letting go of overloaded lives that have been imposed upon us by external social pressures and capitalist mindsets of profit, competition, and accumulation. It is a letting go of exhausting and unsatisfying achievements, of advertising-driven consumption, and of feeling pressured to ignore our own sense of what is just and fair for ourselves and for others. Juliet Schor (2010) calls for a similar trajectory when noting in the title of her book that "true wealth" is one that is "time-rich, ecologically light, small-scale" and that achieves "high-satisfaction." Letting go also requires shifting from the personal to the collective: personal gain is hollow if others have to work harder for less pay, less dignity, and less free time in a toxic or risky environment. In the spirit of community-based global citizenry, letting go requires the release of excess and injustice where we live, work, study, and play, so that others may live justly in safe and clean environments. It is prioritizing a more balanced and rewarding life—for everyone.

Letting go also calls for a shift from "radical self-transformation" to "radical social transformation" (King 2012, 69). The violence of oil and food underscores the importance of this shift and reflects the universality and sense of global interconnectedness that is required to consistently link the self with the wider society. With food and oil in mind, the practice and perspective of letting go ask us to stop striving for and within a global, corporate, capitalist economic model that injures and disrupts individuals, workers, communities, and eco-systems; to imagine a reality that decouples consumption from destruction; to advocate politically and socially for healthy alternatives for producers and consumers; to question, discuss, and challenge the political economy of oil and the industrialization of food; to resist the diversions of new recipes and new cars that conceal human, social, and ecological injuries; and to enjoy and embrace pleasurable times with family, friends, neighbors, and new acquaintances.

None of us can do all of these at once, but some of us can start to do some of them. The practice of letting go embraces a more globally aware way of life that benefits the majority of people and ecosystems rather than the advantaged few. As budding global citizens we may appear constrained in our abilities and unaware of our capabilities to let go, but we are not; we are capable of rejecting some items and demanding political and economic leaders reject them as well, as we are capable of adopting and promoting a more rewarding life for ourselves, for the world's residents, and for planet Earth. Extending environmental, social, and economic empathy beyond the self and one's immediate social network to universal social and ecological justice begins to enable others to live a life well, in dignity and with time for everyone to explore and create, to retreat and relax, and to enjoy pleasurable moments—but also with a commitment to change the political and economic systems that undermine this humane and sustainable direction.

NOTES

A draft of a portion of this essay was presented at the University of Pittsburgh, March 2012, entitled "Just & Unjust Movements: Oil & Food in Ecuador & Florida," and at the annual meeting of the Society for the Study of Social Problems, August 2012, entitled "Unjust Movements for Justice: Oil & Food Conflicts."

1. If interested in the sugar side of production, see the documentary *The Sugar Babies* (2007) on the experience of Haitian sugar cane workers in the Dominican Republic.
2. For the US farmworker, a domestic Fair Trade label and the domestic Food Justice Certification program are still not well established or known. In October 2014, CIW launched a "Fair Food Consumer Powered Worker Certified" label in the United States.

REFERENCES

Arakan Oil Watch. 2008. *Blocking Freedom: A Case Study of China's Oil and Gas Investment in Burma.* Chiang Mai, Thailand: Arakan Oil Watch.

Bales, Kevin. [1999] 2004. *Disposable People: New Slavery in the Global Economy.* Berkeley: University of California Press.

Bales, Kevin, and Ron Soodalter. 2010. *The Slave Next Door.* Berkeley: University of California Press.

Burgwald, Jon. 2012. "Russia's Oil Leaks—A Forgotten Disaster." *Making Waves Weblog*, Greenpeace.org. May 22. *www.greenpeace.org/international/en/news/Blogs/makingwaves/russias-oil-leaks-a-forgotten-disaster/blog/40557.*

Dauvergne, Peter. 2008. *The Shadows of Consumption: Consequences for the Global Environment*. Cambridge, MA: MIT Press.

———. 2010. "The Problem of Consumption." *Global Environmental Politics* 10 (2): 1–10.

Farmer, Paul. 2003. *Pathologies of Power: Health, Human Rights, and the New War on the Poor*. Berkeley: University of California Press.

Giagnoni, Silvia. 2011. *Fields of Resistance*. Chicago: Haymarket Books.

Kandel, William. 2008. *Economic Research Service Report Summary: Profile of Hired Farmworkers: A 2008 Update*. Economic Research Report No. (ERR-60), July. Washington, DC: USDA.

King, Donna. 2012. "Toward a Feminist Theory of Letting Go." *Frontiers* 33 (3): 53–70.

Molotch, Harvey. 1970. "Oil in Santa Barbara and Power in America." *Sociological Inquiry* 40 (Winter): 131–44.

Oil Watch. 1999. *The Oil Flows, The Earth Bleeds*. Quito, Ecuador: Oil Watch.

Rees, William E., and Laura Westra. 2003. "When Consumption Does Violence: Can There Be Sustainability and Environmental Justice in a Resource-limited World?" In *Just Sustainabilities: Development in an Unequal World*, edited by Julian Agyeman, Robert D. Bullard, and Bob Evans, 99–124. Cambridge: MIT Press.

Schor, Juliet B. 2010. *True Wealth: How and Why Millions of Americans Are Creating a Time-Rich, Ecologically Light, Small-Scale, High-Satisfaction Economy*. New York: Penguin.

Slavery: A Global Investigation. 2000. Documentary Film. Directed by Brian Edwards and Kate Blewett. Produced by True Vision of London. *vimeo.com/39383629*.

Speth, James Gustave. 2008. *The Bridge at the Edge of the World: Capitalism, the Environment, and Crossing from Crisis to Sustainability*. New Haven: Yale University Press.

Urry, John. 2010. "Consuming the Planet to Excess." *Theory, Culture & Society* 27 (2-3): 191–212.

Widener, Patricia. 2011. *Oil Injustice: Resisting and Conceding a Pipeline in Ecuador*. Lanham MD: Rowman & Littlefield.

———. 2013. "A Protracted Age of Oil: Pipelines, Refineries and Quiet Conflict." *Local Environment: The International Journal of Justice and Sustainability* 18 (7): 834–51. doi:10.1080/13549839.2012.738655.

17

Growing Food, Growing Justice
Letting Go by Holding On to the Feminine Principle

Leontina Hormel and Ryanne Pilgeram

> There is something really powerful about your
> relationship with the land and the earth and dirt. . . .
> I really do feel inspired by the work we do.
> —Polly, a Northwest farm woman

Introduction & Roadmap

In the United States, farmers' markets, CSAs (Community Supported Agriculture) and backyard gardening have become increasingly important ways for people to access food. In Ukraine, small-scale food cultivation gained popularity during World War II and became even more commonplace as the country experienced dramatic social and economic changes in the 1990s. With household gardening's resurgence in a variety of places like these, we wanted to understand the purpose and meaning motivating people's, and particularly women's, participation. Despite the different cultural and economic contexts women and their families navigate in these different places, we find they hold on to similar ethical tenets incompatible with a global market order that prioritizes growth. Instead, they are guided by values supporting social and ecological sustainability, illustrated in the women's stories we describe here.

Our work spans two continents. Leontina's story of women gardeners' battle to eradicate the Colorado beetle on their *dachas* (tiny plots of land in the countryside that urban residents use to grow food) is derived from observations and interviews during eight months of research in central Ukraine where she explored community responses to post-Soviet social change. On the other side of the world, Ryanne looked at issues of inclusion, with a particular focus on gender, race, and class in alternative agriculture. She visited dozens of sustainable farms in the Northwestern United States while interviewing the women who operate or co-operate them.

Part of Ryanne's research takes place in the Palouse, a rich grain-yielding region located along the eastern edge of Washington State, flowing into north-western parts of Idaho. Leontina worked in central Ukraine, which is renowned as part of the breadbasket region because of its high-yielding grain production. Both places, coincidentally, are prized for their thick, rich topsoil, but mass tillage and chemical inputs have degraded both places over the past decades (Reeves 2006; Duffin 2007). Some consider this industrial approach to agriculture as part of a uniquely Western scientific approach that is also strongly associated with Western notions of masculinity, what we call in this paper masculinist agriculture (Shiva 1989; Salatin 2006). Joel Salatin, an alternative agricultural farmer and activist, described it this way at a 2006 colloquium:

> In the Western scientific cult, nature does not speak. Besides, to listen to nature is decidedly feminine. What macho farmer feels empowered if he comes into his beloved's embrace after a long day and to her idyllic question, "Well, my big hunk, what did you do all day?" He exclaims, "Oh, dear, I made the cows happy!" Somehow, to a culture that idolizes pig iron under male thighs, such a day's activity scarcely embodies the Western notion of manliness. A much more manly response is, "Oh, I ripped up 500 acres, killed 2 million earthworms, sprayed 20 pounds of lethal insecticide, and sent 500 tons of topsoil tumbling down the river. I am a man!" (2–3)

In the following pages, we illustrate that as the women we interviewed (and often by extension their families) try to "let go" of the thinking and practices leading to social and ecological degradation associated with masculinist agriculture, they must at the same time "hold on" to an alternative ethic. We argue that Indian activist Vandana Shiva's "feminine principle" offers an effective framework for understanding how families can seek ways to work with community and nature.

The Feminine Principle Defined

When we (Leontina and Ryanne) shared our stories from Ukraine and the Pacific Northwest, we started seeing similarities in our research experiences. Our conversations revealed the people we met during our research were farming and gardening in ways that put Shiva's feminine principle into practice, despite marked differences in their lives. In our experiences, a significant number of people wanted to let go of the notion that masculinist agricultural practices are the most advanced means for food production. Yet, in doing so they had to also hold on to a sense of greater purpose in their food cultivation that was premised on harmony, care, and stewardship—hallmarks of the feminine principle.

The feminine principle as a concept embodies activities and forms of knowledge that privilege a thoughtful relationship with the natural world. Qualities of the feminine principle—harmony, care and stewardship—must each be present. Harmonious relationships with land and communities establish the possibility that all living forms comprising the natural world (not exclusively humans) may be agents for conservation and sustainable change. Caring invokes the emotional connection necessary in legitimating this agency of all living forms, forging a deep commitment to their sustained health. Stewardship, which is typically concerned with managing and protecting the land and the community, when combined with harmony and care illuminates our human responsibility to sustain coexistence with all living forms. In this intimate relationship, nature (as it is commonly perceived), and not just humans, reaps rewards from human communities and thus cares for human communities. These three qualities must work together and be present in order to enact the feminine principle.

While the individuals we feature here happen to be women, we are not arguing (nor is Shiva) that only women are capable of understanding and practicing the feminine principle. As is evident in Joel Salatin's quote, as well as the various men we have met and worked with in the course of our projects, all people are capable of recognizing that industrial agricultural practices are not sustainable. In fact, the success of alternative agriculture is premised on the idea that all people have the capacity to actively reconsider a different kind of relationship with the land. Industrial agriculture which centers on *man*-the-farmer being in constant conflict with nature, a conflict that requires man to dominate nature through the use of fertilizer, pesticides, and perhaps above all else sheer "manpower" (realized through agriculture's increasing mechanization) is often successfully practiced by women (see Beus and Dunlap 1990; Meares 1997; Little 2002; Salatin 2006). Our focus on women food cultivators seeks to illustrate women's perspectives and agency in the larger movement to build new agricultural philosophies and practices.

With the feminine principle guiding them, the women we describe here were primarily interested in producing food safe to grow and eat. They were concerned more with their relationships to their land, neighbors, and families than with profit and growth. In both the United States and Ukraine small-scale, low-input food production is subversive and works outside of the current system. And in the process of holding on to a feminine principle that calls for emotional attachments to natural and social worlds, these women were able to let go of many of the social pressures that often tie one's sense of self to economic growth and materiality.

Notes from Leontina: Battling Frankenbug in Ukraine

I have been interested in understanding how ordinary women and men make ends meet in an economy reeling from massive factory closure and government indebtedness as a consequence of the Soviet Union's collapse (Hormel 2011; Hormel and Southworth 2006). From 2002 to 2003 I spent time in Komsomolsk,

Ukraine, looking at "off-the-books" work (e.g., summer gardening, street bartering, temporary work migration, and garment sweatshops). Of these different work arrangements, laboring on summer gardens (called dachas in Ukraine and Russia) was most common. In a citywide survey I conducted at the time, over 50 percent of Komsomolsk's households reported working summer gardens, and 90 percent of those said their harvests contributed meaningfully to the family budget. National statistics indicate household garden plots can be credited for feeding Ukraine's people throughout the 1990s. For example, households—not industrial agricultural firms—raised 98 percent of Ukraine's potatoes (State Statistics Committee of Ukraine 2002). Yet, despite the evidence of its critical role in feeding the country, policy experts from Western Europe and the United States tend to treat household gardening as a symptom of desperate times, something that will and should wither away as it is replaced by a modern agricultural market. For example, one report by a policy expert argues:

> The Ukrainian rural family is, on average, better off than urban families at the moment. However, that well-being is very much the result of the ability of the rural resident to supply his [sic] own family's needs from his household plot. In that sense, the relative well-being of the villager indicates how far the Ukrainian economy has broken down. In a functioning market economy the vast majority of rural residents would keep gardens to provide themselves fresher food than they could purchase or simply as a hobby, not because they needed it to survive. (Van Atta 1998, 24)

In the above passage, the author assumes families only raise crops to survive a broken down economy. Yet I have met gardeners in Ukraine who also want to provide themselves food without relying on the market. Even the author notes rural families "keep gardens to provide themselves fresher food than they could purchase." And I have found even if households begrudge the immense amount of labor expended on summer gardens, one of the things they value is the ability to keep their foods organic (*ekologicheskie chistii*) by refusing to use chemicals in their gardens. In their view, markets sell poisoned produce, because it is raised on farms applying intensive, chemical-dependent agricultural practices. Thus while policy at the state-level has been wed to the masculinist agricultural model, I encountered household gardeners who questioned its ethics and consciously followed practices embodying their ideals of stewardship, care, and harmony. How people resisted the pressure to participate in the market in their gardening practices was most striking in my encounters with the following women's efforts to control Colorado beetle populations.

The Colorado beetle could also be called masculinist agriculture's Frankenbug, referenced in scientific literature as such a serious threat to potato crops it is "largely responsible for creating the modern insecticide industry" and was among the first pests DDT was used to control (Alyokhin et al. 2008, 398). Unfortunately for potato gardeners in Ukraine, the Colorado beetle (or *Koloradskii Zhuk*) is thriving there. The strategies to control these insatiable bugs came up in conversation often among folks who gardened in Komsomolsk's surrounding countryside. Conversations typically compared the costs and benefits of using store-bought pesticides versus manual practices. A significant number of my acquaintances felt the labor involved in summer gardening was justified since they knew the food they produced was not exposed to chemicals. For this reason, pesticides bought in stores (regularly described as imports from the United States) were viewed negatively and as a sign of Ukraine's social decline. Two women's experiences capture the dilemma Ukraine's summer gardeners face as they try to hold on to the incalculable value of raising ecologically pure food to keep the country's population healthy.

Raisa, a forty-five-year-old state worker, tended a plot she and her husband owned (given in lieu of wage payments from the local mine in the early 1990s) that was located a half-hour bus ride from Komsomolsk. We talked a lot about Ukrainian dachas when working together in town, which eventually led to an invitation to join Raisa in weeding her garden. The early June sun was hot, and the nearby Psol and Dnepr Rivers' steamed the air. Raisa grumbled under her breath as she inspected her potato plants for Colorado beetle larvae, the hungry culprits who—like the adults—are capable of completely defoliating potato plants. Colorado beetle larvae are usually no larger than the tip of a person's pinky, but since their bodies are mostly a reddish-orange color, they are fairly easy to spot with the naked eye. Sure enough, she found an abundant population of them and proceeded to pick larvae off of each plant's leaves and drop them in her red plastic bucket. When satisfied she had removed the bulk of them, she tromped off to the gravel roadway running adjacent to her little plot. She poured the soft-bodied larvae on to the ground and stomped on them repeatedly for a couple of minutes. All the while, I watched Raisa's efforts from where I stood in the middle of the strawberry patch and remarked, "That is a gruesome job. The creatures don't have any chance with you, do they?" Raisa patiently explained that this is the best way to eradicate the beetles without poisoning her garden, which not only killed other creatures but people too. For her, if she was going to go through the effort of raising food, she was going to make sure it worked in harmony with the people and nature around her.

When Ryanne and I talked about how farmers' and gardeners' practices might undermine masculinist agriculture, this experience with Raisa popped immediately to my mind. She didn't enjoy gardening per se (after all, it is not terribly appealing to handle squirming bugs and squish them en masse), but she nonetheless wished to follow responsible practices (i.e., stewardship) that enabled the local ecology, including human communities, to be healthy. Because this was a significant burden added to her busy life, her efforts also showed she cared a great deal about this connection between being a steward and ensuring harmony between humans' and nature's activities. Without caring, it would be difficult to sustain her work.

Another acquaintance of mine, Victoria, was a fifty-six-year-old retired elementary school principal. She worked a deal to lease part of a plot of land her elderly friend, Larissa, tended. A seventy-eight-year-old widow living alone in Dimitrovka, a small village we reached via a twenty-minute train ride or forty-minute bus ride, Larissa merely asked Victoria to run errands in Komsomolsk and to help her mind her health in exchange for using her land. I accompanied Victoria to Larissa's place on several occasions, during which we often talked about Victoria's views of gardening and how economic and political changes affected her. Victoria lamented the increasing dominance of the market in Ukraine, since local products were being beat out by cheap imports, many of which she felt were bad for Ukrainians' health. Among the imports she couldn't stand were sugary soda beverages, but also on the top of her list were chemical pesticides. With a background in botany in her college education, Victoria knew these chemicals were bad for the local ecology (plants, bugs, and water) and peoples' health.

During one summer visit to Larissa's house, the three of us called upon a neighbor, Lara, to celebrate her birthday with tea, moonshine, and cake. We sat around a table situated at a window, lending us a perfect view of Lara's neighbors working their garden. Victoria watched carefully and after a while complained, "Pfff! He is spraying pesticide on their plants, on their food!" The other two women nodded, remarking that more and more people used chemicals as it seemed the easiest way to try to get rid of Colorado beetles, among other pests. To this Victoria rebuffed that they had managed without these chemicals just fine before they began to import them from the United States. When I later checked the accuracy of Victoria's charges, I found that even though Ukraine had a history of industrially producing highly toxic chemical pesticides, domestic production dropped after the Soviet Union's collapse. By 2002, Ukraine imported 115 million dollar's worth of pesticides, and US companies DowAgroSciences, DuPont, Cargill, and Crompton Uniroyal Chemical were the main suppliers ("Total value" 2002).

The story of the Colorado beetle in Ukraine shows how efforts to work in sync with ecological processes are persistently challenged by the systemic quest for profit growth through the vehicle of ever-expanding markets. In Ukraine, household gardening is the new niche for chemical pesticides whose corporations sell the idea of faster, easier pest control. After all, if pest control is easier, a household can grow more food without expending much labor or time. What is also implied is that chemical pesticide use signals scientific advance and human progress. According to the women I (Leontina) encountered this was too good to be true.

The above experiences can be tied back to Shiva (1991), who observes that without the feminine principle as a guide, the rise of industrial agriculture creates more poverty than plenty. Tracing the decline of subsistence agriculture to the imposition of masculine science onto agricultural practices, she notes that where at one time peasants and small farmers gardened with renewable inputs like manure and compost, the Green Revolution set in motion a complex system dependent on non-renewable inputs such as factory produced fertilizers and machinery that degraded ecological and social health (96–97).[1] Furthermore, as Ryanne has described it elsewhere, "the exportation of the Green Revolution from the United States was in part an explicit tool used to control the economies and by extension political ideologies of developing nations that could possibly 'fall' to communism" (Pilgeram 2013, 125). As such, input-intensive agriculture requires not only participation in a highly interdependent and broad-reaching economy, but also larger and larger plots of land to subsidize the expensive equipment used to produce the food.

The feminine principle is not simply reflected in any type of small-scale system. For example, while peasant culture in Ukraine arguably raised food using more sustainable practices, it was also structured within patriarchal relations inconsistent with the tenets of harmony and care (Worobec 1990). Thus the ethics motivating agricultural practice, not just the scale of food production, is critical in posing a true alternative to masculinist agriculture.

Notes from Ryanne: Gardening in the Midst of Wheat

Interviewing farmwomen on the Palouse is not for the faint of heart. Most interviews begin with a trek to the farm with directions that inevitably involve something like, "yeah, take a left past the small barn, I don't think the road itself has a name." Besides roads that are unnamed, unmarked, and occasionally impassable, the trip itself is an important reminder of the challenges faced by people choosing alternative farming methods, methods that are clearly at odds with their neighbors' conventional choices. The dominance of the masculinist agriculture system here is literally written on the land. Fields are alternately planted in dryland wheat or legumes and stretch on beyond the horizon in every direction. And so to farm anything other than these commodity crops on the Palouse requires fortitude and an almost foolhardy sense of the importance of the work you do. It certainly requires letting go of the trappings that signal success in a growth-driven market.

The homes I visit are often humble and in various states of repair or disrepair. Kitchens are mounded with boxes of garlic, or onions, or zucchinis the size of a child's whiffle bat (destined for chicken feed during the winter). But the women I interview, without fail, feel deeply fulfilled by the work they do, work that is dirty, physically demanding, and low paying. In my interview with Alice, a thirty-five-year-old mother of two, she described these demands as well as the negative judgment from her well-to-do family about her choice to farm. Yet she was adamant that the work she was doing would change the world. She stressed the importance of teaching people, especially children, to produce their own food as a way of subverting industrial agriculture and ultimately pro-growth capitalism. She quoted the Dalai Lama–"the world will be saved by the Western woman"—to make her point.[2] Throughout the interview Alice embraced her life and work as deeply meaningful because it produced one of the few things humans really need—food—using methods that protected the environment and, in the process, people.

The desire and ability to let go of not only masculinist farming methods but also the financial successes that come with it requires a long-term vision for the land and people. It implicitly relies on the feminine principle of harmony, care, and stewardship of people, animals, and land. Another farm woman, fifty-three-year-old Polly, was similarly guided by the feminine principle. Despite raising over twenty thousand pounds of pumpkins and gourds a year, she wasn't sure she would consider herself a farmer. Nonetheless, in our discussion of farming she shared her motivation to grow food by noting, "There is something really powerful about your relationship with the land and the earth and dirt. . . . I really do feel inspired by the work we do."

The most powerful examples, however, were the ways the principle was put into practice on the farms and in their relationships with other farmers. I was frequently impressed with how freely the farmers shared information and even resources among themselves. During a monthly food coalition meeting for the community, this was illustrated when two women spoke about the challenges of finding a place to process food for the farmers' market. The lack of a commercial kitchen in town, coupled with strict FDA laws, has been a source of constant frustration. As a consequence one farmer borrowed money from her parents to build a small commercial kitchen on the farm and is now letting people who need it rent it out. Someone pressed the farmer about how much she is renting the kitchen out for, and she quietly said, "$30 a month" before adding that she doesn't need the kitchen every day, all day, so it only makes sense to share the space. A member of the business community seemed frustrated and taken aback by this low fee and pressed her to explain how she was going to grow her own business if she didn't charge more—and offered up an example of a local hummus maker who recently sold out to Starbucks—as a sort of gold standard. Her response was measured, and she made it clear that her goal was to provide food for her community, to help the other woman provide food to the community, and that her aspirations did not involve selling anything to Starbucks.

In another example of the feminine principle in practice, Hillary, a sixty-two-year-old woman who raised sheep, discussed the lengths she went to raise healthy animals without any chemicals—these included wormers or vaccines.

She told the story of a neighbor who had moved to the Palouse and called Hillary up to introduce herself and talk about the sheep. Hillary recalled:

> I don't know how she got my number, but she called me up and said she wanted introduce herself to me because she's been driving by my place for months now and those sheep look like they're cared for by a woman. I just thought, yes! She knew what she was talking about, she knew sheep, and she knew what she was looking at. There's a difference. There's a glow about them. Of course I'm prejudiced, but that's for raising livestock. In produce I think all the same qualities carry over. Women are nurturers by nature. The chemical approach is not a real, true, shortcut. That's what it was sold as in the forties and fifties and it's not a shortcut. There are no shortcuts. Women intuitively know this.

These examples suggest there are real alternatives to masculinist farming that embrace and value nurturing and caring for the land and for the community. Because these traits are popularly understood as feminine in the United States, it is not surprising some women would be attracted to them, but the women I interviewed were passionate and opinionated. Some were angry, some were quiet, but they all were deeply motivated to do good work for their communities. These were not women who took a back seat on their farms. While most had male partners, these women were central to the success of their farms. They did the dirty work of caring for livestock and did backbreaking labor year round. They also understood how important they were not only on their farms but also within a larger movement to change the structure of the US food system.

Women Food Growers Holding On while Letting Go

The practice of growing food links our (Leontina and Ryanne's) research. Though Ryanne has yet to be offered a cup of moonshine during an interview, we nonetheless share experiences of watching women labor to produce food for their communities. We've spent cold wet springs in the fields with our informants while they tended seedlings, and hot steamy summer days helping them fight pests and weeds. Across thousands of miles these women's stories are linked by their desire to connect with the land for their own good and the good of their communities.

Of course, the market is clearly pushing back in powerful ways that destabilize the work these women and many, many others like them are doing. In Ukraine, dachas are described as old-fashioned, burdensome, and unnecessary in contemporary society. Instead of a means for independence, they are treated as symptoms of an ailing economy. Western policy reports encourage families to put away their shovels and to let mass food production and the market handle food provisioning. Progress is measured by the number of families buying it all in grocery stores, not by their ability to avoid shopping trips. Those that continue to grow food are bombarded with cheap imported pesticides dominating stores' shelves and advertisement space. In such an exhausting practice of traveling to the countryside and laboring in gardens during families' precious free time, the ease and convenience of artificial pest control is difficult to refuse. Yet, the women that Leontina describes did refuse.

Women in the United States face a different, but equally powerful, pressure. As the alternative food system becomes more potent in the United States, it risks being co-opted into consumer culture or creating a system where women feel pushed into gardening as part of the regime of the "perfect" mother or woman, even when their talents and interest lie elsewhere. When the Pottery Barn begins selling bee keeping kits and gardening clogs become fashionable, we'll know the danger of turning household gardening into a hip consumer trend is a reality— blurring the point at which such practices are about systemic change versus personal choice. Forget bringing home the bacon and frying it up in the pan (and never, ever letting him forget he's a man)—there is a danger that on top of this women are now supposed to raise the damn pig and serve it with homegrown arugula too. In the age of the yummy mummy urban farmer blogger, where a deluxe chicken coop seems to be equivalent to a bigger diamond ring in some circles, there is a real danger in the United States of the alternative food movement being co-opted. There is a danger of alternative farming practices being added to the never-ending list of things the perfect woman does.

Furthermore, there is a great deal of pressure on alternative farmers to protect "their" share of the market, which is why farmers' market boards often face contentious battles about what a "farmer" is and what "local" means. This is evident in practices such as plowing under edible food in order to increase the food's value at the farmers' market and prohibiting nonprofit food bank farms from selling their surplus at the farmers' market to raise money for improvements (Pilgeram 2011). Thus, while the farming practices themselves may be expressions of a deep concern for the health of ecological processes on the land, the pressure to produce a profit—over distributing food from these small-scale farms—often occurs at the expense of human communities that are also central to the feminine principle.

Despite these very real risks of alternative agriculture's co-optation by the market or through efforts making their work seem old-fashioned, we are convinced that, if we could bring together the women we describe here, they would remind us they are aware of these risks but refuse to be defined by them. They would tell us that they are too busy doing the work of growing food, too busy lambing or battling the Frankenbug to spend their energies worrying about "market forces." These women are not terribly nostalgic or romantic about the work they do, but they find it rewarding because they are doing it right. If we could bring them together they would be intrigued by each other, they would talk about their jobs and their families, and they would spend days talking about how to coax the last tomatoes and eggplants of the season to ripen or discussing the various techniques for trapping slugs and catching grasshoppers without relying on pesticides.

The women we describe live in places with different histories and markets, and yet they share the desire to produce food using methods consistent with their values. They share an understanding that there ought to be, and there is, an alternative to masculinist agriculture. We contend this alternative puts the tenets embodying the feminine principle—care, harmony, and stewardship—into action, which distinguishes it from small-scale food systems that don't let go of systems that subordinate women and nature. These women share a principle that what they do is valuable, even if it doesn't generate income, and that they can use their hands, their heads, their backs, and perhaps even their hearts to let go of at least some of the demands of growth-driven capitalism. In advanced capitalist economies where everything is for sale and everything has a price, where things go quickly in and out of fashion, growing a potato from one saved by your neighbor and shared over a potluck dinner is a revolutionary act. We are convinced these women are able to let go of some of these demands of material culture because they are guided by the feminine principle that offers something meaningful to hold on to.

NOTES

Authors are listed in alphabetical order, authorship is equal. Email contact information: *lhormel@uidaho.edu* and *rpilgeram@uidaho.edu*.

1. The Green Revolution has been credited for advancing the mass production of food throughout the world and was set in motion in the 1960s by technological advances in areas of agricultural machinery, chemicals, and plant sciences. Critics like Shiva point out that the revolution has also produced many costs to both the human and natural worlds.

2. The Dalai Lama is reported to have delivered this quote during the Vancouver Peace Summit, which opened on Sunday, September 27, 2009. *www.dharmacafe.com/ index.php/news-briefs/articlethe-dalai-lama-the-world-will-be-saved-by-the-western-woman*.

REFERENCES

Alyokhin, Andrei, Mitchell Baker, David Mota-Sanchez, Galen Dively, and Edward Grafius. 2008. "Colorado Beetle Resistance to Insecticides." *American Journal of Potato Research* 85 (6): 395–413.

Beus, Curtis E., and Riley E. Dunlap. 1990. "Conventional Versus Alternative Agriculture: The Paradigmatic Roots of the Debate." *Rural Sociology* 55:590–616.

Duffin, Andrew P. 2007. *Plowed Under: Agriculture and Environment in the Palouse.* Seattle: University of Washington Press.

Hormel, Leontina M. 2011. "Gender, Class, and Garment Work Reorganization in Ukraine." *GENDER. Zeitschrift für Geschlecht, Kultur und Gesellschaft* Special Issue 1:10–25.

Hormel, Leontina M., and Caleb Southworth. 2006. "Eastward Bound: A Case Study of Post-Soviet Labor Migration from a Rural Ukrainian Town." *Europe-Asia Studies* 58 (4): 603–23.

Little, Jo. 2002. "Rural Geography: Rural Gender Identity and the Performance of Masculinity and Femininity in the Countryside." *Progress in Human Development* 23:437–42.

Meares, Alison C. 1997. "Making the Transition from Conventional to Sustainable Agriculture: Gender, Social Movement Participation, and Quality of Life on the Family Farm." *Rural Sociological Society* 62 (1): 21–47.

Pilgeram, Ryanne. 2011. "'The Only Thing That Isn't Sustainable . . . Is the Farmer': Social Sustainability and the Politics of Class Among Pacific Northwest Sustainable Farmers," *Rural Sociology* 76:375–93.

———. 2013. "The Political and Economic Consequences of Defining Sustainable Agriculture in the US." *Sociology Compass* 7 (2): 123–34.

Reeves, D. Wayne. 2006. *Why Take the No-Till Path?* USDA Agricultural Research Service, September 6. Watkinsville, GA: J. Phil Campbell Sr. Natural Resource Conservation Center.

Salatin, Joel. 2006. "Holy Cows and Hog Heaven." Paper presented for the Program in Agrarian Studies Colloquium Series, 2005–2006, Yale University, New Haven, CT, January. *www.yale.edu/agrarianstudies/colloqpapers/14salatin.pdf.*

Shiva, Vandana. (1989) 1991. *Staying Alive: Women, Ecology and Development.* Atlantic Highlands, NJ: Zed Books.

State Statistics Committee of Ukraine. 2002. Статистичний Шорічник України 2001 (*Statistical Yearbook of Ukraine 2001*). Kyiv: Tekhnika.

"Total Value of Pesticide Imports to Ukraine Will Be $115mln," August 14, 2002, *www.fruit-inform.com/en/news/4628.*

Van Atta, Don. 1998. *Ukrainian Rural and Urban Residents' Incomes and Expenses, 1996–97. Staff Analysis Series, Number 47.* Kyiv, Ukraine: Center for Privatization and Economic Reform in Agriculture.

Worobec, Christine D. 1990. "Temptress or Virgin? The Precarious Sexual Position of Women in Postemancipation Ukrainian Peasant Society." *Slavic Review* 49 (2): 227–38.

Part Five

Visionary Feminism

18

Dig Deep
Beyond Lean In

bell hooks

A year ago [in 2012], few folks were talking about Sheryl Sandberg. Her thoughts on feminism were of little interest. More significantly, there was next-to-no public discussion of feminist thinking and practice. Rarely, if ever, was there any feminist book mentioned as a bestseller and certainly not included on the *New York Times* Best Seller list. Those of us who have devoted lifetimes to teaching and writing theory, explaining to the world the ins and outs of feminist thinking and practice, have experienced that the primary audience for our work is an academic subculture. In recent years, discussions of feminism have not evoked animated passion in audiences. We were far more likely to hear that we are living in a post-feminist society than to hear voices clamoring to learn more about feminism. This seems to have changed with Sandberg's book *Lean In* (2013), holding steady on the *Times* Best Seller list for more than sixteen weeks [at the time of this writing].

No one was more surprised than long-time advocates of feminist thinking and practice to learn via mass media that a new high priestess of feminist movement was on the rise. Suddenly, as if by magic, mass media brought into public consciousness conversations about feminism, reframing the scope and politics through an amazing feat of advertising. At the center of this drama was a young, high-level corporate executive, Sheryl Sandberg, who was dubbed by Oprah Winfrey and other popular culture pundits as "the new voice of revolutionary feminism." *Forbes Magazine* proclaimed Sandberg to be one of the most influential women in the world, if not the most. *Time Magazine* ranked her one of a hundred of the most powerful and influential world leaders. All over mass media, her book *Lean In* has been lauded as a necessary new feminist manifesto.

Yet Sandberg confesses to readers that she has not been a strong advocate

Originally published in *The Feminist Wire*, October 28, 2013.
Reprinted with permission. *thefeministwire.com*.

of feminist movement, that like many women of her generation, she hesitated when it came to aligning herself with feminist concerns. She explains:

> I headed into college believing that the feminists of the sixties and seventies had done the hard work of achieving equality for my generations. And yet, if anyone had called me a feminist I would have quickly corrected that notion. . . . On one hand, I started a group to encourage more women to major in economics and government. On the other hand, I would have denied being in any way, shape, or form a feminist. None of my college friends thought of themselves as feminists either. It saddens me to admit that we did not see the backlash against women around us. . . . In our defense, my friends and I truly, if naively, believed that the world did not need feminists anymore.

Although Sandberg revised her perspective on feminism, she did not turn toward primary sources (the work of feminist theorists) to broaden her understanding. In her book, she offers a simplistic description of the feminist movement based on women gaining equal rights with men. This construction of simple categories (women and men) was long ago challenged by visionary feminist thinkers, particularly individual black women/women of color. These thinkers insisted that everyone acknowledge and understand the myriad ways race, class, sexuality, and many other aspects of identity and difference made explicit that there is not now and never was a simple homogenous gendered identity that we could call "women" struggling to be equal with men. In fact, the reality was and is that privileged white women often experience a greater sense of solidarity with men of their same class than with poor white women or women of color.

Sandberg's definition of feminism begins and ends with the notion that it's all about gender equality within the existing social system. From this perspective, the structures of imperialist white supremacist capitalist patriarchy need not be challenged. And she makes it seem that privileged white men will eagerly choose to extend the benefits of corporate capitalism to white women who have the courage to "lean in." It almost seems as if Sandberg sees women's lack of perseverance as more the problem than systemic inequality. Sandberg effectively uses her race and class power and privilege to promote a narrow definition of feminism that obscures and undermines visionary feminist concerns.

Contrast her definition of feminism with the one I offered more than twenty years ago in *Feminist Theory from Margin to Center* ([1984] 2000) and then again in *Feminism Is For Everybody* (2000). Offering a broader definition of feminism, one that does not conjure up a battle between the sexes (i.e., women against men), I state: "Simply put, feminism is a movement to end sexism, sexist exploitation, and oppression." No matter their standpoint, anyone who advocates feminist politics needs to understand the work does not end with the fight for equality of opportunity within the existing patriarchal structure. We must understand that challenging and dismantling patriarchy is at the core of contemporary feminist struggle–this is essential and necessary if women and men are to be truly liberated from outmoded sexist thinking and actions.

Ironically, Sandberg's work would not have captured the attention of progressives, particularly men, if she had not packaged the message of "let's go forward and work as equals with white male corporate elites" in the wrapping paper of feminism. In the "one hundred most influential people in the world" issue of *Time Magazine,* the forty-three-year old Facebook COO was dubbed by the doyen of women's liberation movement, Gloria Steinem, in her short commentary, "feminism's new boss." That same magazine carried a full page ad for the book *Lean In: Women, Work, and The Will to Lead* that carried the heading "Inspire the graduate in your life" with a graduating picture of two white females and one white male. The ad included this quote from Sandberg's commencement speech at Barnard College in 2011: "I hope that you have the ambition to lean in to your career and run the world. Because the world needs you to change it." One can only speculate whether running the world is a call to support and perpetuate first world imperialism. This is precisely the type of feel-good declaration Sandberg makes that in no way clarifies the embedded agenda she supports.

Certainly, her vision of individual women leaning in at the corporate table does not include any clear statements of which group of women she is speaking to and about, and the "lean in" woman is never given a racial identity. If Sandberg had acknowledged that she was primarily addressing privileged white women like herself (a small group working at the top of the corporate hierarchy), then she could not have portrayed herself as sharing a message, indeed a life lesson, for *all* women. Her basic insistence that gender equality should be important to all women and men is an insight that all folks involved in feminist movement agree is a central agenda. And yes, who can dispute the facts Sandberg offers as evidence; despite the many gains in female freedom, implicit gender bias remains the norm throughout our society. Patriarchy supports and affirms that bias. But Sandberg offers readers no understanding of what men must do to unlearn sexist thinking. At no point in *Lean In* does she let readers know what would motivate patriarchal white males in a corporate environment to change their belief system or the structures that support gender inequality.

Readers who only skim the surface of Sheryl Sandberg's book *Lean In* will find much they can agree with. Very few, if any, professional women will find themselves at odds with a fellow female who champions the cause of gender equality, who shares with us all the good old mother wisdom that one of the most important choices any of us will make in life is who we will partner with. And she shares that the best partner is one who, she tells readers, will be a helpmeet—one who cares and shares. Sandberg's insistence that men participate equally in parenting is no new clarion call. From its earliest inception, the feminist movement called attention to the need for males to participate in parenting; it let women and men know that heteronormative relationships where there was gender equality not only lasted but were happier than the sexist norm.

Sandberg encourages women to seek high-level corporate jobs and persevere until they reach the top. For many individual women, Sandberg telling them that they would not be betraying family if they dedicated themselves to work was affirming. It is positive in that it seemed to be a necessary response to popular antifeminist backlash, which continually suggests that the feminist push to place more women in the workforce was and is a betrayal of marriage and family.

Unfortunately her voice is powerful, yet Sandberg is for the most part not voicing any new ideas. She is simply taking old ideas and giving them a new twist. When the book *Lean In* began its meteoric rise, which continues to bring fame and notoriety to Sandberg, many prominent feminists and/or progressive women denounced the work, vehemently castigating Sandberg. However, there was just one problematic issue at the core of the anti-Sandberg movement; very few folks attacking the work had actually read the book. Some of them had heard sound bites on television or had listened to her TED Talk presentation. Still others had seen her interviewed. Many of these older female feminist advocates blatantly denounced the work and boldly announced their refusal to read the book.

As a feminist cultural critic, I found the eagerness with which Sandberg was viciously attacked disheartening. These critiques seem to emerge from misplaced rage not based solely on contempt for her ideas, but a rage bordering on envy. The powerful white-male-dominated mass media was giving her and those ideas so much attention. There was no in-depth discussion of why this was the case. In the book Sandberg reminds readers that "men still run the world." However, she does not discuss white male supremacy. Or the extent to which globalization has changed the makeup of corporate elites. In Mark Mizruchi's (2013) book *The Fracturing of the American Corporate Elite*, he describes a corporate world that is made up of a "more diverse crowd," one that is no longer white and male "blue chip dudes." He highlights several examples: "The CEO of Coca-Cola is Muhtar Kent, who was born in the United States but raised in Turkey; PepsiCo is run by Indra Nooyi, an Indian woman who came to America in her twenties. Burger King's CEO is Brazilian, Chryslers's CEO is Italian, and Morgan Stanley's CEO is Australian. Forget about influencing policy; many of today's leading US CEO's can't even vote here." Perhaps, even in the corporate world, imperialist white supremacist capitalist patriarchy is ready to accept as many white women as necessary to ensure white dominance. Race is certainly an invisible category in Sandberg's corporate fantasy world.

Sandberg is most seductive when sharing personal anecdotes. It is these true-life stories that expose the convenient lies underlying most of her assertions that as more women are at the top, all women will benefit. She explains: "Conditions for all women will improve when there are more women in leadership roles giving strong and powerful voice to their needs and concerns." This unsubstantiated truism is brought to us by a corporate executive who does not recognize the needs of pregnant women until it's happening to her. Is this a case of narcissism as a potential foundation for female solidarity? No behavior in the real world of women relating to women proves this to be true. In truth, Sandberg offers no strategies for the building of feminist solidarity between women.

She makes light of her ambivalence toward feminism. Even though Sandberg can humorously poke fun at herself and her relationship to feminism, she tells readers that her book "is not a feminist manifesto." Adding as though she is in a friendly conversation with herself, "okay, it is sort of a feminist manifesto." This is just one of the "funny" folksy moments in the book, which represent her plain and ordinary approach—she is just one of the girls. Maybe doing the book and talking about it with cowriter Nell Scovell provides the basis for the conversational tone. Good humor aside, cute quips and all, it is when she is taking about feminism that many readers would have liked her to go deeper. How about just explaining what she means by "feminist manifesto," since the word implies "a full public declaration of intentions, opinions or purposes." Of course, historically the best feminist manifestos emerged from collective consciousness raising and discussion. They were not the voice of one individual. Instead of creating a space of female solidarity, Sandberg exists as the lone queen amid millions of admirers. And no one in her group dares to question how she could be heralded as the "voice of revolutionary feminism."

How feminist, how revolutionary can a powerful rich woman be when she playfully admits that she concedes all money management and bill paying to her husband? As Sandberg confesses, she would rather not think about money matters when she could be planning little Dora parties for her kids. This anecdote, like many others in the book, works to create the personal image of Sandberg. It is this "just plain folks" image that has been instrumental in her success, for it shows her as vulnerable.

This is not her only strategy. When giving filmed lectures, she wears clothes with sexy deep V-necks and stiletto heels and this image creates the aura of vulnerable femininity. It reminds one of the popular television advertisement from years ago wherein a sexy white woman comes home and dances around singing: "I can bring home the bacon, fry it up in the pan and never let you forget you're a man . . . 'cause I'm a w-o-m-a-n!" Sandberg's constructed image is not your usual sexist misogynist media portrayal of a feminist. She is never depicted as a man-hating, ball-busting feminist nag.

Instead, she comes across both in her book and when performing on stages as a lovable younger sister who just wants to play on the big brother's team. It would be more in keeping with this image to call her brand of women's liberation *faux feminism*. A billionaire, one of the richest women in the world, Sandberg deflects attention from this reality. To personify it might raise critical questions. It might even have created the conditions for other women to feel threatened by her success. She solves that little problem by never speaking of money in *Lean In*; she uses the word once.

And if that reality does not bring to her persona enough I'M EVERY-WOMAN appeal, she tells her audiences: "I truly believe that the single most important career decision that a woman makes is whether she will have a life partner or who that partner is." Even though most women, straight or gay, have not seen choosing a life partner as a "career decision," anyone who advocates feminist politics knows that the choice of a partner matters. However, Sandberg's convenient use of the word partner masks the reality that she is really speaking about heteronormative partnerships, and even more specifically marriages between white women and white men. She shares: "Contrary to the popular notion that only unmarried women can make it to the top, the majority of the more successful female business leaders have partners." Specifically, though not directly, she is talking about white male husbands. For after telling readers that the most successful women at the top are partnered, she highlights the fact that "of the twenty-eight women who have served as CEO's of Fortune 500 companies, twenty- six were married, one was divorced and only one was never married." Again, no advocates of feminism would disagree with the notion that individual women should choose partners wisely. Good partners, as defined by the old-style women's liberation movement and reiterated by Sandberg (who makes it seem that this is a new insight), are those who embrace equality, who care and share. One of the few radical arguments in *Lean In* is that men should come to the table—"the kitchen table." This is rarely one of the points Sandberg highlights in her media performances.

Of course, the vast majority of men in our society, irrespective of race, embrace patriarchal values; they do not embrace a vision or practice of gender equality either at work or in the domestic household. Anyone who acts as though women just need to make right choices is refusing to acknowledge the reality that men must also be making the right choice. Before females even reach the stage of life where choosing partners is important, we should all be developing financial literacy, preparing ourselves to manage our money well, so that we need not rely on finding a sharing partner who will manage our finances fairly. According to *More Magazine*, American women are expected to control 23 trillion dollars by the end of the decade, which is "nearly twice the current amount." But what will this control mean if women lack financial literacy? Acquiring money and managing money are not the same actions. Women need to confront the meaning and uses of money on all levels. This is knowledge Sandberg the Chief Operating Officer possesses even if she coyly pretends otherwise.

In her 2008 book *The Comeback*, Emma Gilbey Keller examines many of the issues Sandberg addresses. Significantly, and unlike Sandberg, she highlights the need for women to take action on behalf of their financial futures. One chapter in the book begins with the epigram: "A woman's best production is a little money of her own." Given the huge amounts of money Sandberg has acquired, ostensibly by paying close attention to her financial future, her silence on the subject of money in *Lean In* undermines the call for genuine equality. Without the ability to be autonomous, in control of self and finances, women will not have the strength and confidence to lean in.

Mass media (along with Sandberg) is telling us that by sheer strength of will and staying power, any woman so inclined can work hard and climb the corporate ladder all the way to the top. Shrewdly, Sandberg acknowledges that not all women desire to rise to the top, asserting that she is not judging women who make different choices. However, the real truth is that she is making judgments about the nature of women and work—that is what the book is fundamentally about. Her failure to confront the issue of women acquiring wealth allows her to ignore concrete systemic obstacles most women face inside the workforce. And by not confronting the issue of women and wealth, she need not confront the issue of women and poverty. She need not address the ways extreme class differences make it difficult for there to be a common sisterhood based on shared struggle and solidarity.

The contemporary feminist movement has not concentrated meaningful attention on the issue of women and wealth. Rightly, however, the movement highlighted the need for gender equity in the workforce—equal pay for equal work. This economic focus exposed the reality that race was a serious factor over-determining women's relationship to work and money. Much feminist thought by individual visionary women of color (especially black women thinkers) and white female allies called for a more accurate representation of female identity, one that would consider the reality of intersectionality. This theory encouraged women to see race and class as well as gender as crucial factors shaping female destiny. Promoting a broader insight, this work laid the ground for the formation of genuine female solidarity—a solidarity based on awareness of difference as well as the all-too-common gendered experiences women share. It has taken many years of hard work to create basic understandings of female identity; it will take many more years for solidarity between women to become reality.

It should surprise no one that women and men who advocate feminist politics were stunned to hear Sandberg promoting her trickle-down theory: the assumption that having more women at the top of corporate hierarchies would make the work world better for all women, including women on the bottom. Taken at face value, this seems a naive hope given that the imperialist white supremacist capitalist patriarchal corporate world Sandberg wants women to lean into encourages competition over cooperation. Or as Kate Losse (2012), author of *The Boy Kings: A Journey into the Heart of the Social Network*, which is an insider look at the real gender politics of Facebook, contends: "By arguing that women should express their feminism by remaining in the workplace at all costs, Sandberg encourages women to maintain a commitment to the workplace without encouraging the workplace to maintain a commitment to them." It is as though Sandberg believes a subculture of powerful elite women will emerge in the workplace, powerful enough to silence male dominators.

Yet Sandberg spins her seductive fantasy of female solidarity as though comradely support between women will magically occur in patriarchal work environments. Since patriarchy has no gender, women leaning in will not automatically think in terms of gender equality and solidarity. Like the issue of money, patriarchy is another subject that receives little attention in Sandberg's book and in her many talks. This is ironic, since the vision of gender quality she espouses is most radically expressed when she is delineating what men need to do to work for change. It is precisely her avoidance of the difficult questions (like how will patriarchal thinking change) that empowers her optimism and the overall enthusiastic spirit she exudes. Her optimism is so affably intense, it encourages readers to bypass the difficulties involved in challenging and changing patriarchy so that a just moral and ethical foundation for gender equality would become the norm.

Women, and our male allies in struggle, who have been on the frontlines of feminist thinking and practice, see clearly the fairytale evocation of harmonious solidarity is no easy task. Given all the forces that separate women and pit us against one another, solidarity is not an inevitable outcome. Sandberg's refusal to do anything but give slight mention to racialized class differences undercuts the notion that she has a program that speaks to and for all women. Her unwillingness to consider a vision that would include all women rather than white women from privileged classes is one of the flaws in the representation of herself as a voice for feminism. Certainly she is a powerful mentor figure for fiscally conservative white female elites. The corporate infusion of gender equality she evokes is a "whites only" proposition.

To women of color young and old, along with antiracist white women, it is more than obvious that without a call to challenge and change racism as an integral part of class mobility she is really investing in top level success for highly educated women from privileged classes. The call for gender equality in corporate America is undermined by the practice of exclusivity, and usurped by the heteronormative white supremacist bonding of marriage between white women and men. Founded on the principles of white supremacy and structured to maintain it, the rites of passage in the corporate world mirror this aspect of our nation. Let it be stated again and again that race, and more importantly white supremacy, is a taboo subject in the world according to Sandberg.

At times Sandberg reminds readers of the old stereotypes about used car salesmen. She pushes her product and she pushes it well. Her spiel is so good, so full of stuff that is obviously true, that one is inclined to overlook all that goes unspoken, unexplained. For example, she titles a chapter "You Can't Have It All," warning women that this idea is one of the most dangerous concepts from the early feminist movement. But the real deal is that Sandberg has it all, and in a zillion little ways she flaunts it. Even though she epitomizes the "have it all kinda girl"—white, rich, and married to a wonderful husband (like the television evangelist Joyce Meyer, Sandberg is constantly letting readers know how wonderful her husband is lest we forget)—she claims women can't have it all. She even dedicated the book to her husband "for making everything possible"—what doesn't she have? Sandberg confesses that she has a loving family and children, more helpers in daily life than one can count. Add this to the already abundant list, she is deemed by the larger conservative media to be one of "the most influential," most powerful women in the world. If this is not another version of the old game show "Queen for a Day," what is? Remember that the women on the show are puppets and white men behind the scenes are pulling the strings.

Even though many advocates of feminist politics are angered by Sandberg's message, the truth is that alone, individually, she was no threat to the feminist movement. Had the conservative white male dominated world of mass media and advertising not chosen to hype her image, this influential woman would not be known to most folks. It is this patriarchal male dominated reframing of feminism, which uses the body and personal success of Sheryl Sandberg, that is most disturbing, and yes threatening, to the future of visionary feminist movement. The model Sandberg represents is all about how women can participate and "run the world." But of course the kind of world we would be running is never defined. It sounds at times like benevolent patriarchal imperialism. This is the reason it seemed essential for feminist thinkers to respond critically, not just to Sandberg and her work, but to the conservative white male patriarchy that is using her to let the world know what kind of woman partner is acceptable among elites, both in the home and in the workplace.

Feminism is just the screen masking this reframing. Angela McRobbie (2009) offers an insightful take on this process in her book *The Aftermath of Feminism: Gender, Culture, and Social Change*, explaining:

> Elements of feminism have been taken into account and have been absolutely incorporated into political and institutional life. Drawing on a vocabulary that includes words like "empowerment" and "choice," these elements are then converted into a much more individualistic discourse and they are deployed in this new guise, particularly in media and popular culture, but also by agencies of the state, as a kind of substitute for feminism. These new and seemingly modern ideas about women and especially young women are then disseminated more aggressively so as to ensure that a new women's movement will not re-emerge.

This is so obviously the strategy Sandberg and her supporters have deployed. McRobbie then contends that "feminism is instrumentalized. It is brought forth and claimed by Western governments, as a signal to the rest of the world that this is a key part of what freedom now means. Freedom is re-vitalized and brought up to date with this faux feminism." Sandberg uses feminist rhetoric as a front to cover her commitment to Western cultural imperialism, to white supremacist capitalist patriarchy.

Clearly, Sandberg, with her website and her foundation, has many female followers. Long before she was chosen by conservative mass media as the new face of faux feminism, she had her followers. This is why I chose to call my response "dig deep," for it is only as we place her in the overall frame of female cultural icons that we can truly unpack and understand why she has been chosen and lifted up in the neoliberal marketplace. Importantly, whether feminist or not, we all need to remember that visionary feminist goal which is not of a women running the world as is, but as women doing our part to change the world so that freedom and justice, the opportunity to have optimal well-being, can be equally shared by everyone—female and male.

REFERENCES

hooks, bell. (1984) 2000. *Feminist Theory From Margin to Center*. Cambridge, MA: South End Press.

———. 2000. *Feminism is for Everyone: Passionate Politics*. Cambridge, MA: South End Press.

Keller, Emma Gilbey. 2008. *The Comeback*. New York: Bloomsbury.

Losse, Kate. 2012. *The Boy Kings: A Journey into the Heart of the Social Network*. New York: Free Press.

McRobbie, Angela. 2009. *The Aftermath of Feminism: Gender, Culture, and Social Change*. London: Sage.

Mizruchi, Mark S. 2013. *The Fracturing of the American Corporate Elite*. Cambridge, MA: Harvard University Press.

Sandberg, Sheryl. 2103. *Lean In: Women, Work, and the Will to Lead*. New York: Knopf.

Contributors

Tracy B. Citeroni is associate professor of sociology at the University of Mary Washington in Fredericksburg, VA. She is a feminist scholar with a PhD from the University of Texas at Austin and specializes in the study of gender and health using qualitative research methods.

Deborah J. Cohan is assistant professor of sociology at the University of South Carolina-Beaufort, where she teaches about domestic and sexual violence, feminist theory and practice, and service learning and civic engagement. She is currently working on two projects, about intimacy and violence, and caring for an ill and elderly parent.

Kevin J. Delaney is professor of sociology and vice dean for faculty affairs in the College of Liberal Arts at Temple University. He is author of *Public Dollars, Private Stadiums: The Battle over Building Sports Stadiums*; *Strategic Bankruptcy: How Corporations and Creditors Use Chapter 11 to Their Advantage*; and *Money at Work: On the Job with Priests, Poker Players and Hedge Fund Traders*.

Steven Farough is associate professor of sociology at Assumption College in Worcester, MA. His recent publications include "White Masculinities in the Age of Obama: Rebuilding or Reloading?" in *American Identity in the Age of Obama* and "The End of Men?" in *Understanding and Managing Diversity: Readings, Cases, & Exercises*. He is currently writing a book on stay-at-home fathers.

Haley Gentile is a graduate student in the department of sociology at Florida State University, where her research interests include social movements, mass media, sexualities, processes of inequality, and political sociology. She is coauthor of "Moral Identity in Friendships between Gay, Lesbian, Bisexual Students and Straight Students in College" in *Symbolic Interactionism*.

Roxanne Gerbrandt is associate professor of sociology at Austin Peay State University in Clarksville, TN, where she teaches and conducts research on national and global systems of stratification. She is coauthor of "Hearing Social Structure: A Musical Exercise in Teaching Introduction to Sociology," and coauthor of a chapter in *Sociology for the Curious: Why Study Sociology*.

bell hooks is distinguished professor in Appalachian Studies at Berea College in Berea, KY. She is a noted cultural critic, commentator, and feminist, and author of over thirty books, including *Ain't I a Woman?*, *Feminist Theory from Margin* to Center, *All About Love*, *Writing Beyond Race*, and *Appalachian Elegy: Poetry and Place*.

Leontina Hormel is associate professor of sociology at the University of Idaho where she teaches and conducts research on gender and class inequalities, international political economy, and environmental sociology. She has published in *Critical Sociology*, *Europe-Asia Studies*, *Humanity & Society*, *GENDER: Zeitschrift für Geschlecht, Kultur und Gesellschaf*, and in several edited volumes.

Shirley A. Jackson is professor of sociology and founder and co-coordinator of the Ethnic Studies minor at Southern Connecticut State University. She is editor of *The Routledge International Handbook of Race, Class, and Gender* and is currently working on an analysis of race, gender, nationality, and violence in editorial cartoons during WWII, the Civil Rights era, and post-9/11.

Robert Jensen is professor in the School of Journalism at the University of Texas at Austin and board member of the Third Coast Activist Resource Center in Austin. He is author of *Arguing for Our Lives: A User's Guide to Constructive Dialogue*; *Getting Off: Pornography and the End of Masculinity*; and *The Heart of Whiteness: Confronting Race, Racism and White Privilege*.

Donna King is professor of sociology and associate department chair at the University of North Carolina Wilmington, where she teaches courses in media and popular culture. She is author of *Doing Their Share to Save the Planet: Children and Environmental Crisis*, and coeditor of *Men Who Hate Women and Women Who Kick Their Asses: Stieg Larsson's Millennium Trilogy in Feminist Perspective*.

Liza Kurtz graduated from Austin Peay State University with a BS in Sociology in 2011. She is a doctoral student in global health at Arizona State University, where she studies emergency and disaster.

Diane E. Levy is professor of sociology at the University of North Carolina Wilmington where she was founding director of the Honors Scholars program. Her most recent publication is a chapter in *Men Who Hate Women and Women Who Kick Their Asses: Stieg Larsson's Millennium Trilogy in Feminist Perspective*.

David R. Loy is a professor, writer, and Zen teacher. He focuses primarily on the encounter between Buddhism and modernity, and is especially concerned about social and ecological issues. His latest book is *A New Buddhist Path: Emptiness, Ecology, and Ethics in the Modern World*.

Anthony C. Ocampo is assistant professor of sociology at California State Polytechnic University Pomona, one of the most racially diverse campuses in the nation. A graduate of Stanford University and the University of California Los Angeles, he is currently finishing his first book, *The Latinos of Asia: How Filipinos Break the Rules of Race*.

Ryanne Pilgeram is assistant professor of sociology at the University of Idaho where she teaches on food systems and sustainability in addition to courses on race, gender, and class. Her work on issues of social inclusion and social justice within sustainable agriculture has recently appeared in *Race, Class & Gender*, *Rural Sociology*, and *Environmental Communication*.

Jennifer Randles is assistant professor of sociology at California State University, Fresno. Her research explores how social and economic inequities affect American family life and has appeared in *Gender & Society*, the *Journal of Policy Analysis and Management*, the *Journal of Contemporary Ethnography*, *Contexts*, and *Sociology Compass*. She is author of *Learning and Legislating Love: Marriage Education, Politics, and Inequality in America*.

Deana A. Rohlinger is associate professor of sociology at Florida State University. She has published articles in *Social Problems*, *Sociological Theory*, *Mobilization*, *The Sociological Quarterly*, *Sociological Spectrum*, *Research in Social Movements*, *Conflicts and Change*, *The American Behavioral Scientist*, and *Journal of Women and Aging* as well as several book chapters. Her most recent book is *Abortion Politics, Mass Media, and Social Movements in America*.

Janine Schipper is professor of sociology at Northern Arizona University. She is author of *Disappearing Desert: The Growth of Phoenix and the Culture of Sprawl* and "Toward a Buddhist Sociology: Its Theories, Methods and Possibilities" in *American Sociologist*. Her current work focuses on the connections between Eastern philosophies, sociology, and sustainable communities.

Meghan M. Sweeney is associate professor of English at the University of North Carolina Wilmington, where she teaches courses on children's and adolescent literature. Her current work addresses the ways that wedding culture is sold to girls through books, films, magazines, and toys. She has published in journals including *The Lion and the Unicorn* and *Children's Literature in Education* and for the series *Critical Insights*.

Catherine (Kay) G. Valentine is professor emerita of sociology and founding director of women's studies at Nazareth College in Rochester, NY. Her publications appear in *Symbolic Interaction*, *Teaching Sociology*, and *Urban Life* as well as various anthologies, including most recently *Men Who Hate Women and Women Who Kick Their Asses: Stieg Larsson's Millennium Trilogy in Feminist Perspective*. She is coeditor of *The Kaleidoscope of Gender: Prisms, Patterns, and Possibilities*.

Patricia Widener is associate professor of sociology at Florida Atlantic University and author of *Oil Injustice: Resisting and Conceding a Pipeline in Ecuador*. She is currently studying how activists in New Zealand are mobilizing against new oil proposals in a time of known disasters and climate awareness.

Index

academia, 51, 113–22
academic feminism, 16, 171n4
    class bias within, 168–70
    middle class privilege in, 162–63
    problems with success model of, 161–71
    and shift to neoliberalism, 161–62
    See also neoliberal feminism; working
        class feminists
achievement mandates
    colonizing realm of illness, 127
    divesting, 71–72
    letting go of, 24, 29, 54–56, 71–72, 106,
        110–11, 207–8
    and limitations of grit, 119
    performance expectations and, 16–17,
        25–28, 53, 98–99
    in retirement, 107–8
    and unproductive time, 27–28, 49
    See also letting go; neoliberalism;
        nonwork; productivity
aging
    capitalist mandates regarding, 175
    having fun and, 175, 181–82
    as opportunity, 181
    redefining for women, 173–82
    See also letting go; Red Hat Society
agriculture
    alternatives to masculinist, 221
    cooptation of alternative, by market, 220
    and feminine principle, 212–13
    gender, race, and class in, 211
anatta, 36, 188, 193–95, 196, 197n3. *See also*
    Buddhism: delusion of separate self

anti-pornography movement, 58. *See also*
    radical feminism

bardo, 97. *See also* being
being
    vs. doing, 27–28, 49, 50, 51–52, 54
    space between states of, 97
biospheric consciousness, 187–88, 193,
    195–96. *See also* environmental crisis;
    feminism: and feminine principle
body
    finding peace in, 127
    as fragmented and chaotic, 94–95
    and illness, 92, 132–33, 137
    listening to, 17–18, 25, 30, 52, 71–72
    neoliberal demand for controlled, 129
    See also self-care
"bright-sided," 28–29, 30, 30n4
Buddhism
    critiquing capitalism, 18–19
    delusion of separate self, 33, 34, 35,
        36–37, 44, 193–95, 197n3
    and environmental crisis, 187–97
    freedom, 35
    impermanence, 188–89
    instructions for dying, 97
    interdependence, 5, 193–94
    lack, 37–38, 44
    noble eightfold path, 190–95
    precepts, 35, 44n2
    socially engaged, 18–19, 39, 189–90
    in sociology, 188, 195
    Thich Nhat Hanh, 189–90

Buddhism, *continued*
    three marks of reality, 188–95
    three poisons or roots of evil, 33, 34,
        37–39, 41, 189
    Zen and letting go, 17–19, 28–29
    See also meditation; mindfulness;
        suffering
Butler, Judith, 3, 100n9

capitalism
    and aging women, 175
    and alternative agriculture, 220
    and feelings of alienation, 163
    second-wave feminist shift, 137–38
    visionary feminism challenging, 225–34
    See also Eisenstein, Hester; hooks,
        bell; liberal feminism; neoliberal
        feminism; neoliberalism; visionary
        feminism
care and compassion
    and Buddhist path, 40
    as central concerns of feminism, 3,
        16–19, 30, 55, 128
    in economic systems, 40
    for Mother Earth, 203
    political economy of, 16, 18
    social support systems of, 3, 30, 54–56,
        140–41
    vulnerability and, 3, 29–30
    See also care work; empathy; feminism:
        and feminine principle; self-care
care work, 8, 49, 50, 54, 55, 119
    as career choice for women, 151–52,
        159–60
    de-gendering, 147–48
    and food production, 211–22
    and occupational sorting, 151, 153
    revalued, 137
    stay-at-home fathers and, 139–48
    See also essentialism; family-friendly
        policies; second shift; work-life
        balance
cervical cancer
    ending treatment for, 135–37
    HPV and stigma in, 131–32

and loss of fertility, 134–35
and oppressive beauty standards, 133
and rhetoric of battle, 129–30
sociological insights into, 127–38
and uncompromising optimism, 128,
    136–37
See also "bright-sided"; chronic illness;
    grief; letting go; pain; suffering;
    vulnerability
choice feminism. *See* liberal feminism;
    neoliberal feminism
chronic illness, 17
    critical reflections on, 91–100
    living with, 19–30, 52–53, 127–38
    narratives of embodied subjectivity,
        19–20; 91–100; 127–38
    restitution and recovery tropes, 127–28
    See also body; care and compassion; grief;
        letting go; pain; stigma; suffering;
        transformation; vulnerability
climate change, 187, 197n1, 204. *See also*
    environmental crisis
closure, 85
Colorado potato beetle, 211, 214–16, 220
community supported agriculture (CSAs),
    211
competition
    masculine, 61, 139, 140
    risks for LGBT, 72
    women letting go of, 28, 108, 109–10,
        175
    See also achievement mandates; letting
        go
consumerism, 16, 37, 44, 129
    as act of violence, 201–8
    and alternative food systems, 220
    as cause of suffering, 201–8
    credit counseling and, 158
    feminist collaboration with, 137–38,
        161–62
    letting go of, 207–8
    mandates regarding aging, 174–75
    marketing dissatisfaction, 37, 129, 173
    See also lack; letting go; neoliberalism;
        self; suffering

control
  benefits of relinquishing, 129
  illusions of, 28, 51, 109
  letting go of, 29, 109
  and masculine identity, 139–40
  men's patriarchal, 7, 58–61
  neoliberal myth of, 2
covering
  as challenge for chronically ill, 72
  letting go of, 73–75, 78
  and LGBT community, 71
  as social strategy, 70
  See also stigma
credit counseling
  as act of resistance, 153–55
  as career change, 151–60
  and hyper-consumerism, 158
  and occupational sorting, 151, 153
  structural limitations of, 155–59
  See also care work

dachas, 211, 214–17, 219
domestic masculinity. *See* stay-at-home
  fathers
*Dude, You're A Fag: Masculinity and
  Sexuality in High School* (Pascoe), 71,
  77
dukkha, 18, 188, 190, 193. *See also*
  Buddhism; suffering
Dworkin, Andrea, 58
dying
  ending treatment for terminal cancer,
    135–37
  instructions for, 97
  and permission to let go, 137–38
  and recovery and restitution narratives,
    127–30
  stillness and quiet necessary for, 86, 88
  See also being; grief; letting go;
    Sedgwick, Eve

economic crisis, 25, 36
  credit counseling, 155–58
  Great Recession, 107, 175
Eisenstein, Hester, 16–17, 30, 72, 148, 161

empathy
  and biospheric consciousness, 193, 196,
    208
  at heart of care, 3
  and qualities associated with women,
    151
  for workers exposed to hardships, 206
  See also biospheric consciousness; care
    and compassion
environmental crisis
  and biospheric consciousness, 187–88,
    193
  applying Buddhist principles to, 187–97
  and feminine principle, 211–21
  and interconnectedness, 5, 194–95, 202,
    206–8
  and oil production and consumption,
    202–3
  threats to the environment, 42–43
  and Western values, 188–89
essentialism, 7, 16
  and biological motherhood, 134–35
  de-gendering as a radical act, 147–48
ExxonMobil
  Exxon *Valdez*, 42, 202
  funding climate change denial, 42–43

fag discourse, 71, 77. See also *Dude, You're
  a Fag*
Family and Medical Leave Act (FMLA),
  97–98, 105. *See also* maternity leave
family-friendly policies, 47, 51, 96–98, 141,
  147–48. *See also* care work; maternity
  leave; work-life balance
fatigue, 17–18, 22–25. *See also*
  neoliberalism: values; rest
faux feminism. *See* neoliberal feminism
feminism, 6–8, 111nn1–3
  backlash against, 163
  and classism, 170
  and feminine principle, 211–22
  fourth wave, 111
  as gift to men, 57–64
  and Red Hat Society, 181–82
  See also specific types; letting go

Feminism and Disability (Hillyer), 17, 19, 29–30

Feminism Seduced: How Global Elites Use Women's Labor and Ideas to Exploit the World (Eisenstein), 16, 17, 30, 72

Frankenbug, 211, 214–16, 220

Fraser, Nancy, 137

free-market feminism. *See* neoliberal feminism

gender wage gap, 9n3, 49, 151, 163

Goffman, Erving, 70

Goldman Sachs, 39–42

good-enough, 25–28

Great Recession, 107,

grief
    and being in touch with one's limitations and vulnerability, 30
    and the capacity for joy, 64
    over ecological destruction, 190, 203
    as transformative pedagogical practice, 89–90, 95–96
    See also *Feminism and Disability* (Hillyer)

having-it-all myth. *See* superwomen

Hochschild, Arlie, 49, 52, 54, 55. *See also* second shift

homosexuality. *See* covering; *Dude, You're A Fag*; fag discourse; identity politics; letting go: and masculinity

hooks, bell, 25–26, 170, 225–34

hospice, 135–36. *See also* dying; letting go

identity politics
    and critique of capitalism, 137
    and intersectionality, 111n3, 231

impermanence. *See* Buddhism

inequality
    in academic feminism, 161
    between producers and consumers, 201–8
    credit counselors aware of, 158–59
    dead-end jobs, 16, 25
    destabilizing practices, 147–48

and fight to dismantle patriarchy, 226–27

gap between rich and poor, 34, 35–40, 44n1, 44n3

and *Lean In*, 226

and oppression, 3–4

See also care work

intensive mothering, 48, 55

interconnectedness, 5, 194–95, 201–8. *See also* biospheric consciousness; Buddhism; letting go

Iyer, Pico, 93

Journal of a Solitude (Sarton), 27

joy, 30, 55, 63–64, 93, 122, 174. *See also* aging: having fun and

King, Donna, 50, 71, 99, 106, 111, 128, 138, 153, 163, 203, 207–8

Lacan, Jacques, 94–95

lack, 37–38. *See also* Buddhism; consumerism; *dukkha*; self; suffering

Lean In: Women, Work, and the Will to Lead (Sandberg), 2, 4, 9, 47, 50, 72, 98–99, 104–5, 225–34
    Black and poor women left out of, 118, 227–28, 231
    and conservative white females, 232–33
    as faux feminism, 228–29
    on *New York Times* bestseller list, 2, 48, 225

leisure, 175. *See also* aging; joy; nonwork; Red Hat Society

letting go
    as act of resistance, 153–55
    aging and, 106–7, 175
    of being mom, 108–9
    competition, 28, 108, 109–10, 175
    of covering or straight-acting, 69–78
    of delusion of separate self, 33, 34, 35, 37, 188
    and ecological crisis, 188–89, 213
    and feminine principle, 211–22

and growing close, 109–110
of harmful consumption, 207–8
and having fun, 173–83
and illness, 127–38
of illusion of control, 28–29, 51, 109, 140
main dilemma in, 53
of masculinist agriculture, 211–21
and masculinity, 57–64, 69–78, 139–40,
    145–48
of neoliberal values, 1, 2, 5, 16, 19, 50,
    52, 54, 56, 71, 72, 78, 98, 104, 110–11,
    127, 163, 168, 181
of normal, 57–64
of oil, 203–4
of oppressive beauty standards, 133
and redefinition of the self, 99
as a revolutionary act, 55–56
self-awareness and, 1, 5–6
self-care and, 1, 54–56
as self-help-y pursuit, 91
social responsibility and, 5, 206–7
and stillness, 86
and success, 106, 108, 152, 161–72
Zen and art of, 17–19
liberal feminism, 6
    choice feminism, 105–6
    and critique of capitalism, 137–38
    and existing social systems, 226
    second wave, 103–4, 111n1
    See also neoliberal feminism
liberal humanism, 142–44
Listening Below the Noise: The
    Transformative Power of Silence
    (LeClaire), 86
Living with Chronic Illness: Days of Patience
    and Passion (Register), 17, 20, 23, 25–27
Losse, Kate, 48–49, 99, 100n7, 231–32
Loy, David, 18, 33–45, 188–89

mainstream feminism. See liberal feminism;
    neoliberal feminism
masculinities
    and agriculture, 212, 221
    Connell, R. W., 146
    gay, 71–73

hegemonic, 69, 139, 145–48
king-of-the-hill, 61–63
patriarchal, 59–60
toxic, 62–63
See also competition; control; letting
    go; patriarchy; stay-at-home fathers;
    vulnerability
maternity leave, 4, 97, 108
    Family and Medical Leave Act
        (FMLA), 97–98, 105
    and parental leave, 6, 47
    See also family-friendly policies;
        paternity leave
medical industrial complex, 93
meditation
    in corporations, 39–41
    insight meditation instructions,
        196–97
    as path to social transformation, 5,
        189–90, 195–96
    as self-care practice, 5
    Vipassana, 196
    See also Buddhism; mindfulness
mindfulness, 35, 171, 193, 195
    insight meditation instruction, 196–97
    in service of profit, 39–44
    and Engaged Buddhism, 189–90
mommy wars, 105–6

neoliberal feminism, 1, 30n1
    care-lite, 3–5
    choice feminism, 105–6
    cooptation of Eastern spirituality, 9n4
    faux feminism, 3–5, 9, 228–29
    free market feminism, 16, 19
    radical individualism of, 1, 2–3, 105–6,
        161
    and social justice, 137–38
    trickle-down approach, 3, 9n3
neoliberal individualism, 71, 161
neoliberalism, 9n2
    capitalism and, 1–2, 8, 16, 55, 59
    emphasis on extrinsic value, 108
    imperialist logic of, 5
    and mindfulness movement, 39–44

neoliberalism, *continued*
  and US health care system, 128–29
  values, 1, 2, 8, 24–25
nonwork, 49–50, 54
normal, 57, 59, 63–64
nothing special, 16, 106
Novartis, 41

pain
  living with, 20–22, 127–28
  as pathway to transformation, 72, 97,
    127–28
Parsons, Talcott, 52–53
Pascoe, C. J., 71, 77, 147. See also
  Dude, You're a Fag; fag discourse;
  masculinities
paternity leave, 147–48. *See also* family-
  friendly policies; maternity leave;
  work-life balance
patriarchy, 6–7, 57–58,
  and visionary feminism, 226–27, 232
  See also visionary feminism
pleasure. *See* joy; nonwork
poverty, 4
  credit counseling and, 158–59
  ignored in *Lean In*, 231
  negligible empowerment in, 171n1
  of US farmworkers, 204
  for women over 65, 107
productivity, 99
  demands to push past limits, 16–17, 51
  liberation from performance
    expectations, 17, 54, 110–11
  and need for non-productive pastimes,
    27–28, 48, 49
  retirement and, 108
  See also achievement mandates; being;
    nonwork

racism, 114, 117–18, 151
radical feminism, 6–7, 57–59, 62–63
Red Hat Society, 173–83
  cultivating sisterhood, 175–78
  empowering women, 178–80
  letting go and having fun, 180–82

*Rejected Body, The: Feminist Philosophical
  Reflections on Disability* (Wendell), 17,
  21, 23, 24, 28–29
rest, 17–18, 27–28, 99
Ricoeur, Paul, 100n1
Rifkin, Jeremy, 187–88, 193. *See
  also* biospheric consciousness;
  environmental crisis

Sandberg, Sheryl. See *Lean In: Women,
  Work, and the Will to Lead*
second shift, 52, 141, 153. *See also*
  Hochschild, Arlie.
Sedgwick, Eve, 92, 96, 97, 99, 100
self
  aging, 181
  cervical cancer and, 127–38
  as consumer, 37–38, 173
  delusion of separate, 33, 34, 35, 37
  embracing redefinition of, 99
  finding peace in, 127
  myth of unified, 94–95, 100n4
  and no-self, 193–95, 197n3
  transformation, 159
  See also anatta; Buddhism; Lacan,
    Jacques; letting go; self-care
self-care, 1, 54–56
  achievement mandates and, 71–73,
    98–99
  Black women's need for, 5, 113–22
  as resistance to capitalist health care,
    137–38
  See also body; meditation
Serenity Prayer, 28, 30n3
Shiva, Vandana, 212–13, 217, 221n1. *See
  also* environmental crisis: and feminine
  principle
sick role, 52–53
social democracy, 4
social justice, 18, 33–38, 44
  feminism, 2–3, 47, 49, 54–56
  growing food and growing, 211–22
socialist feminism, 7–8, 162. *See also* Fraser,
  Nancy
Sociological Imagination, The (Mills), 51

stay-at-home fathers
and domestic sphere, 144–45
lived experiences of, 141–42
and masculine identity, 139, 140, 145–46
and masculine privilege, 146–48
number in the US, 140
rational economics of 142–44
stigma
of angry Black woman stereotype, 117
and covering, 70
and family leave, 163
HPV and, 131–32, 137
for stay-at-home fathers, 141
See also covering; racism
striving. *See* achievement mandates; letting
go; productivity
suffering
and acceptance, 127–28
alleviating, 195–96
economic injustice and, 35–39
of environmental crisis, 190
feminist explorations of, 92
food production workers and, 204–6
freedom from, 16, 18, 20–22, 33, 44, 52,
188, 190–91
gendered compliments that amplify, 133
greed, hatred, and delusion as causes of,
33–39, 44, 190
making sense of, 137–8, 195
oil and food consumption and, 201–8
resisting forces that increase, 137–38
See also Buddhism; care and
compassion; *dukka*; letting go
supercrip, 29
supergay, 71–72
superwomen
African American, 113
benefits to capitalism, 55

having-it-all myth, 47–48, 51, 104–5,
106, 173
risks of trying to be, 19, 29–30, 50,
71–72, 220
See also liberal feminism; neoliberal
feminism

transformation
by changing careers, 159
of environmental crisis, 187–88, 193
link between personal and social, 5,
29–30, 33–44, 188–89, 193–95, 207–8
pain as pathway to, 20–22, 72
of reality through letting go, 188–89
social forces and, 8

visionary feminism, 9, 225–34
and fight to dismantle patriarchy,
226–27
and financial literacy for women, 229–31
and gender identity, 226
and intersectionality, 231
vulnerability
in classroom, 74, 78, 90, 91–92
and finding significance, 2, 28, 30, 62, 78

"Warning" (Joseph), 174, 182n1
white supremacist society, 59
work-life balance, 49. *See also* Hochschild,
Arlie
working class, 163, 171n1
working class feminists
bias against, 168–70
in academy, 163–64
passing as middle class, 170
Writing a Woman's Life (Heilbrun), 85

Zen. *See* Buddhism; letting go